The Truth Seeker's Guide to the Bible

by

Christopher Mark Hanson

Bloomington, IN   authorHOUSE®   Milton Keynes, UK

AuthorHouse™
1663 Liberty Drive, Suite 200
Bloomington, IN 47403
www.authorhouse.com
Phone: 1-800-839-8640

AuthorHouse™ UK Ltd.
500 Avebury Boulevard
Central Milton Keynes, MK9 2BE
www.authorhouse.co.uk
Phone: 08001974150

© *2007 Christopher Mark Hanson. All rights reserved.*

No part of this book may be reproduced, stored in a retrieval system, or transmitted by any means without the written permission of the author.

First published by AuthorHouse 7/18/2007

ISBN: 978-1-4259-6863-2 (sc)

Printed in the United States of America
Bloomington, Indiana

This book is printed on acid-free paper.

Dedication.

With devotion to my spiritual teacher K.B.N. May this small offering be instrumental in guiding at least a few sincere seekers into the presence of their God-chosen Guides.

Declaration & Foreword.

I must begin by 'coming clean' as it were. This is not the work of a person sitting on the fence. Neither is it an objective study of the scripture of my childhood in an attempt to prove its authenticity or to rediscover myself. I already believe in a supreme state of Being, or God if you like, and have spent long years studying the teachings of the various Schools and meditating under the loving care of an enlightened spiritual Guide.

It appears to me that anyone who has considered deeply who and what they are, or studied the beauty, intricacy and carefully crafted processes of nature in any detail, cannot possibly believe that such wonders could have sprung up by trial and error (evolution) or by chance mutation. Indeed, the real answers to what we are and where Creation came from are in the Bible for anyone to find.

I believe that biblical teachings have been sidelined temporarily by the public simply because of difficulties in understanding the language of the prophets and the relevance of spiritual matters to our everyday lives. The message all saints and prophets have brought to mankind is that **Spirit is and always has been the very foundation of life and cannot and should not be left out of every day decision-making.** Those who declare that spiritual teachings should be kept apart from such daily activities as business, politics, economics, the workplace and family life, and relegated to one hour on Sunday morning, clearly do not understand what religion is all about. True Religion teaches people how to live their everyday lives and how to use such daily activity to discover their full potential as divine children of God.

In this journey around the Bible, I have adopted the King James Version not just because it was the text of my youth but because many of the subtler meanings have become obscured or distorted in other versions. I cringe when I think of how much information must have been lost already from biblical texts during the translations from Hebrew, German, Greek and Latin. Nevertheless, a reasonable facsimile of the original meanings can be brought to light by comparing the biblical accounts with the unchanging message brought to the world throughout the ages by Enlightened Teachers of all eras and cultures.

The biblical quotations that appear at the end of each of the sections of text have been carefully selected to support the main contention of this work that there is but One Universal Truth that has been brought to the world at different times whenever mankind has forgotten the real purpose of life: to find the Path back to God.

Today, perhaps more than at any time during our history, man is challenging the existence of a Supreme Being. But whether God exists or not is a question that no amount of rationalising, debate or collection of facts can satisfactorily answer. To pursue such lines of intellectual enquiry merely cloud the issue even further. Indeed it is a question that no one can solve for anyone else. Since the beginning of time, the saints have advised that the purpose of life can be discovered only in the silence of one's own soul. A person either believes or does not believe according to his/her own nature and the degree of effort they are prepared to invest in their spiritual development.

The saving grace of humanity is that whatever so-called 'rational man' concludes in the clinical halls of science, his heart will always yearn to discover the answer to the most important question in life: "Who am I?"

Contents

Declaration & Foreword. vii

Part 1. The Human Dilemma. 1
1 Asking the Right Questions. 3
2 The Problem with Religion. 5
3 Clearing the Way. 7
4 The Language of the Saints. 10
5 The Accidental Structure of the Bible. 12

Part 2. The Nature of God & the World. 15
1 God the Father. 17
2 The Purpose of Creation. 25
3 Forming Creation. 31
4 The Captivity. 44

Part 3 The Nature of Mankind. 75
1 Perfect & Imperfect Man. 77
2 The Higher Spiritual Centres. 89
3 The Tree of Life. 107
4 What is Intuition? 118

Part 4. Starting on the Journey. 129
1 Paths to God. 131
2 Qualities of the Truth-Seeker. 145
3 How to Identify False Teachers. 159
4 The Nature of Enlightened Ones. 167
5 The Functions of Enlightened Ones. 186

Part 5. The Knowledge. 207
1 What is Knowledge? 209
2 The Word. 222
3 The Divine Light. 242
4 The 'I AM HE'. 253
5 The Nectar. 262

Part 6. How to Escape the World. 273
1 Initiation into the Path. 275
2 Meditation. 289

3 Qualities for Success...312
4 Enlightenment. 335
The Final Word. 352
Acknowledgements..355
Recommended Reading. 357
Recommended Sources of Spiritual Information........................359

Part 1.

The Human Dilemma.

1

Asking the Right Questions.

Man comes into this world not knowing where he came from, not understanding why he is here, and completely mystified as to the origin and purpose of Creation. These are great and important questions to which we have the right to know the answers.

The reason we don't know the answers already is because we don't ask the right questions of the right people. Instead of approaching Enlightened Spiritual Guides to provide the solutions to our deep metaphysical questions, we prefer, oddly enough, to approach members of the scientific community, the very people who are most poorly equipped to answer them. Material Science, by definition, cannot understand the Spiritual Experience because it cannot measure non-material phenomena.

This is not to say that an unbridgeable gulf exists between science and spirituality, at least not from the point of view of the Truth-Seeker. Far from it! In reality the two subjects are entirely compatible. Spiritual teachings hold that matter cannot exist of itself; that it arises out of the interaction between a series of layers of increasingly subtle energies, the finer levels of which cannot be measured by man-made instruments. These energies are so fine that they can be experienced only through the subtle instruments of mind and intuition. Material science, using much coarser instruments, is gradually discovering the physical laws governing the grosser manifestations of nature, the superficial cloak of Reality. Should material science wish to delve into the realms out of which matter evolves and reach the root of consciousness itself, it will have to adopt the tools of the spiritual scientist: mind and intuition. If and when material science is able to make this shift, the complete compatibility between science and spirituality will be more widely understood and today's apparent division between the two will melt away.

One of the most fundamental metaphysical questions facing mankind is 'What is Truth?' This is the very question Pontius Pilate demanded of Jesus two thousand years ago and though Jesus refused to answer because he knew that the worldly Pilate had absolutely no chance of understanding the subject, the urge to know the answer has not gone away. If anything, it has intensified over the centuries.

Since the question is essentially a metaphysical one, the most sensible place to look for the answer is in the spiritual teachings of the world's Enlightened Ones: those who have delved deeply into the non-material roots of nature and discovered – nay become united with – the Source from which man and all matter have originated. Those who sincerely wish to know (and experience) this Truth can find it hidden within the texts of all the major scriptures of the world, or can seek it first hand from the mouth of any Enlightened One alive on earth today.

Jesus could have explained to Pilate that though there are many relative truths, there is only one Absolute Truth, a Truth which the Enlightened Ones of all times, races and creeds have taught to mankind and will continue to do so until every last one of us has 'entered the kingdom of heaven'. For want of a better name let it be called 'The Perennial Philosophy'. The Perennial Philosophy teaches that the only Absolute Truth that exists and has ever existed in this world is that there is One God who is that eternal consciousness in the image of which we, ourselves, are made. Man is, in reality, an eternal soul encased in a human body, part of the unchanging essence behind the changing panorama of life. It is from Spirit we came and to Spirit we have to return. Spirit is what we are and the reason why we are here on earth, right now, is to find our way back to our original state. The 'how to get there' occupies the rest of this book.

As soon as one of God's children begins earnestly to seek Him, the Path opens before that devotee in a most mysterious and divine way. As if from nowhere, the most appropriate information and people begin to manifest before him and lead him to the goal he so desires. This has been the experience of every sincere seeker throughout all time and many there are who will attest to this Truth.

2

The Problem with Religion.

    Enlightened spiritual teachers do not teach religion. Buddha made no mention of Buddhism nor did Jesus claim to be bringing Christianity to the world. Though they will have been born into particular cultures and religions, authentic spiritual guides have risen above any such limited identification. Indeed they have no teachings they claim to be their own or to be the province of any particular chosen group. From age to age they come to bring the Perennial Philosophy, spiritual teachings which are the property of all peoples of all times, teachings which come directly from the Eternal Father whose sole wish is to bring His lost children back to Him. These guides have come on earth time and time again throughout the ages whenever the world has forgotten the real purpose of life and the Truth has become smothered by illusion.

    Such was the situation when Jesus appeared. The Dark Ages were sweeping in. People had become steeped in ignorance. Cruelty and exploitation were rampant and compassion in short supply. He came bearing the Eternal Truth, the Perennial Philosophy, offering the harassed people of his time a way out of their misery. Few there were who recognised his stature and the priceless gift he was offering to them. Indeed, the world at large is still unaware of the great common spiritual heritage we all share.

    The majority of people living in the West revere the Bible even though its content is mostly incomprehensible to them. Somewhere deep within the human psyche lurks the feeling that there must be considerably more hidden within its pages than superficial study can reveal. Indeed, it must be admitted that the spiritual seeker has to dig very deep to expose the real meanings behind the verses of the Old and New Testaments. But they will not be disappointed when they make the effort to discover the real 'identity' of Jesus and the prophets and the importance of the message they were bringing to mankind. Anyone with an acute thirst for spiritual knowledge and an open mind can start on the greatest adventure of their existence: the journey to discover the limitless potential that lies hidden within the biblical texts and within themselves.

The greatest value can be got out of this work by first reading the text and then going through the list of biblical quotations given at the end of each section. These quotations should be regarded as samples selected from the general text of the Bible to support the main teachings of the Enlightened Ones. Interpretations have been provided to clarify the language used by Christian prophets and saints and thereby assist the reader in interpreting any other verses he/she might wish to look up. It is hoped that enough quotations have been provided under each section to substantiate that the teachings of the prophets and saints of the Old and New Testaments correspond exactly with the teachings brought by the saints of all times and cultures and that the same teachings are being propagated today by their modern counterparts, any differences being limited to the particular languages of the saints and the times in which they lived.

For earnest spiritual seekers wishing to discover the Truth for themselves, lists of suitable literature and contact details of some authentic spiritual organisations are given at the end of this book.

3

Clearing the Way.

It is unfortunate that during the course of Christianity's long history, it has collected many fearful words designed to discourage enquiring minds from asking troublesome questions. Before starting on this exploration of the Bible it would be wise to put some of these bogies to rest.

Blasphemy: blasphemies are expressions that are considered to defame the Church, its religious figures, or its teachings. But, since the vibratory force of the Holy Ghost (see the section on 'The Word') is the real power behind all speech, a blasphemy is actually any word or expression that creates an inharmonious vibration and, consequently, obscures or upsets the lawful operation of the Holy Ghost or Word in its work of maintaining the body and mind in a healthy condition, and of leading man back to his Creator.

Dogma: a dogma is a fixed belief. Since this world and everything in it is in a state of flux, the idea that such a thing as an unchanging rule can exist is a total myth. In spiritual terms the only unvarying essence is the One Spirit from which all Creation has evolved, unchanging, ever constant, totally reliable God. That is why God is called Truth.

God: God is not what you think He/She/It is. As soon as the word 'God' enters the mind, a web of misconceptions rises to obscure the Truth. Everyone wants God to fit his or her own treasured image of that Indefinable Absolute. If you want to find God, throw away everything you ever thought that you knew about Him. Stop telling Him what He is. Let Him reveal Himself to you.

Heresy: heresy is a word that has no real spiritual value. It is simply a word dreamed up to frighten people into accepting, without question, the Church's religious dogmas.

Logos: though the literal translation of the Greek word logos is 'Word', 'Sound' would be more in keeping with the teachings of the saints.

Man: this term stretches back to the Mother of all languages: Sanskrit. It originates from the Sanskrit word 'manas' meaning mind. Thus, man is the creature with the distinguishing feature of having a developed mind or 'manas'. In its original usage the word 'manas' had no gender implications. The term 'man' has been adopted throughout this book in its original genderless context.

Meditation: is just another word for the process Christians call 'contemplation', an inner concentration leading to divine ecstasy. Meditation is not a negative process of emptying the mind but of stilling it so that God can fill it with Himself: "Be still and know that I am God."

Religion: means much more than its conventional interpretation as a particular set of rituals, ceremonies and beliefs. The word is derived from the Latin verb religare meaning to tie back or bind fast (to one's origin). Since all mankind came from the same Source, there can be only one true religion universal to all. That religion is Love.

Repentance: to repent is not to say sorry to God in words or to merely promise to be good in future. The word 'repentance' has much deeper implications. A better interpretation would be 'to turn in the other direction'. In this context, since our attention is normally fixed on the world around us, to repent means to turn the attention away from the outward world of matter to the spiritual realms that lie within ourselves.

Sin: 'sin' was originally translated from the Greek word harmartia, an archery term meaning 'to miss the target'. In spiritual terms one misses the target when one's actions deviate from one's soul nature. Thus, in its true sense, a 'sin' is simply an action that runs contrary to the purity of the soul and thus obscures our vision of it. Sins are actions that keep our focus engaged in the unreal: fixed on the world and its events. The opposite of sin is repentance: a turning away from the world outside to the world inside.

Soul: the soul is not a separate entity from God in the same sense that an artist and her painting are two different things, though one certainly created the other. In the case of the soul, a better analogy would be between the sun and the sunbeam. The sun can exist without the sunbeam but the sunbeam cannot exist without the sun. Even so, the sunbeam has all the qualities of the sun and is not essentially different from it in kind.

Yoga: is an eastern expression encompassing practices that lead to union with God. Thus it has exactly the same meaning as 'religion'.

4

The Language of the Saints.

The Enlightened Ones of past eras often cloaked their teachings in allegory, metaphor and symbolism. Many Old Testament stories and the parables of Jesus provide clear examples of spiritual teachings being conveyed in this way. The reason Jesus and other Enlightened Ones of past times delivered their messages in obscure language or hidden within seemingly simple stories was explained by Jesus to his disciples:

> *Because it is given unto you to know the mysteries of the kingdom of heaven, but to them it is not given.*
> (Matthew 13: 11)

In other words, though his disciples were advanced enough to understand his teachings, the general public of the time were not. On other occasions he expressed the same opinion more succinctly saying:

> *He that hath ears to hear, let him hear.*
> (Matthew 11: 15)

Scriptural truths have been hidden behind allegory since ancient times. The writings of the Enlightened Ones of India, which pre-date Christianity by thousands of years, are replete with such instances. For example the Hindu Scripture called the Bhagavad Gita, the Song of God, though appearing on the surface to be an account of an historical battle between two opposing armies, in actual fact is a description of the inner battle each person must face in order to be reunited with God. Even today the Bhagavad Gita is considered to be the foremost treatise on the Path to God of any of the world's scriptures.

Though modern saints might, on occasion, adopt obscure means of expression for reasons similar to their ancient counterparts, more often than not their language appears unclear simply because of the difficulty of translating direct spiritual experience into words. As the Master K.B.N says:

> *There is a power that we call God. That Power is all-beautiful. It is all-shining. It is ever-blissful. It is Eternal Truth, the source of this Creation and it is **indescribable**.*

In view of these difficulties associated with the language employed by the saints, it is not surprising that most people go through life not understanding the scripture of their culture and without finding anyone who can answer their questions adequately. This situation is bound to continue until they have studied and meditated for a sufficient length of time under an Enlightened Teacher who can express scriptural truths in the common language of the times and who can give them a direct experience of the indescribable. Anyone wishing to climb to the spiritual heights would be wise to find someone who has already reached the summit and can show them the Path or Way.

The glorious message the prophets of the Old Testament brought to mankind was often in the form:

> *And it shall come to pass in the last days, that the mountain of the Lord's house shall be established in the top of the mountains, and shall be exalted above the hills; and all nations shall flow unto it.*
> (Isaiah 2: 2)

Today's Enlightened Ones might deliver the same message in a more direct way:

> *Wake up! Wake up! Shake off the illusions of this world. Claim your rightful divine heritage. Meditate!*

5

The Accidental Structure of the Bible.

The structure of the Holy Bible broadly follows the spiritual journey of mankind right from the very beginning to its inevitable end. In Genesis we see the Creator making not just this Earth but the entire Cosmos, with mankind first appearing in the heavenly realms before manifesting in the flesh on earth.

The claim made by the early church as to the time-frame of Creation being in days, though rightly rubbished by the scientific community at the start of the 20th century, can be transformed into a different and more realistic scale by comparison with the Hindu scriptures which relate how God makes and destroys Creation in alternate cycles of one 'day' (manifestation) and one 'night' (the period of dissolution), each of which is billions of years long. The time scales intended by the writer of Genesis are not known but it is safe to say that the author was not thinking in terms of earthly days and nights but of very, very, long periods of time.

Soon after man's appearance in the physical form in the ideal world of the 'Garden of Eden', Genesis describes how he used his freewill to separate himself from his Creator. Thereafter, the entire Old Testament is given over to accounts of man's adventures in the world of matter, sometimes stumbling through a wilderness of ignorance of his own making, sometimes reaching for his state of original purity.

This long and arduous journey peaks with the advent of the Messiah who God has chosen to begin a new era, to bring a new covenant (the old teaching refreshed) to His children. This is the point every person must eventually reach and is described by Jesus in his parable of the Prodigal Son wherein, having exhausted himself chasing the things of this world, man eventually realises that he was much better off before he separated from his Holy Father. With the dawn of that realisation, he decides to return home. The advent of the Master or Messiah is vital to this journey as he is the one who is destined to show the prodigal son the Way. Thus the New Testament occurs in the Bible in just the right place.

All that the good book needs now to be fully complete is a concluding section relating man's return journey to God. And it has one: the Revelation of St. John the Divine. But, ironically, because of difficulties in understanding the esoteric content of this fabulous spiritual treatise, this wonderfully rich and informative inner experience of St. John has long been accepted as a doomsday prophesy. This is an unfortunate misconception. Revelation is not a prophetic work at all. It is not a forecast of frightful events that are about to engulf the world. It is quite the opposite! In reality it is a glorious message of hope and encouragement to all mankind. Revelation relates the direct spiritual experiences of St. John when he turned towards his inner Self and, in doing so, witnessed the 'New Jerusalem': the realm of God Consciousness from whence he, Creation, and all mankind originally came.

Thus, the structure of the Bible completely reflects mankind's epic journey, starting with his freewill decision to leave his celestial home, his trials and tribulations in the world of matter, the seemingly miraculous appearance of an Enlightened One just at the right time and, as the final chapter, the inner journey he must make to unite once more with his ever-loving Father.

Part 2.

The Nature of God & the World.

1

God the Father.

*O Lord, there is none like thee,
neither is there any God beside thee,
according to all that we have heard
with our ears.*
                    (I Chronicles 17: 20)

*There is only one religion: the religion of love.
There is only one language: the language of the heart.
There is only one caste: the caste of humanity.
There is only one God, and He is omnipresent.*
                    (Sri Sathya Sai Baba)

Enlightened Ones do not come to divide but to unite. Often, they begin their teachings by emphasising that there is and can ever be only one Creator, one Father, even though the adherents of different religions call Him by various names: God, Allah, Jehovah, Brahman and so on. The saints take great care to point out that just as each language has a different word for the same substance 'water', the outwardly different names of God are all referring to the same Creator.

Viewed in this light, it is clear that the 'God' of the Bible is not the Supreme Father of just one particular section of the population who have adopted the term 'God'. To the Creator, to the formless, the name allocated to Him by any particular sect is not the essential factor. He knows that He has always been 'One' and will always be so. The first challenge facing the spiritual aspirant, therefore, is to open his/her mind to this fact.

Even in Judeo-Christian literature the Creator is called by an array of different names: Lord, Jehovah, Redeemer, Saviour, God, Yahweh, Father and so on. But the selected biblical quotations given at the end of this section show clearly that the authors of the texts had only One Essence in mind. This being the case, Christian communities should have no difficulty in accepting that all religions are worshipping the same Supreme Being irrespective of the name they have adopted for Him.

But it is one thing to give the Creator a name and quite another to describe the qualities of that Supreme Being. Perhaps the clearest descriptions are given in the Hindu Scripture, written originally in poetic Sanskrit verses and aptly called the Bhagavad Gita: the Song of God.

In the Bhagavad Gita, God or Brahman's basic qualities are identified as Sat, Chit, Ananda. Brahman is 'Sat', or Truth, because He is the Eternal Essence, the Formless behind all forms, the Unchanging in the midst of change, the One Reality behind all the apparent diversity of forms in Creation. He is the subtle substratum from which all Creation has sprung forth and into which it is withdrawn at the end of its prescribed cycle of manifestation at the end of the 'Day of Brahman'. The Absolute is also 'Chit', or Conscious Awareness, because He is always aware that He exists. The Eternal Essence has the ability to stand aloof from all the vibrant activity of creation while also being activity engaged in it. The third main quality of Brahman is 'Ananda', or Bliss, which is supreme love-joy experienced as boundless energy and compassion.

In biblical texts, 'Sat' can be clearly recognised as 'God the Father', the Supreme Creator, who announces Himself as

I am Alpha and Omega, the beginning and the ending.
(Revelation 1: 8)

and whose honour and majesty is described by King David in Psalm 104 in the form of an itemised list which bears a distinct similarity to the one provided by Krishna in Chapter X of the Bhagavad Gita.

'Chit' is closely allied to the term 'Spirit' use by St. Paul in his second letter to the Corinthians,

> *Now the Lord is that Spirit: and where the Spirit of the Lord is, there is liberty.*
> (II Corinthians 3: 17)

an expression which infers a Being that is consciously aware, an Essence that is non-material and eternally free.

And the quality of 'Ananda' is comparable to Lord's 'loving kindness' mentioned by the prophet Isaiah,

> *I will mention the lovingkindnesses of the Lord, and the praises of the Lord, according to all that the Lord hath bestowed on us,...and according to the multitude of his lovingkindnesses.*
> (Isaiah 63: 7)

an experience described as 'spiritual ecstasy' by many Christian saints and as 'samadhi' by the Hindus.

The Bhagavad Gita also identifies the three major powers of Brahman as omniscience (all knowing), omnipotence (all powerful) and omnipresence (without boundaries), qualities readily found in biblical verses, though, not surprisingly, in different terminology. For instance, in the book of Job we see the Lord impressing His powers of omnipresence and omnipotence on His trembling devotee by demanding:

> *Hast thou an arm like God? or canst thou thunder with a voice like him?*
> (Job 40: 9)

And, later on, a contrite Job acknowledging God's omnipotence and omniscience in the words:

> *I know that thou canst do every thing, and that no thought can be withholden from thee.*
> (Job 42: 2)

In the literature supporting his child educational programme called Education in Human Values (EHV), the current Indian Avatar, Sathya Sai Baba, provides detailed lists of God's attributes, the contents of which should be of no surprise to biblical scholars. The lists start with five basic divine qualities: love, peace, truth, right conduct and non-violence, all of which are expressed in equally broad terms in the 'Beatitudes' of Jesus found in the Sermon on the Mount. But Sai Baba's literature breaks down each of these five major qualities into what are called sub-qualities within which appear all the additional Christian values: mercy, charity, wisdom, chastity, forgiveness, compassion, understanding and so on. These same values can be identified not only in both the Old and New Testaments but also in the teachings of the Prophet Mohammed, in Buddhist texts and just about every other religion that exists. It is clear, therefore, that the many different religions are not only worshipping the same Creator but also agree on the nature of that Supreme Being.

Differences occur, of course, but these are not as great as they may seem on the surface. It is often claimed for instance that the Hindus worship many gods. At a cursory glance this may seem to be true. Effigies and holy pictures of a vast array of divine figures can be seen in Hindu homes and temples throughout the world. But each icon merely symbolises one of Brahman's (God's) qualities and is not intended to depict a separate entity at all. The ancient spiritual leaders of India, understanding the inability of man to grasp the concept of a formless God, put 'flesh' on His qualities and encouraged their followers to worship God through these pictures and symbols. Thus the elephant-headed god, Ganesh, represents the ability of the Creator to remove obstacles from the spiritual aspirant's path so that he can make rapid progress to the Godhead. Similarly, the goddess Kali with her six arms represents God, or Brahman, as Cosmic Nature.

In the same vein, it is often claimed, even by Buddhists, that Buddha was an atheist. This is a regrettable misunderstanding. Spiritual teachers of Buddha's eminent stature not only express themselves obliquely they also aim their teachings at the level of spirituality already attained by their followers. Thus, readers of the teachings of that great southern Indian saint Ramana Maharshi will discover that although he talked to some of his new devotees in the dualistic terms of God as an entity apparently separate from themselves, he would teach non-dualism to his more advanced students.

> *If the first person "I" exists, then the second and third persons "you" and "he" will also exist. By enquiring into the nature of the "I", the "I" perishes. With it "you" and "he" also perish. The resultant state, which shines as the Absolute Being, is one's own natural state, the Self.*

(Adapted from Forty Verses on Reality by Sri Ramana Maharshi)

Non-dualists hold that it is a metaphysical error to talk about God as a separate entity (from ourselves) since there is in reality only 'One' of which everything is a part. The Buddha was one of the greatest of the non-dualistic teachers. Thus, whether an Enlightened One talks in terms of God or does not mention God at all is not a reflection of the validity of his teachings, but of the level of understanding of his devotees.

What the Bible Says About God The Father.

The Bible confirms that though mankind may call the Creator by many different names, there is only one God whose powers and qualities are universally recognised.

Genesis 1: 1 The Universe and everything in it was created and is not accidental.
"In the beginning God created the heaven and the earth." See also John 1: 1-3 in the section called 'Forming Creation'.

Exodus 6: 3 God tells Moses that one of the names to which He answers is Jehovah.
"And I appeared unto Abraham, unto Isaac, and unto Jacob, by the name of God Almighty, but by my name JEHOVAH was I not known to them."

Deuteronomy 32: 4 Moses describes the basic qualities of God as Truth.
"He is the Rock, his work is perfect: for all his ways are judgement: a God of truth and without iniquity, just and right is he."

I Chronicles 17: 20 The Creator is unique and there is only one of Him.
"O Lord, there is none like thee, neither is there any God beside thee, according to all that we have heard with our ears."

I Chronicles 29: 11 There is only One Reality behind the diversity of Creation.
"Thine, O Lord, is the greatness, and the power, and the glory, and the victory, and the majesty: for all that is in the heaven and in the earth is thine; thine is the kingdom, O Lord, and thou art exalted as head above all."

Job 40: 9 The Lord makes a point to Job about His omnipresence and omnipotence.
"Hast thou an arm like God (Can you be everywhere in Creation at the same time)*? or canst thou thunder with a voice like him* (or have you His power)*?"* See the section called 'The Word' for the meaning of the 'voice' of God.

Job 42: 2 Two of the three main powers of the Lord are omnipotence & omniscience.
"I know that thou canst do every thing (are all-powerful, omnipotent), *and that no thought can be withholden from thee* (are all-knowing, omniscient)*."*

Psalm 56: 1 The Lord is also merciful in all circumstances.
"Be merciful unto me, O God: for man would swallow me up; he fighting daily oppresseth me."

Psalm 85: 2 The all-powerful God is eternally forgiving.
"Thou (God) *hast forgiven the iniquity of thy people, thou hast covered all their sin."*

Psalm 104: 24 The third of the three main powers of the Lord is omnipresence.
"Oh Lord, how manifold are thy works (Thou art everywhere, omnipresent)*! in wisdom hast thou made them all: the earth is full of thy riches."* In Psalm 104 David gives an exhaustive list of the works of the Creator that closely echoes the list given by Krishna in the Bhagavad Gita, Chapter X, Verses 19–40.

Proverbs 8: 14 The Lord, through Solomon, says that wisdom is a divine quality.
"Council is mine, and sound wisdom: I am understanding; I have strength."

Isaiah 43: 3 The Lord uses 'Holy One' and 'Saviour' when referring to Himself.
"For I am the Lord thy God, the Holy One of Israel, thy Saviour: I gave Egypt for thy ransom, Ethiopia and Seba for thee." See the section called 'The Captivity' for the symbolic meaning of Egypt.

Isaiah 43: 10 The Lord identifies Himself to Isaiah as the one and only God.
"Ye are my witnesses, saith the Lord, and my servants whom I have chosen: that ye may know and believe me, and understand that I am he: before me there was no God formed, neither shall there be after me."

Isaiah 44: 24 God had no other god to help Him create. He alone did it all by Himself.
"Thus saith the Lord, thy redeemer, and he that formed thee from the womb, I am the Lord that maketh all things; that stretcheth forth the heavens alone; that spreadeth abroad the earth by myself;"

Isaiah 45: 5 The Lord confirms yet again that He is the only One.
"I am the Lord, and there is none else, there is no God beside me: I girded thee, though thou hast not known me:"

Isaiah 48: 17 The Lord identifies Himself to Isaiah as the 'Redeemer' and 'Holy One'.
"Thus saith the Lord, thy Redeemer, the Holy One of Israel; I am the Lord thy God which teacheth thee to profit, which leadeth thee by the way that thou shouldest go."

Isaiah 63: 7 The Lord is eternally loving and kind.
"I will mention the lovingkindnesses of the Lord, and the praises of the Lord, according to all that the Lord hath bestowed on us,...and according to the multitude of his lovingkindnesses."

Matthew 10: 29 Jesus refers to the power of omniscience of God who knows all things.
"Are not two sparrows sold for a farthing? and one of them shall

not fall on the ground without your Father (without His omniscient knowledge)."

Mark 12: 29 & 32 There is only one God, one Creator, for the whole of mankind.
"And Jesus answered him, The first of all commandments is, Hear, O Israel; The Lord our God is one Lord:"
"And the scribe said unto him, Well, Master, thou hast said the truth: for there is one God; and there is none other but he:"

II Corinthians 3: 17 Spirit is closely allied to 'Chit' one of the three main qualities of God mentioned in Hinduism.
"Now the Lord is that Spirit: and where the Spirit of the Lord is, there is liberty."

Philippians 4: 7 St. Paul refers to the divine quality of supreme peace.
"And the peace of God, which passeth all understanding, shall keep your hearts and minds through Christ Jesus."

James 1: 17 St. James speaks of the reliability and constancy of God.
"Every good gift and every perfect gift is from above, and cometh down from the Father of lights, with whom is no variableness, neither shadow of turning."

Revelation 1: 8 God expresses all-embracing power by quoting the first and last letters of the Greek alphabet.
"I am Alpha and Omega, the beginning and the ending, saith the Lord, which is, and which was, and which is to come, the Almighty."

Revelation 19: 6 God's omnipotence is expressed through the power of 'God-the-Holy Ghost'.
"And I heard as it were the voice of a great multitude, and as the voice of many waters, and as the voice of mighty thunderings, saying Alleluia: for the Lord God Omnipotent reigneth." For the meaning of 'voice' see the section on 'The Word'.

2

The Purpose of Creation.

For thus saith the Lord that created the heavens; God himself that formed the earth and made it; he hath established it, he created it not in vain, he formed it to be inhabited: I am the Lord; and there is none else.
(Isaiah 45: 18)

I was a hidden treasure and I wanted to be known, so I created the world.
(Divine utterance, Islam)

How is it possible for the limited mind of man to understand the motives of the Infinite Intelligence that created him? To try to do so is akin to a child at nursery school attempting to fathom the intellect of a university professor. Nevertheless the mind demands answers that are within the scope of its abilities to grasp intellectually and that the heart can empathise with emotionally, and so some explanation must be given.

The Masters have many ways of explaining God's purpose in making mankind and placing him within Creation. One of them is that prior to Creation nothing existed. God was alone and realised His condition. Over the eons, a desire grew within Him to have companions and, eventually, He divided himself into trillions of individual entities so that He could love and be loved in return. To each of these souls He gave free will: the freedom to either love Him or not, for He wished to be loved without compulsion or it would not be love at all. To have free will infers that some form of competition must be on offer, some opposing attraction; and so God provided the world and all its various diversions to serve that very purpose.

Creation, the Masters say, is God's great game of hide-and-seek with His children. The One who has made Himself the Many hides behind the multiple forms of His making. He sleeps in the mineral kingdom, thrusts heavenward in the plants, rushes busily hither and thither in the animal realm, and constantly seeks to reunite with Himself through mankind.

In his excellent treatise called The Second Coming of Christ, page 143, one of the major Avatars of this age, Paramahansa Yogananda, explains that God did not mean man to be trapped on earth indefinitely. The Divine Scheme was that after spending some time enjoying the delights of God's Creation, man would, of his own free will, choose to return to his celestial home; but this ideal plan was foiled by man using his free will to turn away from his Creator.

This concept of a delightful creation is supported by the story of the Garden of Eden, the paradise God made for man to enjoy while on earth. During their early days in the world, the archetypal Adam and Eve lived a blissful life, having been given everything they needed. The story tells of how they were banished from the garden after they had ignored the voice of God within them. The point at which they first disobeyed the inner voice and hid themselves from God is recorded in Genesis:

> *And they* (Adam and Eve) *heard the voice of the Lord God walking in the garden in the cool of the day: and Adam and his wife hid themselves from the presence of the Lord God among the trees of the garden.*
> (Genesis 3: 8)

However, the Old Testament has very little else to say on God's purpose in forming Creation. The book of Isaiah merely records God confirming that He formed the earth with the specific intention of it being inhabited

> *For thus saith the Lord that created the heavens; God himself that formed the earth and made it; he hath established it, he created it not in vain, he formed it to be*

> *inhabited: I am the Lord; and there is none else.*
> (Isaiah 45: 18)

and, in Proverbs, we see Solomon counselling the people of Israel to be wise and ascend back into the heavenly realms 'above', which is a much better place than the comparative 'hell' of earthly life.

> *The way of life is above to the wise, that he may depart from the hell beneath.*
> (Proverbs 15: 24)

With little to go on from the Old Testament, it is to Jesus' teachings in the New Testament that we must turn in order to get a fuller picture of God's divine purpose.

In his allegorical story known as the Parable of the Prodigal Son, Luke 15: 11-32, Jesus describes how errant man (the younger son of the household) decided to leave his contented existence in his father's house (the heavenly realms where he lived with God), taking with him his inheritance (taking with him the divine qualities that were his natural birthright as a Son of God). After leaving home, the young man journeyed into a far country (the material world, far in consciousness from the heavenly realms), where he wasted (lost) his divine inheritance in riotous living (seduced by the temptations of the world). When he had lost ever bit of his divine inheritance (had forgotten that he is a Son of God and believed himself to be a mortal being), a great famine arose in the land (the world began to appear more and more empty and meaningless to him and a spiritual hunger began to stir within him). Eventually he found himself looking after a herd of swine and in danger of eating the same food as them because no one would feed him (he had fallen to a dangerously low level of morality and nothing could satisfy his spiritual hunger). At last the young man remembered that even the hired servants in his father's house were well looked after (he remembered how contented he had been in the heavenly realms where those who serve God are 'fed' on Divine Bliss). And so he decided to return home (to make the spiritual journey back to his Father's house). The rest of the story tells of God's great pleasure in seeing His errant child return and the Lord's willingness to forgive His offspring all his transgressions.

In this colourful story of the Prodigal Son, Jesus explains that though it may be in our nature to want to leave our celestial home and experience the world of matter, we soon find that we cannot be happy on earth. Having lost so much in leaving our heavenly abode, the paltry pleasures of earth, seemingly irresistible at first, cannot satisfy us and we constantly yearn to get back to our original spiritual state. Thus, Jesus' story implies that since Creation is imperfect by comparison to 'heaven', it serves the purpose of making us dissatisfied so that we will seek out our divine inheritance and return home to God the Father.

What the Bible Says About God's Purpose.

Creation was made out of the love of God so that man would use his God-given free will wisely and find his way back to his Celestial Home. Man came from God and to God he is destined to return.

Genesis 3: 8 Archetypal Man & Woman were banished from the Garden of Eden because they disobeyed God.
"And they (Adam and Eve) *heard the voice of the Lord God walking in the garden in the cool of the day: and Adam and his wife hid themselves from the presence of the Lord God among the trees of the garden."* See the section called 'The Tree of Life' for the meaning of 'trees of the garden'.

I Kings 8: 60 God created the world with the specific purpose of leading all His children back to Him.
"That all people of the earth may know that the Lord is God, and that there is none else."

Proverbs 15: 24 The wise aim to rise in consciousness to heaven so that they may escape from the hell of earth–life.
"The way of life is above to the wise, that he may depart from hell beneath."

Isaiah 45: 5 & 6 The Lord formed this wonderful Creation as proof of His existence.
"I am the Lord, and there is none else, there is no God beside me: I girded thee, though thou hast not known me:
"That they may know from the rising of the sun, and from the west, that there is none beside me. I am the Lord, and there is none else."

Isaiah 45: 18 & 22 We all came out of God and must go back to Him.
"For thus saith the Lord that created the heavens; God himself that formed the earth and made it; he hath established it, he created it not in vain, he formed it to be inhabited: I am the Lord; and there is none else."
"Look unto me, and be ye saved, all the ends of the earth: for I am God, and there is none else."

Zechariah 1: 3 The Lord sums up the entire purpose of life: turn to God and return to the Godhead.
"Therefore say thou unto them, Thus saith the Lord of hosts; Turn ye unto me, saith the Lord of hosts, and I will turn unto you..."

Matthew 6: 33 Jesus states unequivocally that our first priority is to seek God and all else will work out right.
"But seek ye first the kingdom of God, and his righteousness; and all these things (all your material needs) *shall be added unto you* (shall be given to you by the power of God's creative laws)*."*

Luke 15: 11-32 In his parable of the prodigal son Jesus tells the story of mankind: how we decided to leave our celestial home for life on earth, taking all our divine inheritance with us. On descending into body-consciousness we then 'spent' all our divine inheritance in riotous living (lost our divine qualities). Eventually, after many trials and tribulations, we began to dimly remember our celestial home and that we were much better off there. But, at the very moment we get an earnest desire to return home, the Good Father responds (by sending one of His saints to lead us) and comes rushing to greet us and welcomes us into His house. In this story the other son represents those children of God who did not set out on the great earthly adventure but decided to remain in Cosmic Consciousness, united to the Father.

John 3: 16 & 17 God made the world out of love so that we would return back to Him out of love.
"For God so loved the world, that he gave his only begotten Son (God gave the Christ Consciousness, His only beloved offspring, part of His own consciousness out of which the world was made), *that*

whoseover believeth in him should not perish, but have everlasting life (that whoever seeks Him shall realise the immortality of their souls).

"For God sent not his Son into the world to condemn the world (God did not create the world through His Son, the Christ Consciousness, to entrap mankind); *but that the world through him might be saved* (but so that His children might return back to Him via the same route that they descended into matter: through the Christ Consciousness)."
See the section on 'Forming Creation' for the meaning of 'Christ Consciousness' and 'Only Begotten Son'.

II Corinthians 3: 17 & 18 St. Paul points out that the purpose of mankind is to be changed back into Spirit.

"Now the Lord is that Spirit: and where the Spirit of the Lord is, there is liberty.

"But we all, with open face beholding as in a glass the glory of the Lord, are changed into the same image from glory to glory, even as by the Spirit of the Lord (Turning to God in purity of heart and mind, we become identical to Him)."

Ephesians 4: 13 St. Paul identifies the purpose of man: to become perfect as a Son of God.

"Till we all come in the unity of the faith, and of the knowledge of the Son of God, unto a perfect man, unto the measure of the stature of the fullness of Christ (Till we all achieve the highest potential possible to human beings as perfect Sons of God, united to the Christ Consciousness)."

Colossians 4: 12 St. Paul points out that perfection means our little human will becoming one with God's Will.

"Epaphras, who is one of you, a servant of Christ, saluteth you, always labouring fervently for you in prayers, that ye may stand perfect and complete in all the will of God."

3

Forming Creation.

And the great dragon was cast out, that old serpent, called the Devil, and Satan, which deceiveth the whole world: he was cast out into the earth, and his angels were cast out with him.
(Revelation 12: 9)

Spirit, by eclipsing Itself in cosmic delusion, appears as myriad ever-changing material phenomena. It is by this process, this malevolent delusive medium, that Spirit recreates Itself from the macrocosmic Infinitude to infinitesimal, microcosmic, almost unendingly divisible ions of energy.
(God Talks With Arjuna, page 446).

In his book 'The Second Coming of Christ', page 202, Yogananda, deviates momentarily from his interpretation of the New Testament to explain the process of creation outlined in Geneses 1: 1-9. He points out that Verse 2

And the earth was without form, and void

refers to what today's Enlightened Teachers call the **Causal World**, the ideational world holding the blueprints of creation: God's thought-plans; and, in the next stage, God sent forth Divine Light, the basic energy behind all matter, Verse 3,

And God said, Let there be light: and there was light.

Yogananda continues his explanation by explaining that God then separated or created a spiritual division between the Causal World and the realm of light energy, Verse 4,

> *and God divided the light from the darkness.*

and followed this by creating a 'firmament', Verse 6, a subtle, etheric, multidimensional screen upon which His play of creation was to be cast and made to appear real. This etheric layer also provided a barrier between the earthly realm and the heavens so that earth-bound souls could not see the heavenly realms and vice versa.

> *And God said, Let there be a firmament in the midst of the waters, and let it divide the waters from the waters.*

Verse 7 then records God dividing the Divine Light into two parts: the upper one being the subtler **Astral World** of light energy, and the lower being the grosser world of matter, the **Physical World**:

> *And God made the firmament, and divided the waters* (elemental energies) *which were under the firmament* (the Physical World) *from the waters which were above the firmament* (the Astral World)*: and it was so.*

In the New Testament, Jesus himself explicitly mentions these three main divisions. When referring to his coming resurrection he tells those demanding proof of his spiritual status that he will revive the temple of his crucified body back to life again in three 'days' or, rather, in three stages: physical, astral and causal.

> *Jesus answered and said unto them, Destroy this temple, and in three days, I will raise it up.*
> (John 2: 19)

Again, when Mary Magdalene saw Jesus' apparition outside the sepulchre after his crucifixion, the Bible records him asking her not to touch him because he had not yet completed his ascension through these three realms to God and back again.

> *Jesus sayeth unto her* (to Mary), *Touch me not; for I am not yet ascended to my Father: but go to my brethren* (to my disciples), *and say unto them, I ascend unto my Father, and your Father; and to my God, and your God.*
> (John 20: 17)

In the opening verses to his Gospel, St. John, the disciple who best understood the stature and teachings of his God-chosen Master, provides us with an informative insight into how God made these three realms of Creation:

> *In the beginning was the Word, and the Word was with God, and the Word was God. The same was in the beginning with God. All things were made by him; and without him was not any thing made that was made.*
> (John 1: 1-3)

This passage states that absolutely everything that exists in the Universe, including our human bodies and souls, has been created out of God's consciousness vibrated into energy waves (The Word). Clearly this act of creation differs in essence from that of a sculptor who takes a piece of clay and moulds it into a recognisable shape. The artist in the latter case creates a work of art out of something that is separate from himself, whereas St. John clearly says that God made everything directly out of Himself.

The above distinction is of vital importance when trying to understand the nature of creation and mankind. God is as much in the stone as He is in the plant, the animal and the human being, the only difference between each of these four categories is in the degree to which each is able to reflect or manifest its divinity; with man, the 'crown of creation', being the only one having the ability to manifest full divine potential.

The above biblical verses from Genesis and St. John also reveal the creative process of God. Firstly, the Divine Artist visualised the entire cosmos and its workings down to the last detail. This ideational schema or thought-plan became the Causal World. Next, the Lord vibrated His thought-consciousness into light energy so forming the Astral World. Finally He lowered the vibration even further to transform invisible energy into visible matter. It is interesting too to realise that man, created in the image of God, uses the same processes as the Creator when he creates. We begin by thinking (the Causal World of the process). We then input the energy of action into the system (the Astral World). Finally, the finished object appears (the Physical World of the process).

It is this apparent step-by-step creative process that has given rise to the concept of the Christian Trinity, expressed by Jesus in the following verse:

> *Go ye therefore, and teach all nations, baptising them in the name of the Father, and of the Son, and of the Holy Ghost.*
> (Matthew 28: 19)

Here we see, for reasons of theological understanding, the artificial division of the One Absolute God into God-the-Father, God-the-Son, and God-the-Holy Ghost. God-the-Father is infinite and not limited to Creation alone. Being infinite, He is not diminished or circumscribed by His involvement in Creation. God-the-Son, on the other hand, as God within Creation, is limited to Creation and is the intelligence that guides all things to comply with scientific laws. This God-force is called the 'Only Begotten Son of God' because it was the first-born manifestation of God when He conceived Creation and lies within the womb of Nature along with the Holy Ghost. The Holy Ghost is none other than the Word mentioned by St. John, the vibratory power out of which all matter is formed under the guidance of God as the Son. Other modern names for these forces are: Cosmic Consciousness (the Father), Christ Consciousness (the Son) and the Word (Holy Ghost).

The expression of God as three entities is not unique to Christianity. In the Bhagavad Gita the same Trinity is expressed as Sat, Tat, Aum. 'Sat' meaning Truth, God the Father of Creation; 'Tat' meaning That, the Son or Krishna Consciousness; and Aum is the Word, the vibratory power of God in Creation.

Another important point enjoying scriptural agreement is that God, being perfect, created a potentially flawless Universe

> *As for God, his way is perfect; the word of the Lord is tried: he is a buckler to all them that trust him.*
> (II Samuel 22: 31)

yet the world clearly is far from perfect in practice. Some contrary power is indisputably active.

> *O God, how long shall the adversary reproach? shall the enemy blaspheme thy name forever."*
> (Psalm 74: 10)

Enlightened Ones explain that as the Holy Ghost descended from God beyond Creation, its inherent God-perfection was 'reflected' in its purest form in the Causal and Astral Worlds but, when passing into the Physical World of matter, the Divine Creative Light of the Holy Ghost became corrupted or distorted by the Satanic Force of duality: the power that divides the One into many different forms. This is what Jesus was referring to when he said:

> *I beheld Satan as lightning fall from heaven;*
> (Luke 10: 18)

In the Gospel of St. John, Jesus fills in some extra details of this same force when referring to it as a murderer and a liar from the beginning of the world because of its ability to hide the One Truth behind a screen of illusion:

> *He* (Satan) *was a murderer from the beginning, and abode not in the truth, because there is no truth in him.*
> (John 8: 44)

The belief in a contrary force is by no means limited to Christianity. In Islam Satan, known as Iblis, is also presented as the personification of the cosmic macro-force in Creation that makes things appear to be separate from God. And similarly, in Hinduism, the same Satanic Force is called Maya, the hypnotic spell that hides God from the eyes of man and makes this world seem real and attractive.

Originally, the function of the Cosmic Satan was solely to make the Universe possible because it cannot exist without the One appearing as the multitude of different forms that we see around us. But Satan, having been given free will just as we humans have, rebelled against God and decided to use his considerable powers to keep mankind earthbound for as long as he could.

> *And moreover I saw under the sun* (under the power of the Divine Light) *the place of judgement, that wickedness was there* (that even though perfect judgement exists in the world, the Satanic Force was there too); *and the place of righteousness, that iniquity was there* (and that Righteousness and the Satanic Force came from the same source).
> (Ecclesiastes 3: 16)

This does not mean that Satan has power over God. The Creator could force the disaffected Satanic Power back into line if He so wished. Instead, He prefers to outwit Satan by using the Adversary's own powers against him. In the Divine Game of hide-and-seek, Satan has merely become an additional hurdle challenging our perception, persistence and courage in the struggle to discern Truth from illusion and find our way back to the Godhead. It is said by the saints that Satan sees only the material, angels see only the spiritual, but man lies in between these two extremes with the potential to see both.

There are several mentions in the Bible that God creates and destroys His Creation in repeated cycles,

> *And, Thou, Lord, in the beginning hast laid the foundation of the earth; and the heavens are the works of thine hands: They shall perish; but thou remainest; and they all shall wax old as doth a garment; And as a vesture shall thou fold them up, and they shall be changed: but thou art the same, and thy years shall not fail.*
> (Hebrews 1: 10-12)

a fact well known to the authors of India's most ancient scriptures called the Vedas, and common knowledge to all liberated Masters (God Talks With Arjuna, page 448).

The Masters also refer to the phenomena of 'partial dissolutions' wherein large events destroy parts of the earth or universe. The great flood of Noah's time would fall into this category as well as the sudden disappearance of solar systems when their stars turn into super novae. Less acknowledged perhaps is that, at the same time as this disintegration is going on, other solar systems are appearing in space seemingly out of nowhere.

It is the field of astronomy that the findings of modern day science are beginning to coincide most closely with teachings of the Enlightened Ones. In the last 50 years science has discovered that not only is the once inviolable law of the schoolroom 'matter cannot be created or destroyed' incorrect but also its successor 'energy cannot be created or destroyed' is a fallacy too. In fact by studying the comings and goings of stars and galaxies modern astronomers have come to the same conclusion as the ancient scriptures: matter and energy appear and disappear out of and into the void. But while the material scientist is still puzzling over the nature of this void, the spiritual scientist is aware that the origin and destination of all things is the Cosmic Consciousness of God.

What the Bible Says About the Nature of Creation.

All Creation is made out of God's consciousness. First of all He formed the Causal World of God-ideas, then the Astral World of energy as light and, finally, the gross Physical World of matter. To produce the diversity of realms and objects He divided His one consciousness into the Trinity and introduced the principle of separateness, Cosmic Satan.

Genesis 1: 1-9 Out of His one consciousness God formed the three worlds: Causal, Astral & Physical.

"*In the beginning God created the heaven and the earth.*

"*And the earth was without form, and void* (was pure creative consciousness, the Causal World); *and darkness was on the face of the deep* (only God's pure creative consciousness existed). *And the Spirit of God moved* (began to create) *upon the face of the waters* (using His fluid creative energies).

"*And God said* (sent out the primal energy of creation), *Let there be light: and there was light* (God manifested His creative vibratory Light out of which all energy and matter appeared).

"*And God saw the light, that it was good: and God divided the light* (divided His creative vibration, the basis for the Astral and Physical Worlds) *from the darkness* (from His pure creative consciousness, the Causal World).

"*And God called the light Day, and the darkness he called Night. And the evening and the morning were the first day* (the first stage leading to the manifestation of solid Creation).

"*And God said, Let there be a firmament* (an etheric screen) *in the midst of the waters* (creative forces), *and let it divide the waters from the waters* (let it hide the Astral World from the Physical).

"*And God made the firmament, and divided the waters which were under the firmament* (the Physical World) *from the waters which were above the firmament* (the Astral World): *and it was so.*

"*And God called the firmament Heaven* (the Astral World). *And the evening and morning were the second day* (the second stage leading to manifested Creation).

"And God said, Let the waters (creative energies) *under the heaven be gathered together unto one place* (the Physical World), *and let the dry land appear: and it was so."*

II Samuel 22: 31 Since God is perfect His Creation must be perfect also.
"As for God, his way is perfect; the word of the Lord is tried: he is a buckler to all them that trust in him."

Psalm 74: 10 The prophet understands that the work of Cosmic Satan is to 'split' the Name into many forms.
"O God, how long shall the adversary reproach? shall the enemy blaspheme thy name forever (for how long shall the satanic force of Duality divide the One Consciousness into the many different material forms that make up Creation).*"* See the section called 'The Word' for the meaning of 'name'.

Proverbs 3: 19 The Lord made the astral heavens and the physical earth out of His wisdom and understanding.
"The Lord by wisdom hath founded the earth; by understanding hath he established the heavens." Wisdom and understanding are qualities inherent in the Christ Consciousness.

Proverbs 16: 4 All Creation is God's play. He even created Satan and the temptations of the world.
"The Lord hath made all things for himself: yea, even the wicked for the day of evil."

Proverbs 25: 2 Though God conceals Himself behind the diversity of His Creation, pure souls find Him.
"It is the glory of God to conceal a thing: but the honour of kings (kingly souls) *is to search out a matter* (to discover the way back to Him).*"*

Ecclesiastes 3: 11 & 16 Cosmic Satan and desires are endemic in an otherwise perfect world.
"He (God) *hath made every thing beautiful in his time: also he hath set the world in their heart* (created worldly desires), *so that no man can find out the work that God maketh from the beginning to the end* (so that the Truth is hidden from those who fall prey to desire).*"*
"And moreover I saw under the sun (under the power of the Divine

Light) *the place of judgement, that wickedness was there* (that even though perfect judgement exists in the world, the Satanic Force is there too); *and the place of righteousness, that iniquity was there* (and that Righteousness and the Satanic Force come from the same source)."

Ecclesiastes 3: 14 God's actions last forever and are complete in every way.
"I know that, whatsoever God doeth, it shall be forever: nothing can be put (added) *to it, nor can anything be taken* (removed) *from it: and God doeth it, that men should fear* (be in awe) *before him."*

Isaiah 45: 7 The Lord says that both good and evil emerge from His One Consciousness.
"I form the light, and create darkness: I make peace, and create evil: I the Lord do all these things."

Isaiah 60: 2 The Lord talks to Isaiah about the temporary influence of Cosmic Satan and ignorance in man.
"For, behold, the darkness shall cover the earth (the delusive force of Duality, the Cosmic Satan, will cover the world in spiritual darkness), *and gross darkness the people* (gross individual ignorance will affect the people): *but the Lord shall arise upon thee, and his glory shall be seen upon thee* (but God will manifest Himself to you and will be your Saviour)."

Apocrypha, The Wisdom of Solomon 12: 1 Creation is potentially pure in spite of the Cosmic Satan.
"For thine incorruptible spirit is in all things."

Matthew 28: 19 Jesus identifies the Trinity, listing them in order of descent of Spirit into matter.
"Go ye therefore, and teach all nations, baptising (initiating) *them in the name of the Father, and of the Son, and of the Holy Ghost* (giving them the Holy Vibration and the Divine Light):" See the sections on 'The Word' and 'The Divine Light' for details of the Holy Ghost, and the section called 'Initiation into the Path' for the meaning of baptism.

Luke 10: 18 Jesus refers to the Satanic Power that distorts God's perfect Creation, hiding the One behind the many.
"And he (Jesus) *said unto them, I beheld Satan as lightning fall from*

heaven (descending from the heavenly causal and astral realms to distort the pure power of the Holy Ghost manifesting in the physical realm)."

John 1: 1-3 St. John identifies the Word of God as the origin of all Creation.
"In the beginning was the Word, and the Word was with God, and the Word was God.
"The same was in the beginning with God.
"All things were made by him; and without him was not any thing made that was made." See the section on 'The Word' for the meaning of the Word in the above context. 'Word' is one of the many different terms used by the saints to describe the Holy Ghost.

John 1: 10 The Ultimate Unity of the Godhead remains hidden behind the multiplicity of forms in creation.
"He (God) *was in the world, and the world was made by him, and the world knew him not."*

John 1: 14 The Holy Ghost is the basis of matter and is directed intelligently by the Christ Consciousness.
"And the Word (the Holy Ghost) *was made flesh* (into matter), *and dwelt among us* (exists in the midst of us as matter), *and we beheld his glory* (we marvelled at God's creation), *the glory of the only begotten of the Father* (the glory of the Christ Consciousness), *full of grace and truth."* See the section on 'The Word' for the meaning of the 'Holy Ghost'.

John 2: 19 Jesus refers to the importance of the three worlds in resurrecting his body.
"Jesus answered and said unto them (those demanding proof of his spiritual status), *Destroy this temple* (my body, the temple of God), *and in three days* (in three stages: causal, astral and physical), *I will raise it up* (I will resurrect it)."

John 3: 35 God is the origin beyond creation and the Son is the guiding power of God in Creation.
"The Father loveth the Son (Cosmic Consciousness is Love and therefore loves Himself as the Christ Consciousness, His offspring), *and hath given all things into his hand* (and the Son, the Christ

Consciousness, is the intelligent guiding force of God within Creation)."

John 5: 26 Jesus spells out clearly that God is life and has given life to the Christ Consciousness.
"For the Father hath life in himself (God as the Absolute Father beyond Creation is the source of life and law); *so hath he given to the Son to have life in himself* (and this life and the associated laws appear within Creation through the agency of God as the Son, the Christ Consciousness);"

John 8: 44 Cosmic Delusion is the father of our imperfections and prevents us from recognising Great Souls.
"Ye (those seeking to kill me, Jesus) *are of your father the devil* (the cosmic principle of delusion), *and the lusts* (the power of attachment to material things) *of your father ye will do. He* (Cosmic Satan) *was a murderer* (of spiritual perceptions) *from the beginning* (from the moment Creation was made), *and abode not in the truth* (created the illusion of separate forms in God's one consciousness), *because there is no truth in him* (he is an unchanging, in-built cosmic lie). *When he speaketh a lie, he speaketh of his own* (he is the father of the lie that solid matter is the only reality): *for he is a liar, and the father of it* (for the principle of Duality is inherent in the Cosmic Satan and therefore is an endemic part of Creation itself)."

John 14: 2 Jesus refers to the Astral Heavens and its many vibrational divisions.
"In my Father's house (in the heavenly realms above this earth) *are many mansions* (are many different levels of vibration): *if it were not so, I would have told you. I go to prepare a place for you."* See the section on 'The Captivity' for further details of the function of the different vibrational levels in the Astral World.

John 20: 17 Jesus resurrected his body in three phases: physical, astral and causal.
"Jesus sayeth unto her (Mary), *Touch me not; for I am not yet ascended to my Father* (I have not yet raised myself through the three stages, physical, astral and causal, necessary to be united to Cosmic Consciousness): *but go to my brethren* (to my disciples), *and say unto them, I ascend unto my Father, and your Father* (I am

going into Cosmic Consciousness); *and to my God, and your God."*
See also John 2: 19 quoted earlier in this section.

Hebrews 1: 10-12 The unchanging God makes and destroys Creation in cycles.
"And, Thou, Lord, in the beginning hast laid the foundation of the earth; and the heavens are the works of thine hands:
"They shall perish; but thou remainest (You are everlasting and do not change); *and they all shall wax old as doth a garment;*
"And as a vesture shalt thou fold them up (You will 'roll up' the heavens and the earth when the time comes), *and they shall be changed: but thou art the same, and thy years shall not fail."* See also Psalm 102: 25-28 which is almost identical to St. Paul's version above.

Revelation 12: 9 Satan, the principle of cosmic duality, was 'cast down' into the world at the time of Creation.
"And the great dragon was cast out, that old serpent, called the Devil, and Satan, which deceiveth the whole world: he was cast out into the earth, and his angels (supporting energetic forces) *were cast out with him."*

4

The Captivity.

Awake, awake, stand up, O Jerusalem, which hast drunk at the hand of the Lord the cup of his fury; thou hast drunken the dregs of the cup of trembling, and wrung them out.
(Isaiah 51: 17)

As long as the body's storehouse
Abounds with the hoard
Of lust and anger,
Of ego and greed,
The learned and the lout
Are no doubt the same.
(Kabir, 15th century Muslim saint)

Though the Satanic Force creates duality and the temptations of the world, mankind has free will and can choose whether to be fooled or not. Adam, the archetypal man, fell from Grace as soon as he chose not to be guided by the voice of God within him and began to see the world as an independent reality separate from his Lord.

When man chooses to believe that the world he is experiencing with his senses is the ultimate reality, he is said to be living in ignorance. Enlightened Ones also refer to this state variously as 'death', 'darkness', 'sleep' or 'dreaming' and constantly call on humanity to Wake up! Wake up! In the Vedas of India this condition is called 'avidya' meaning individual delusion. It is this individual delusion that creates ego as the pseudo-soul. Under the thrall of the vanity of the ego, the 'silent voice of spirit' within man is eclipsed and he begins to think of himself only as a bodily instrument. Thus, King Solomon wryly observes:

> *Surely vain are all men by nature, who are ignorant of God, and could not out of the good things that are seen know him that is: neither by considering the works did they acknowledge the workmaster;*
> (Book of Apocrypha, The Wisdom of Solomon 13: 1)

Immediately an incarnate being turns away from Spirit to matter, a wide array of temptations come into view. The world is full of attractions, each promising that much sought after property of permanent happiness. Attractions give rise to desires, thwarted desires give rise to anger and anger destroys judgement. It is largely because of the combination of these three 'enemies' of man that his soul becomes shrouded in ignorance and he loses his awareness of his real nature. Somewhere during our journey through life we should take time to calmly analyse the world and realise that it never, ever, fulfils its promises.

That the prophets of old were aware of this connection between desire, anger and ignorance is quite evident. In Ecclesiastes the Preacher points out that desires hide God from us,

> *He* (God) *hath made every thing beautiful in his time: also he hath set the world in their heart* (created desires), *so that no man can find out the work that God maketh from the beginning to the end.*
> (Ecclesiastes 3: 11)

and Solomon clearly agrees, pointing out that anger from thwarted desires leads to further errors in judgement:

> *An angry man stirreth up strife, and a furious man aboundeth in transgression.*
> (Proverbs 29: 22)

Solomon was also aware, however, of the irony that it is these same desires, when constantly thwarted, that eventually lead many of us to question the reality of the world:

> *Through desire a man, having separated himself* (from God), *seeketh and intermeddleth with all wisdom* (seeks to unite with God: the Source of wisdom).
> (Proverbs 18: 1)

Transgressions against the perfection of the Spirit within us are what the Buddhists and Hindus call 'karma'. Karma actually means action, which can be either good or bad depending on the quality of the action. Every schoolboy is aware of this law as Newton's Third Law of Motion which states 'to every action there is a reaction which is equal and in the opposite direction to that action'. But in actuality the extent of this law is not confined to mere motion. In spiritual circles the Law of Karma, meaning the unbroken chain of cause and effect, is recognised as one of the most important laws governing life, extending to man's every thought, word and deed.

Thought is the most important part of this cause-effect chain for it is the root of action. No action can take place without a thought behind it. Jesus emphasised the importance of thought as a karma-producing factor when he said:

> *Ye have heard that it was said by them of old time, Thou shalt not commit adultery: But I say unto you, That whosoever looketh on a woman to lust after her hath committed adultery with her already in his heart.*
> (Matthew 5: 27 & 28)

Karmas represent the debts man owes to the world through his egotistical actions. These debts can be incurred by individual action, or by the collective actions of groups, governments and nations. The world population in general collects what are called 'world karmas'. These are global in nature such as changes in world climate as a result of widespread pollution of the atmosphere, and world wars.

The Enlightened Ones tell us that man cannot escape from this material sphere and go back to the Godhead until he has paid off all these debts and is abiding by the laws of healthful living, moral behaviour and engaging in spiritual practices under the guidance of an Enlightened Teacher.

It is important for those on the spiritual path not to view the Law of Karma in a totally negative light: solely as a means by which God punishes mankind. Far from being solely punitive in intention, this law has been created out of Divine Love with the express purpose of guiding mankind on to the right track so that he can eventually reach 'the peace that passeth all understanding' (Philippians 4: 7).

> *My son, despise not the chastening of the Lord; neither be weary of his correction: For whom the Lord loveth he correcteth; even as a father the son in whom he delighteth.*
> (Proverbs 3: 11 & 12)

Being such an important law it is not surprising that the Bible abounds with references to it, with the first unambiguous reference to karmic law appearing early in the book of Genesis:

> *Whoso sheddeth man's blood, by man shall his blood be shed: for in the image of God made he man.*
> (Genesis 9: 6)

with further clear expositions being provided by biblical prophets and saints in the form of sayings concerning 'sowing and reaping':

> *They* (the enemies of the Lord) *have sown wheat, but shall reap thorns:*
> (Jeremiah 12: 13)

> *Be not deceived; God is not mocked: for whatsoever a man soweth, that shall he also reap.*
> (Galatians 6: 7)

an analogy favoured by many of the saints of other cultures:

> *Whatever thou hast sown,*
> *the same shalt thou reap;*
> *No change in it shall there be.*
> *Throw aside the rubbish,*
> *And devote thyself to the Lord's Holy Feet;*
> *Thy cycle of birth and death shall cease for thee.*
> (Guru Ravidas, 15th century Indian saint)

It is apparent also that the Old Testament prophets were referring to this law every time they warned the people to 'fear the Lord' as shown by the considerable number of biblical quotations given at the end of this section. Clearly the prophets could not have been suggesting that mankind should 'fear' the Divine Father since He is the embodiment of Love. But there is every good reason for man to fear a law that hides from him his immortality in God and binds him to mortal limitation. In fact the prophetic abilities of the Old Testament 'Seers' was due to the fact that they understood karmic law and could foresee the good and evil effects arising from the good and bad actions of the Israelites, a talent that all Enlightened Ones share even today.

Recognition of the Law of Karma does not in any way suggest that a lack of compassion should be shown to sufferers. We are all suffering, some more obviously than others. It is wise to keep in mind that where the obvious sufferer 'stands' we also have stood before and, depending on the quality of our present actions, might well be as unfortunate in future. Also the Law of Karma warns that those who are not compassionate to the suffering of others will reap an appropriate 'reward'.

Mankind is also advised throughout the Bible not to seek revenge for perceived or real crimes committed against him. The saints and prophets have stated many times in the clearest terms that vengeance is the prerogative of the Lord through Karmic Law.

> *Dearly beloved, avenge not yourselves, but rather give*
> *place unto wrath: for it is written, Vengeance is mine; I*

will repay, saith the Lord.
                (Romans 12: 19)

This is not to say that man should not seek redress for wrongs done to him. Saints say quite definitely that man should seek justice through the courts, but without a mind tainted by the sickness of revenge, because holding such corrosive feelings does much harm to one's own body, mind and soul. Victims of felonies should keep in mind that, even if the perpetrator escapes man's justice, he cannot escape God's justice enacted through the Law of Karma.

It is important to realise too that karma is not a fatalistic philosophy but one of hope. Bad actions certainly bring suffering but good ones bring just rewards. By using free will wisely, anyone can avoid doing bad actions and choose to perform good ones. By performing actions that help others and are beneficial spiritually, people can carve out bright futures for themselves. The message of the Enlightened Ones is that Fate is not blind or random. Our future is firmly in our own hands.

Throughout his lifetime, moment by moment, man is paying off some of his accrued karmic debts in the form of the types and frequency of the events he currently experiences; while at the same time adding to his store of debt by the quality of his responses to those events. If his motives are self-centred, as are those of most people, then his store of debt will be increasing every second and, during the 70 or 80 years of his life, he will have amassed an enormous debt far too great to pay off in any one lifetime. Inevitably it requires many lifetimes for man to learn how to stop creating adverse karmas and, in addition, pay off his store of accumulated ones.

It follows therefore that the natural twin of the Law of Karma is that of Reincarnation. Enlightened Teachers point out that the Law of Reincarnation was formulated by the Creator to ensure that perfect justice can be carried out: that the Law of Karma can be satisfied. If the two-fold Laws of Karma and Reincarnation did not exist how could the death of a young child be justified or how could one explain the fact that many cruel dictators live their entire lives in luxury? In the former case, the seemingly premature death of the child flowed from its actions in a previous lifetime and, in the latter case, the despot is surely due to reap his just reward in a future incarnation. The smooth operation of a just world designed by a perfect Creator hangs on these two laws.

The fact that the Bible is full of direct and indirect references to the Law of Karma has been discussed already but the relative paucity of explicit references to reincarnation needs some explanation. Though historical documents show that many Christian sects (including the Essenes, Copts and Gnostics) and many early Christian theologians (such as Alexandria, Origen and St. Jerome) accepted reincarnation as a valid teaching, the subject fell into disfavour during the fourth and fifth centuries AD, and was finally declared heretical at the Second Council of Constantinople in AD 553. This high-handed decision not only affected the content of the Bible in later years but official Church doctrine too, since anyone foolish enough to teach this subject was thereafter in danger of being burnt at the stake, or worse.

Fortunately, in spite of this severe censorship of scriptural material within the corridors of Christian orthodoxy, several pertinent references to reincarnation have managed to slip through the net. Naturally, these are ones that could most easily be explained by the early church in other ways. However, the truth cannot be hidden forever and more and more Christians are digging up the evidence and revisiting the subject with renewed interest.

Perhaps the most direct biblical reference to reincarnation occurs in the case of the prophesy of the coming of John the Baptist. At the very end of the Old Testament the Lord promises, through one of his prophets, that:

> *Behold, I will send you Elijah the prophet before the coming of the great and dreadful day of the Lord.*
> (Malachi 4: 5)

and, in Matthew, Jesus states unequivocally that John the Baptist was none other than the great prophet Elijah in his last life:

> *And if ye will receive it, this* (John the Baptist) *is Elias* (Elijah), *which was for to come* (whose reincarnation

was forecast by the prophets).
(Matthew 11: 14)

That reincarnation was a general teaching in Jesus' world is reflected in the following conversation recorded between the Master and his disciples:

> *When Jesus came into the coasts of Caesarea Philippi, he asked his disciples, saying, Whom do men say that I the Son of man am? And they said, Some say that thou art John the Baptist: some, Elias* (Elijah)*; and others, Jeremias* (Jeremiah)*, or one of the prophets.*
> (Matthew 16: 13 & 14)

It is hard to imagine a discussion of this nature ever taking place if reincarnation had not been a common belief of the times.

Then there are several recorded instances where Jesus, having healed people suffering from infirmities since birth, advised them to 'go their way and sin no more', a situation that can be adequately explained only if Jesus recognised reincarnation and karma as fact. Clearly Jesus knew that these unfortunates were suffering as a result of their sins (karmas) of past lifetimes. They could hardly have sinned in the womb.

In this context, the following conversation between Jesus and his disciples on the occasion the Master healed a man blind from birth is particularly illuminating:

> *And as Jesus passed by, he saw a man which was blind from his birth. And his disciples asked him, saying, Master, who did sin, this man* (in a previous lifetime)*, or his parents* (in this lifetime before the child was born)*, that he was born blind? Jesus answered, Neither hath this man sinned, nor his parents* (neither have sinned in this lifetime)*: but that the works of God should be made manifest in him* (but the blind man has enough good

karma to allow me to heal him through the power of God in me).
(John 9: 1-3)

And Jesus was clearly referring to the principle of reincarnation when he said:

And no man hath ascended up to heaven, but he that came down from heaven (no one has gone up into the astral heavens without first having come down from there to earth), *even the Son of man which is in heaven* (this applies to all unenlightened people).
(John 3: 13)

Again, the book of Revelation makes reference to the principle of reincarnation when describing how to reach immortality in Spirit:

Him that overcometh (overcomes the delusion of separateness imposed by Cosmic Satan and his spiritual ignorance) *will I make a pillar of the temple of my God, and he shall go no more out* (need incarnate into the world no more):
(Revelation 3: 12)

The content of the above sayings also infers that man's soul remains captive in the world until he stops creating new karmas and pays back all of his accumulated karmic debts; a principle Jesus also refers to in Matthew:

Agree with thine adversary quickly, whiles thou art in the way with him (harmonise your behaviour with God's law of right thoughts, words, and deeds as quickly as you can); *lest at any time the adversary* (your wrong behaviour) *deliver thee to the judge* (deliver you to Karmic Law that 'judges' every man), *and the judge deliver thee to the officer* (and your bad karma gives rise to individual delusive ignorance), *and thou be cast into prison* (with

The Truth Seeker's Guide to the Bible

the result that you become doomed to returning time and again to this worldly prison of suffering). *Verily I say unto thee, Thou shalt by no means come out thence, till thou hast paid the uttermost farthing* (You will not escape from this world until you have paid off all your worldly dues down to the smallest item).
(Matthew 5: 25 & 26)

The fact that errant man remains captive in the world of gross matter until he has paid off all his karmic debts was well known to the Old Testament prophets. In the following verse the prophet Isaiah describes how God has sent him to help those fit for the spiritual path (the ego-less, or meek, who are mourning after their lost soul-state) to release themselves from captivity (the recurrent cycles of birth, death and rebirth):

The Spirit of the Lord God is upon me; because the Lord hath anointed me to preach good tidings unto the meek; he hath sent me to bind up the broken hearted, to proclaim liberty to the captives, and the opening of the prison to them that are bound;
(Isaiah 61: 1)

The world's great saints explain that when the body dies, it is left behind in the material world where it disintegrates back into its basic mineral constituents (dust to dust); but the more refined astral body of man 'ascends' into the Astral World (the heavens) where it resides until all its 'good' karmas are spent. When that point is reached, latent earthly desires then become strong enough to pull the soul back into a new birth so that those desires can be worked out. Thus, 'the departed' are only temporary residents of the Astral Heavens and remain captives of their earthly 'sowing and reaping'.

The saints explain that the Astral World has been designed by the Creator with many different vibrational levels to accommodate 'prisoners' of all kinds, from those with relatively good characters to those with distinctly evil natures. At bodily death, evil people are drawn to the lower astral levels, called hell, while those who have made some progress on the Path to God rise to the higher 'heavenly' levels.

In one of his final addresses to his disciples, Jesus gives them an enticing glimpse of these astral levels when he assures them of the many mansions in his Father's house and that he, as their Master, will lead them to their earned level when they have left their mortal bodies.

> *In my Father's house are many mansions: if it were not so, I would have told you. I go to prepare a place for you.*
>
> (John 14: 2)

In view of the necessary existence of the Laws of Karma and Reincarnation in making sense of the world, for perfect justice could not exist without both of them, it is a great pity that Christians have been denied access to this most important spiritual knowledge.

Should man but understand fully the implications of these two divine laws, he would think more carefully about his everyday thoughts, words and actions. People spend hours, days, weeks, cheating others, fiddling tax forms, falsifying claims, backbiting and cutting the heads off others to make themselves look taller. And, ironically, after engaging in all this duplicity the same people continue to wonder why they are unhappy, have no real friends and end their lives in solitary misery and, very often, in poverty. The teachings of the saints reveal that such people are the victims of their own actions, a legacy earned through the combined laws of Karma and Reincarnation. Justice is perfect and complete. No one can escape it.

An understanding of these two spiritual laws would bring the currently much-needed realisation that peace can only be reached through compassion and understanding and not by violence in any form (thoughts, words, or deeds). According to the Law of Karma, like attracts like. To use violence as a means to an end merely generates more violence. Such knowledge would not only radically alter our thought patterns, behaviour, and view of the world, but also entirely change our ideas concerning the real nature of captivity and freedom.

What the Bible Says About Karma & Reincarnation.

All the scriptures of the world declare that the Creator is a God of perfect justice. Perfect justice cannot exist either in the world or beyond it without the Laws of Karma and Reincarnation. Man imprisons himself in the world through making wrong choices and can equally earn freedom for his soul through making right ones.

Genesis 9: 6 God spells out the Law of Karma to Noah in simple terms: like brings like.
"Whoso sheddeth man's blood, by man shall his blood be shed: for in the image of God made he man."

Exodus 21: 23-25 The Lord spells out to Moses the Law of Karma in its simplest form.
"And if any mischief follow, then thou shalt give life for life,
"Eye for eye, tooth for tooth, hand for hand, foot for foot,
"Burning for burning, wound for wound, stripe for stripe."

Deuteronomy 2: 15 The 'hand of the Lord' often refers to good and bad karma.
"For indeed the hand of the Lord was against them, to destroy them from among the host, until they were consumed."

I Samuel 2: 3 Hannah says beware of pride and arrogance because of the Lord's Law of Karma.
"Talk no more so exceedingly proudly; let not arrogancy come out of your mouth: for the Lord is a God of knowledge, and by him actions are weighed (actions are judged through the Law of Karma).*"*

II Samuel 22: 21 David records that the Lord, through the Law of Karma, has rewarded his good actions.

"The Lord rewarded me according to my righteousness: according to the cleanness of my hands (lack of sin) *hath he recompensed me."*

II Kings 2: 23 & 24 In this apparently cruel story of the bear tearing up the children when they teased the prophet Elisha, the fate of these little ones was not brought upon them by the will of Elisha; far from it! A man of God would not wish such a thing on anyone. The 'curse' came naturally through the ripening of the karma of the children resulting from many past-life actions. Their confrontation with the man of God was merely the last straw, the event that caused their past karmas to ripen at that particular moment. See The Second Coming of Christ, pages 72 & 73, for further details.

Job 1: 6-12 These verses encapsulate the function of the Cosmic Satanic Principle that creates the illusion of multiple forms out of the One Consciousness so that the play of creation can take place. At the same time this force clouds humankind's ability to see The One In All. The Book of Job also covers the principle of Individual Delusion which deflects man's consciousness from God to the trinkets of this world which he then chases with seemingly undiminished zeal.

Job 2: 10 In spite of his severe trials Job reminds his disbelieving wife of God's karmic law.

"But he said unto her (Job said to his wife), *Thou speakest as one of the foolish women speakest. What? shall we receive good at the hand of God, and shall we not receive evil* (if we receive good from God then mustn't we also receive evil from the same source)? *In all this did not Job sin with his lips* (his words were true)."

Job 19: 21 & 22 Job laments that karmic law is played out through our close associates in addition to other means.

"Have pity upon me, have pity upon me, O ye my friends; for the hand of God hath touched me.

"Why do ye persecute me as God, and are not satisfied with my flesh (Why do you, my friends, as God's unwitting agents, persecute me through the workings of the Law of Karma. Are you not satisfied that all my worldly possessions have been taken from me)?"

Job 37: 23 No one can escape God's perfect justice meted out by the Law of Causation or Karma.

"Touching the Almighty, we cannot find him out: he is excellent in power, and in judgement, and in plenty of justice: he will not afflict (He will not punish those who do not deserve it)."

Psalm 7: 8 & 11 God's Law of Karma ensures that we receive like for like.
"The Lord shall judge the people: judge me, O Lord, according to my righteousness, and according to mine integrity that is in me."
"God judgeth the righteous, and God is angry with the wicked every day (no action escapes its due reward).*"*

Psalm 7: 12 Karmic law is likened to a sharp sword or to an arrow fired from a bow.
"If he (the wicked) *turn not* (does not turn towards God*), he* (God) *will whet his sword* (the Law of Karma)*; he hath bent his bow, and made it ready* (He is ready to fire His shafts of justice).*"*

Psalm 7: 16 David laconically observes that the actions of the wicked automatically rebound upon them.
"His mischief shall return upon his own head, and his violent dealing shall come down upon his own pate."

Psalm 8: 2 David acknowledges the cause of karma to be the ego-mind.
"Out of the mouth of babes and sucklings (the innocent and humble) *has thou ordained strength because of thine enemies* (have You given the strength to overcome their ego–filled tendencies)*, that thou mightest still the enemy* (calm the mind) *and the avenger* (and keep the Law of Karma at bay).*"*

Psalm 33: 4 David acknowledges that perfect justice reigns in the world.
"For the word of the Lord is right; and all his works are done in truth (the Law of Karma ensures perfect justice).*"* See the section on 'The Word' for the meaning of 'word'.

Psalm 52: 7 Man deludes himself into thinking that his riches will protect him and be lasting.
"Lo, this is the man that made not God his strength; but trusted in the abundance of his riches, and strengthened himself in his wickedness."

Psalm 75: 7 & 8 Even the positions we hold in society are governed by our karmas.
"But God is the judge: he putteth down one, and setteth up another.
"For in the hand of the Lord is a cup (karmic law)*, and the wine is red* (it is active)*; it is full of mixture* (made up of good and evil

actions); *and he poureth out of the same* (and through its operation God dispenses justice): *but the dregs thereof, all the wicked of the earth shall wring them out, and drink them* (no one can escape its effects)."

Psalm 118: 15 David rejoices in the fact that right actions in harmony with divine law are rewarded.

"The voice of rejoicing and salvation is in the tabernacles of the righteous (the bodies of the devotees of God): *the right hand of the Lord* (karmic justice) *doeth valiantly."* See the section on 'The Word' for the meaning of 'the voice of rejoicing and salvation'.

Proverbs 1: 29-31 Those who take no notice of karmic law suffer the fruits of their own actions.

"For that they hated knowledge (spiritual truths), *and did not choose the fear of the Lord* (did not live in awe of God's karmic law):

"They would none of my council (would not listen to good advice): *they despised all my reproof.*

"Therefore shall they eat of the fruit of their own way, and be filled with their own devices (therefore they will suffer the inevitable consequences)."

Proverbs 3: 11 & 12 God formed the Law of Karma out of love to guide His children back to Him.

"My son, despise not the chastening of the Lord; neither be weary of his correction:

"For whom the Lord loveth he correcteth; even as a father the son in whom he delighteth."

Proverbs 11: 18 & 19 Through the Law of Karma, evil brings evil upon the doer and good brings good.

"The wicked worketh a deceitful work: but to him that soweth righteousness shall be a sure reward.

"As righteousness tendeth to life (Just as right behaviour attracts Eternal Life or Enlightenment): *so he that pursueth evil pursueth it to his own death* (so evil behaviour brings spiritual death, ignorance of our real nature)."

Proverbs 11: 23 The righteous desire only to do good but the wicked can expect the wrath of the Law of Karma.

"The desire of the righteous is only good: but the expectation of the wicked is wrath."

Proverbs 15: 33 Fear of the Lord's Law of Karma drives man to seek wisdom and humility.

"The fear of the Lord (God's Law of Karma) *is the instruction of wisdom; and before honour is humility."*

Proverbs 16: 6 By Grace and association with Divine Truth, bad karma is destroyed.

"By mercy and truth iniquity (evil karma) *is purged: and by the fear of the Lord* (by fear of the Lord's Law of Karma) *men depart from evil."*

Proverbs 18: 1 Desires separate man from God and this drives him to seek God again.

"Through desire a man, having separated himself (from God), *seeketh and intermeddleth* (unites or becomes inseparable) *with all wisdom."*

Proverbs 25: 21 & 22 Karmic Law rewards good deeds and punishes unspiritual ones.

"If thine enemy be hungry, give him bread to eat (feed him); *and if he be thirsty, give him water to drink:*

"For thou shalt heap coals of fire upon his head (If he remains an enemy in spite of your kindness he will fall foul of the Law of Karma), *and the Lord shall reward thee* (but God, through the same law, will see to it that your kindness is rewarded)."

Proverbs 26: 10 Solomon speaks of the Law of Karma: What ye sow so shall ye reap.

"The great God that formed all things both rewardeth the fool, and rewardeth transgressors."

Proverbs 29: 22 Anger leads to confusion and to errors that bind man to material consciousness.

"An angry man stirreth up strife, and a furious man aboundeth in transgression."

Ecclesiastes 2: 24 The Preacher understands that good things also come through the Law of Karma.

"There is nothing better for a man, than that he should eat and drink (keep his body healthy), *and that he should make his soul enjoy good in his labour* (enjoy the good things that come from good actions). *This also I saw, that it was from the hand of God* (that good things also come through God's Law of Karma)."

Ecclesiastes 3: 11 & 16 Desires arising out of the Satanic Force obscure man's perception of God.

"He (God) *hath made every thing beautiful in his time: also he hath set the world in their heart* (created desires), *so that no man can find out the work that God maketh from the beginning to the end* (desires hide God from mans' perceptions)."

"And moreover I saw under the sun the place of judgement, that wickedness was there; and the place of righteousness, that iniquity was there (I saw that the 'sun' of the Divine Creative Light held the seeds of both good and evil, and justice through Karmic Law)." See the section on the 'Divine Light' for the meaning of 'under the sun'.

Ecclesiastes 9: 1 The Preacher dips into the causes behind the way we act.

"For all this I considered in my heart even to declare all this, that the righteous, and the wise, and their works, are in the hand of God (Man's good qualities come from God through the Law of Karma): *no man knoweth either love or hatred by all that is before them* (The love and hatred we feel come from our past actions and not intrinsically from the events we are faced with at the time)."

Ecclesiastes 12: 13 & 14 The Preacher warns us to follow the Divine Laws governing Creation.

"Let us hear the conclusion of the whole matter: Fear God, and keep his commandments (Live according to God's Laws): *for this is the whole duty of man.*

"For God shall bring every work into judgement, with every secret thing, whether it be good, or whether it be evil (the Law of Karma is exact and no one and no thing can escape it)."

Isaiah 2: 3 The Law of Karma and the Holy Ghost come out of the Cosmic Consciousness of God.

"...for out of Zion shall go forth the law (the Law of Karma), *and the word of the Lord from Jerusalem."* See the section on 'The Higher Spiritual Centres' for the meaning of 'Zion' and 'Jerusalem'; and the section on 'The Word' for the meaning of 'word of the Lord'.

Isaiah 5: 11-13 A life violating the divine laws of health binds us to the earth.

"Woe unto them that rise up early in the morning, that they may follow strong drink; that continue until night, till wine inflame them!

"And the harp, and the viol, the tabret, and pipe, and wine, are in their feasts: but they regard not the work of the Lord, neither consider the operation of his hands (nor understand the workings of the Law of Karma).

"Therefore my people are gone into captivity (are imprisoned into the cycle of birth, death, and rebirth), *because they have no knowledge* (because they have not been given the knowledge of how to escape the laws of Karma and Reincarnation): *and their honourable men are famished, and their multitude dried up with thirst* (for they are without the spiritual nourishment that would have satisfied them)." See the section on 'What is Knowledge?' for the way to escape from captivity and the meaning of 'knowledge'.

Isaiah 5: 24 Isaiah points out that lack of spirituality leads to individual ignorance and its consequences.

"Therefore as the fire devoureth the stubble, and the flame consumeth the chaff, so their root shall be as rotteness, and their blossom go up as dust: because they have cast away the law of the Lord of host (have disregarded the Law of Karma), *and despise the word of the Holy One of Israel* (sneer at the teachings about the Holy Ghost or Word)." See the section on 'The Word' for the meaning of 'word'.

Isaiah 29: 15 Ignorant people think they can hide their evil deeds and not be punished for them.

"Woe unto them that seek deep to hide their council from the Lord, and their works are in the dark, and they say, Who seeth us? And who knoweth us?"

Isaiah 30: 27 The Holy Name carries within it the Law of Karma that punishes wrong doers.

"Behold, the name of the Lord cometh from far (the Holy Name comes from God beyond Creation), *burning with his anger* (burning with His Law of Karma), *and the burden thereof is heavy: his lips are full of indignation, and his tongue as a devouring fire* (it wreaks havoc on the wicked)." See the section on 'The Word' for the meaning of the 'name of the Lord' in the above verse.

Isaiah 51: 17 God talks to His children through the prophet Isaiah: Wake up to Law of Karma!

"Awake, awake, stand up, O Jerusalem, which hast drunk at the hand of the Lord the cup of his fury (experienced the Law of Karma); *thou hast drunken the dregs of the cup of trembling, and wrung them out* (haven't you learned from your errors?)."

Isaiah 52: 2 & 3 Trapped in the cycles of repeated incarnations by karmic law, man needs to seek God.

"Shake thyself from the dust (escape from the evil of the world); *arise, and sit down, O Jerusalem: Loose thyself from the bands of thy neck* (free yourself from karmic ties that keep you returning to the world like slaves), *O captive daughter of Zion* (O you people imprisoned by your own ignorance and not claiming your true spiritual estate).

"For thus saith the Lord, Ye have sold yourselves for nought (you have sold your souls for nothing and will gain nothing worthwhile): *and ye shall be redeemed without money* (the Path of redemption costs nothing and you will realise that, in reality, you have had to give up nothing to attain enlightenment)." See the section on 'Meditation' for the meaning of 'sit down'.

Isaiah 61: 1 Isaiah declares his Godly duty to be to free people from the Law of Karma that holds them captive.

"The Spirit of the Lord God is upon me; because the Lord hath anointed me to preach good tidings unto the meek (God has asked me to redeem the non-violent of character); *he hath sent me to bind up the broken hearted* (to bring solace to those yearning for God), *to proclaim liberty to the captives* (to show those imprisoned in this world how to escape), *and the opening of the prison to them that are*

bound (to give to Truth-Seekers the Knowledge which will set them free);" See the section on 'What is Knowledge?' for the meaning of 'knowledge'.

Isaiah 66: 14 The Lord speaks to Isaiah of good and bad karma.
"And when ye see this (God's compassion), *your heart shall rejoice, and your bones shall flourish like an herb: and the hand of the Lord* (karmic law) *shall be known towards his servants* (to those who obey divine law), *and his indignation toward his enemies* (you will see that the enemies of the Lord suffer the consequences of their evil actions)."*

Jeremiah 2: 19 Karmic Law is designed so that people will learn the folly of their wrong ways and turn to God.
"Thine own wickedness shall correct thee, and thy backslidings shall reprove thee: know therefore and see that it is an evil thing and bitter, that thou hast forsaken the Lord thy God, and that my fear is not in thee (you do not fear the Law of Karma), *saith the Lord God of hosts."*

Jeremiah 12: 1 & 13 The prophet asks the usual question but soon finds the answer.
"Righteous art thou, O Lord, when I plead with thee: yet let me talk with thee of thy judgements: Wherefore doth the way of the wicked prosper? wherefore are all they happy that deal very treacherously (why do the wicked seem to get away with it)*?"*
"They have sown wheat, but shall reap thorns: they have put themselves to pain, but shall not profit: and they shall be ashamed of your revenues because of the fierce anger of the Lord (I realise now after some conjecture that they shall reap the karmic fruits of their own actions)."*

Ezekiel 33: 2-4 The Lord warns people to listen to the prophets in order to avoid the Law of Karma falling upon them.
"Son of man, speak to the children of thy people, and say unto them, When I bring the sword (of karma) *upon a land, if the people of the land take a man of their coasts, and set him for their watchman* (if the people choose a prophet from their ranks to act as a watchman to warn of pending events coming through the Law of Karma)*:*

"If when he seeth the sword come upon the land (when he sees justice coming as a result of their bad actions), *he blow the trumpet and warn the people;*
"Then whosoever heareth the sound of the trumpet, and taketh not warning; if the sword come (if the Law of Karma exacts its punishment), *and take him away, his blood shall be upon his own head* (it will be his own fault for not heeding the prophet's warning)."
See the section on 'The Word' for the meaning of 'trumpet'.

Micah 1: 13 The Lord warns the people to control their desires or else risk offending the God within.
"O thou inhabitants of Lachish, bind the chariot to the swift beast (reign in your desires): *she is the beginning of the sin to the daughter of Zion* (desire is the beginning of all other evils encompassing the soul): *for the transgressions of Israel were found in thee."* See the section on 'The Higher Spiritual Centres' for the meaning of 'Zion'.

Malachi 4: 5 God promises the reincarnation of Elijah through the prophet Malachi
"Behold, I will send you Elijah the prophet before the coming of the great and dreadful day of the Lord:" For reference to Elijah's (Elias in Greek) reincarnation as John the Baptist see Matthew 17: 12 & 13.

Apocrypha, II Esdras 4: 28 The Lord tells Esdras that punishment for evil acts arrive at some future date.
"But as concerning the things whereof thou askest me, I will tell thee; for the evil is sown, but the destruction thereof is not yet come."

Apocrypha, II Esdras 5: 42 The fruits of karmic action ripen in due course and season, at the right time.
"And he (God) *said unto me* (Esdras), *I will liken my judgement unto a ring: like as there is no slackness of the last, even so there is no swiftness of the first."*

Apocrypha, The Wisdom of Solomon 1: 8 Evil cannot be hidden and will not go unpunished.
"Therefore he that speaketh unrighteous things cannot be hid: neither shall vengeance, when it punisheth, pass by him."

Apocrypha, The Wisdom of Solomon 13: 1 Individual ignorance blinds man to the existence of God.

"Surely vain (lost in ego) *are all men by nature, who are ignorant of God, and could not out of the good things that are seen know him that is: neither by considering the works did they acknowledge the workmaster* (even the glories of Creation do not inspire them to admire the Creative Hand that made them);"

Apocrypha, The Wisdom of Solomon 17: 17 Solomon talks of Group or Collective Karma.
"For whether he were husbandman, or shepherd, or a labourer in the field, he was overtaken, and endured that necessity (the karmic backlash), *which could not be avoided: for they were all bound with one chain of darkness* (the people affected were bound together by their bad karma)."

Apocrypha, Ecclesiasticus 1: 22 Anger leads to greater error.
"A furious man cannot be justified (cannot be free of error); *for the sway of his fury shall be his destruction* (shall cause him to do even worse deeds than before)."

Apocrypha, Ecclesiasticus 7: 1 A cryptic message on karma from the prophet.
"Do no evil, so shall no harm come unto thee."

Matthew 4: 1-11 These verses give an insight into how our good and bad habits become obstacles to our achieving and maintaining Oneness with the Christ Consciousness. Jesus was not only tempted by hunger but by pride and offers of unlimited earthly power as well, but to no avail. See also Luke 4: 1-15. See the section on 'The Higher Spiritual Centres' for the meaning of 'the Christ Consciousness'.

Matthew 5: 25 & 26 Our wrong actions cause karmic reactions that bind us to the prison of this world.
"Agree with thine adversary quickly, whiles thou art in the way with him (harmonise your behaviour with God's laws of right thoughts, words, and deeds as quickly as you can); *lest at any time the adversary* (your wrong behaviour) *deliver thee to the judge* (Karmic Law that 'judges' every man), *and the judge deliver thee to the officer* (individual delusive ignorance), *and thou be cast into prison* (be locked up in this worldly prison of suffering).
"Verily I say unto thee, Thou shalt by no means come out thence, till thou hast paid the uttermost farthing (You will not escape from

this world until you have paid off all your worldly dues down to the smallest item)."

Matthew 5: 27 & 28 Thought is the forerunner of an action and any action can be prevented by checking the thought.
"Ye have heard that it was said by them of old time, Thou shalt not commit adultery:
"But I say unto you, That whosoever looketh on a woman to lust after her hath committed adultery with her already in his heart."

Matthew 7: 1 & 2 Jesus states the Law of Karma very concisely so that no one can be left in doubt.
"Judge not, that ye be not judged.
"For with what judgement ye judge, ye shall be judged; and with what measure ye mete, it shall be measured to you again."

Matthew 9: 2 The illness Jesus cured was the result of the man's transgressions against the Law of Karma.
"And, behold, they brought unto him a man sick of the palsy, lying on a bed: and Jesus seeing their faith said unto the sick of the palsy; Son, be of good cheer; thy sins be forgiven thee (By God's command, I take on to myself your karmic debt).*"* See the section on 'The Functions of Enlightened Ones' for details of the ability of Masters to take on the karmic debts of their disciples.

Matthew 11: 14 Jesus identifies John the Baptist as the reincarnation of Elijah the prophet.
"And if ye will receive it, this (John the Baptist) *is Elias* (Elijah), *which was for to come* (whose reincarnation was forecast by the prophets).*"*

Matthew 11: 28-30 Jesus compares the lightness of the spiritual Path to the heavy burden of karma.
"Come unto me, all ye that labour and are heavily laden (Come to me all you who are loaded with light–extinguishing karma), *and I will give you rest* (I will give you relief by lifting it).
"Take my yoke upon you (adopt my spiritual discipline), *and learn of me* (learn what I have to teach you); *for I am meek* (non–violent) *and lowly* (without ego) *in heart: and ye shall find rest unto your souls* (and you will discover the peace of your souls).

The Truth Seeker's Guide to the Bible

"For my yoke is easy (by comparison to the karmic burden you are carrying), *and my burden is light* (I can carry your karma without it affecting me).*"* See the section on 'The Functions of Enlightened Ones' for details of the ability of Masters to take on the karmic debts of their disciples.

Matthew 12: 36 We are condemned by the Law of Karma for the thoughtless words that bring harm to others.

"But I say unto you, That every idle word (every thoughtless, harmful word) *that men shall speak, they shall give account thereof in the day of judgement* (they will carry the evil effects with them and eventually have to suffer the consequences).*"*

Matthew 13: 3-8 In the Parable of the Sower Jesus describes how ignorance prevents us from listening to and practising the teachings of the Enlightened Ones. See also Luke 8: 4-15.

Mathew 13: 24-30 In the Parable of the Tares Jesus describes how our individual delusions prevent us from reaping the harvest of divine realisations that arise out of meditating on the inner Self. See pages 701-703 in 'The Second Coming of Christ' for a detailed explanation.

Matthew 16: 13 & 14 Jesus asks his disciples who the people say he was in his past life.

"When Jesus came into the coasts of Caesarea Philippi, he asked his disciples, saying, Whom do men say that I the Son of man am?
"And they said, Some say that thou art John the Baptist: some, Elias (Elijah); *and others, Jeremias* (Jeremiah), *or one of the* (other) *prophets."*

Matthew 16: 22 & 23 Peter's words are not in keeping with Divine Will and reflect human delusion.

"Then Peter took him, and began to rebuke him, saying, Be it far from thee, Lord: this shall not be unto thee (It is unthinkable that you should be taken from us and crucified so cruelly).
"But he turned, and said unto Peter, Get thee behind me, Satan: thou art an offence unto me: for thou savourest not the things that be of God, but those that be of men." Jesus did not address these words to Peter but to the Satanic Power that he detected behind Peter's sympathetic words.

Matthew 17: 12 & 13 Jesus and his disciples clearly accepted reincarnation as a fact not a supposition.

"But I (Jesus) *say unto you, That Elias* (Elijah) *is come already* (has already incarnated), *and they knew him not* (the people did not

recognise him in his new body), *but have done to him whatsoever they listed* (have beheaded him). *Likewise shall also the Son of man suffer of them* (they are going to kill me too).
"Then the disciples understood that he spake unto them of John the Baptist."

Matthew 18: 7 Jesus describes the cause and effect cycle of karmic law arising from our actions.
"Woe unto the world because of offences (The world endlessly suffers from men's evil deeds)*! for it needs be that offences come* (Bad things must happen through karmic law because of our past evil deeds)*; but woe to that man by whom the offence cometh* (but the one who harms others will suffer in his turn through the workings of the same karmic law)*!"*

Mark 2: 5 & 10 Jesus identifies past errors, sins, as the cause of sickness brought through the Law of Karma.
"When Jesus saw their faith (the faith of those carrying the sick man)*, he said unto the sick of the palsy, Son, thy sins be forgiven thee* (I will lift the karmic burden which is causing your disease)."
"But (I do this miracle of healing) *that ye may know that the Son of man* (the embodied Master) *hath power on earth to forgive sins."* See also the section on 'The Functions of Enlightened Ones' for the ability of Masters to carry the karmic burdens of their disciples and the people they have healed.

Mark 7: 21-23 Evil tendencies come from within the mind and heart of man.
"For from within, out of the heart of men, proceed evil thoughts, adulteries, fornications, murders.
"Thefts, covertness, wickedness, deceit, an evil eye, blasphemy, pride, foolishness;
"All these evil things come from within, and defileth the man."

Mark 10: 24 & 25 Our desires, especially to be rich, drag us back time and time again to this world.
"And the disciples were astonished at his words. But Jesus answereth again, and saith unto them, Children, how hard it is for them that trust in riches to enter into the kingdom of God!
"It is easier for a camel to go through the eye of a needle, than for a rich man to enter into the kingdom of God."

Mark 14: 34 The Master shows strain under the heavy burden of the karmas he is carrying for those he has healed.

"And (Jesus) saith unto them, My soul is exceedingly sorrowful unto death: tarry ye here and watch."

Mark 15: 34 The Master again shows strain under the heavy karmic burden he is carrying for 'many'.

"And at the ninth hour Jesus cried with a loud voice saying, Eloi, Eloi, lama sabachthani? Which is, being interpreted, My God, my God, why hast thou forsaken me?" Under the extreme pain of crucifixion and the heavy karmic burden he was carrying Jesus momentarily lost his contact with Cosmic Consciousness.

Luke 13: 16 Jesus infers that it is our past evil actions that cause our ailments and trials.

*"And ought not this woman (*bent almost double and in constant pain), *being a daughter of Abraham, whom Satan hath bound* (who has fallen victim to satanic ignorance), *lo, these eighteen years, be loosed from this bond* (be freed from her karmic debt) *on the Sabbath day?"*

Luke 22: 3-5 Judas' individual delusion, arising from past-life bad karmas, leads him to betray his own Master.

"Then entered Satan (Satan-induced individual ignorance) *into Judas surnamed Iscariot, being of the number of the twelve* (one of the twelve disciples).

"And he went his way, and communicated with the chief priests and captains, how he might betray him (Jesus) *unto them.*

"And they were glad, and covenanted to give him money."

Luke 22: 31 & 32 Our karmic bonds create individual delusion and put us into the hands of Satan.

"And the Lord (Jesus) *said, Simon, Simon, behold, Satan hath desired to have you, that he may sift you as wheat* (Peter, your karmas and individual delusion have you in their grip)*:*

"But I have prayed for thee, that thy faith fail not: and when thou art converted, strengthen thy brethren (I, your Master, am supporting you with strong positive vibrations so that when you are purified of all karma you will be a support for the other disciples)."

John 1: 11 God is obscured behind the veils of ignorance (darkness) of unthinking humanity.

"*He* (God) *came unto his own* (as the Creator of all things), *and his own received him not* (mankind could not see Spirit because of the principles of Cosmic Satan and Individual Ignorance)."

John 1: 29 The Master, Jesus, took on the karma of not only his disciples but of everyone he healed.

"*The next day John* (John the Baptist) *seeth Jesus coming unto him, and saith, Behold the Lamb of God, which taketh away the sin* (karmic burden) *of the world.*"

John 3: 13 Jesus states the principle of reincarnation.

"*And no man hath ascended up to heaven, but he that came down from heaven* (No one has gone up into the astral heavens without first having come down from there to earth), *even the Son of man which is in heaven* (this applies to all unenlightened people in the astral heavens)."

John 5: 22 Jesus points out that God does not punish man, man punishes himself through the Law of Karma.

"*For the Father judgeth no man* (God does not judge man directly; it is the Law of Karma that judges), *but hath committed all judgement unto the Son* (Karma is applied on earth through the Christ Consciousness, the Only Begotten Son of the Father):" See the section on 'The Higher Spiritual Centres' for the meaning of 'the Son'.

John 8: 44 Our satanic imperfections obscure our vision and prevent us from recognising Great Souls.

"*Ye* (those seeking to kill me, Jesus) *are of your father the devil* (the principle of Cosmic Delusion and Individual Ignorance), *and the lusts* (the power of attachment to material things) *of your father ye will do. He* (the devil) *was a murderer* (of spiritual perceptions) *from the beginning* (from the moment creation was made) *and abode not in the truth* (he created the illusion of form by dividing God's One Consciousness), *because there is no truth in him* (he, Satan or the devil, is an unchanging, in-built cosmic lie). *When he speaketh a lie, he speaketh of his own* (he is the father of the lie that solid matter is the only reality): *for he is a liar, and the father of it.*"

John 9: 1-3 This story confirms that both Jesus and his disciples believed in the Laws of Karma and Reincarnation.

"And as Jesus passed by, he saw a man which was blind from his birth.

"And his disciples asked him, saying, Master, who did sin, this man (in a previous lifetime), *or his parents* (in this lifetime before he was born), *that he was born blind?*

"Jesus answered, Neither hath this man sinned, nor his parents (neither have sinned in this lifetime): *but that the works of God should be made manifest in him* (but the blind man has enough good karma to allow me to heal him of his past-life sins through the power of God in me)."

John 12: 25 The lover of material life will lose his spirituality.

"He that loveth his life shall lose it (The person who loves material life shall lose his spiritual life); *and he that hateth his life in this world shall keep it unto life eternal* (and he who has had enough of material life and wishes to return to the Godhead shall realise that he is the immortal soul)."

John 14: 2 The Astral Heavens have many vibrational divisions, each suited to the karmic level of the dying person.

"In my Father's house (in the heavenly realms above this earth) *are many mansions* (are many different levels of vibration): *if it were not so, I would have told you. I go to prepare a place for you* (When I leave this body I will lead you, my disciples, to the place in the heavens that is in keeping with the spiritual level you have achieved with me while on earth)."

John 15: 6 Jesus warns his disciples of the power of attraction of the world.

"If a man abide not in me (does not attain the Christ Consciousness), *he is cast forth* (he becomes a victim of worldly temptations) *as a branch, and is withered* (his spiritual life dies); *and men gather them* (they fall prey to the evil in the world), *and cast them into the fire, and they are burned* (and the 'lost ones' become scorched with unquenchable material desires)."

John 15: 18 & 19 Satan–deluded people hate the teachings of the Enlightened Ones and their followers.

"If the world hate you, ye know that it hated me before it hated you.

"If ye were of the world (If you had the same worldly values as the spiritually ignorant), *the world would love his own* (the world would love you): *but because ye are not of the world* (because you do not have worldly values), *but I have chosen you out of the world* (and because you are my disciples), *therefore the world hateth you* (materially-minded people hate you for challenging their values)."

John 15: 22 The karmic reaction is more severe when we are aware that our actions have consequences.

"If I had not come and spoken unto them, they had not had sin (If I, the Master, had not come with my teachings, the karmic backlash on people would be less because of their ignorance of the truth): *but now they have no cloke for their sin* (but now they have heard the truth, they have no excuse for disobeying divine laws)." See the section on 'The Functions of Enlightened Ones' for further details.

John 19: 11 Jesus fell into the hands of Pilate only because he had chosen to take on the karmic burdens of others.

"Jesus answered, Thou (Pilate) *couldst have no power at all against me, except it were given thee from above* (from the Law of Karma): *therefore he* (Judas) *that delivereth me unto thee hath the greater sin* (has committed a greater crime than yourself)."

Romans 1: 18-20 St. Paul points out that we suffer from karma because we offend the purity of our souls.

"For the wrath of God is revealed from heaven against all ungodliness and unrighteousness of men, who hold the truth in unrighteousness (Karma is a divine law that impacts negatively on people who act against the purity of their own souls).

"Because that which may be known of God is manifest in them; for God hath shewed it unto them (for God is inside everyone as the soul and instructs them what to do through their intuition).

"For the invisible things of him from the creation of the world are clearly seen, being understood by the things that are made, even his eternal power and Godhead; so that they are without excuse (Man

has no excuse because the wonders of creation inform him of the existence of God)."

Romans 12: 19 St. Paul states that man should not seek vengeance. This is God's prerogative by Karmic Law.

"*Dearly beloved, avenge not yourselves, but rather give place unto wrath* (allow the Law of Karma to do the necessary action): *for it is written, Vengeance is mine; I will repay, saith the Lord.*" See also Psalm 94: 1; Isaiah 61: 2; Jeremiah 50: 15 & 28; Jeremiah 51: 11 & 36; Ezekiel 25: 14 & 17; Micah 5: 15; Nahum 1: 2; Hebrews 10: 30.

Galatians 6: 7 & 8 St. Paul succinctly sets out the Law of Karma which controls all thoughts, words & deeds.

"*Be not deceived; God is not mocked* (Don't imagine for a minute that God is fooled): *for whatsoever a man soweth, that shall he also reap* (for whatever a man does he will reap like for like through the Law of Karma).

"*For he that soweth to his flesh* (For he whose actions are motivated or driven by bodily desires) *shall of the flesh reap corruption* (shall become ensnared in a web of desires through the Law of Karma); *but he that soweth to the Spirit shall of the Spirit reap life everlasting* (but those whose actions are spiritually motivated shall attain freedom in enlightenment)." See also Job 4: 8; Proverbs 11: 18 & 19; and Hosea 8: 7 for similar references.

Revelation 3: 12 God, through the astral form of Jesus, describes how to be free from the cycle of incarnations.

"*Him that overcometh* (overcomes Cosmic Satan and Individual Ignorance) *will I make a pillar of the temple of my God, and he shall go no more out* (need incarnate no more): *and I will write upon him the name of my God, and the name of the city of my God, which is new Jerusalem, which cometh down out of heaven from my God: and I will write upon him my new name.*" See the section on 'The Word' for the meaning of 'name of my God' and 'The Higher Spiritual Centres' for the meaning of 'new Jerusalem'.

Part 3

The Nature of Mankind.

1

Perfect & Imperfect Man.

Know ye not that ye are the temple of God, and that the Spirit of God dwelleth in you?
          (I Corinthians 3: 16)

*Within your own body resides your Lord,
Why open the outer eyes to look for Him?
Says, Kabir: Listen, O friends,
I found the Lord behind the mole.*
          (Kabir, 15th century Muslim saint)

    The Perennial Philosophy (best expounded in the Bhagavad Gita, the Hindu Scripture, and in the writings of modern Masters) differs from orthodox Christianity in having an upbeat rather than downbeat view of the essential nature of mankind. The elevating message of the Bhagavad Gita and of all Enlightened Ones is that far from being inherently sinful in nature human beings are, at their very core, the complete opposite: perfect in every way. In fact the Bhagavad Gita states:

He, the Indivisible One, appears as countless beings; He maintains and destroys those forms, then creates them anew. The Light of All Lights, beyond darkness; Knowledge itself, That which is to be known, the Goal of all learning, He is seated in the hearts of all.
(God Talks With Arjuna, Ch. XIII: 16 & 17, page 888)

Man is a mirror image of God. Just as God is both the formless and has a form (the Universe), man is both formless spirit and a material body, the sole difference between man and his Maker being that God is the macrocosm while man is the microcosm.

In actuality this teaching of the origin of man has clear biblical support. Genesis records that God 'breathed' Himself into the human form He had created,

> *And the Lord God formed man of the dust of the ground, and breathed into his nostrils the breath of life; and man became a living soul.*
> (Genesis 2: 7)

thus ensuring the perfection of the soul by creating man in His image.

> *So God created man in his own image, in the image of God created he him: male and female created he them.*
> (Genesis 1: 27)

In view of these clear statements, there should be no doubt in minds free of dogma that man is actually Soul, made in the image of the Father and perfect in every way, albeit encased in a human body. This is confirmed in Psalms in the words:

> *I have said, Ye are gods; and all of you are children of the most High.*
> (Psalm 82: 6)

a view repeated by Jesus in the Gospel According to St. John

> *Jesus answered them, Is it not written in your law, I said, Ye are gods?*
> (John 10: 34)

and again by St. Paul in his First Epistle to the Corinthians:

> *What? know ye not your body is the temple of the Holy Ghost which is in you, which ye have of God, and ye are not your own?*
> (I Corinthians 6: 19)

One can hear the incredulity in St. Paul's voice reverberating down the centuries: "Don't you really know who you are?" Yes, why indeed do we Christians not know even to this day what a human being actually is? And this especially when our chosen saviour, Jesus, also asserted this truth with the words:

> *Neither shall they say, Lo here! or, lo there! for, behold, the kingdom of God is within you.*
> (Luke 17: 21)

The principle of human divinity is perhaps the most significant of all scriptural teachings. It declares that each and every soul without exception is an inseparable part of the Divine Creator; that the Essence within the body of man that enlivens it is no different from God in quality, only in quantity. We are rays of the Divine Sun, inseparable from our Source, fed constantly by It and qualitatively identical to It. The saints of all ages say that we have no reality outside of God. This divine principle is the key to understanding not only our true nature but also what the spiritual path is all about.

The process by which the spiritual man operates safely in the world is described in the Bhagavad Gita where Krishna explains to his devotee Arjuna:

> *The senses are said to be superior to the physical body; the mind is superior to the sense faculties; the intelligence is superior to the mind; but he, the Self (soul), is superior to the intelligence.*
> (God Talks With Arjuna, Ch. III: 42, page 414)

Thus the Bhagavad Gita explains that the soul of man should be the divine commander passing its instructions down through the intellect (the decision maker) to the mind (the reporter of external information to the intellect), from the mind to the senses (the sensors of the external world) and thence to the body itself which carries out the necessary physical actions.

But 'Today's Man' is not driven by soul-wisdom but by the desire for the things of this world: possessions, name, fame and fortune. His soul has become body-identified. He thinks that he is a body under the influence of the mind. As a result of this wrong perception the all-perfect, all-powerful soul has become the limited, insecure ego desperately trying to fill the gap of its non-existence (for in reality it is a creation of our imagination) by chasing worldly desires. The pristine soul has become trapped in a web of ego-actions that binds it to recurrent incarnations through the Law of Karma.

For an account of how this came about it is necessary to return once more to the story in Genesis where Adam and Eve are banished from the Garden of Eden. In this allegory, Adam represents the 'male' quality of intellect, Eve the 'female' quality of feeling or emotion and the Garden of Eden is symbolic of the man's state of God Consciousness and ability to communicate directly with his Maker. The account describes how the first people to inhabit Earth allowed their 'Eve-feelings' to overcome their 'Adam-reason' to the extent that they became body-identified (realised that they were naked) and forgot that they were spiritual beings. In perceiving themselves as body and not spirit, the first human beings lost their ability to communicate with God and to be in harmony with Divine Law:

> *Therefore the Lord God sent him* (Adam or reason) *forth from the Garden of Eden* (from God-Consciousness) *to till the ground from whence he was taken* (to toil under the thrall of body-consciousness).
> (Genesis 3: 23)

'Tilling the ground' means that after his fall from Divine Grace, man was condemned forever to 'till' the ground of his material senses in place of the spiritual perceptions he had previously enjoyed. Similar analogies have been employed by the saints of other religions. For example, Kabir says:

> *Woe to him*
> *Who thinks not of God,*
> *Whose mind and heart*
> *Remain absorbed in plowing*
> *The field of the senses.*
>
> (Kabir, 15th century Muslim saint)

The biblical account in Genesis of man's expulsion from God-Consciousness also highlights the important role our thought processes play in determining whether we see ourselves as material or spiritual beings; and, therefore, whether we listen to our own egos or to God's guidance. Indeed, a consistent teaching of the Masters is that man's mind is his greatest friend and greatest enemy. Turned away from God the mind is man's implacable enemy; turned towards God it becomes his greatest friend. Clearly, this being the case, it is important to understand what is meant by 'mind' and this means beginning with the root cause of everything: consciousness.

In its pure state, consciousness, Soul or Spirit, is that Eternal Essence that is absolutely still yet aware that it exists and conscious of everything that is happening. As soon as consciousness has a desire to create, the will to create or 'to do' causes it to vibrate. When stillness is activated we call it 'mind'. Mind fulfils its material desires through the body by means of the organ called the brain. But once the soul becomes body-identified and caught in a web of desires, fears, and expectations, it becomes the ego: the self-centred thinking process in man that reveals itself by constantly declaring 'I am', 'I want', and even ' I am not'. Thus, in actuality, the ego is none other than the limitless soul buried under a mass of self-centred thoughts and emotions. In this condition the soul is like a brilliant diamond hidden beneath layers of mud. All that is needed is to remove the mud and the incorruptible diamond is revealed in all its pristine glory as Krishna assures his devotee Arjuna in the Bhagavad Gita:

> *By diligently following his path, the yogi, perfected by the efforts of many births, is purged of sin and finally enters the Supreme Beatitude.*
>
> (God Talks With Arjuna, Ch. VI: 45, page 652)

Therefore the main goal of the spiritual aspirant is to curb the incessant 'chatter' of the mind and, in the resulting stillness, begin to respond to the guidance of the divine soul within. As the Lord says in the book of Psalms:

> *Be still, and know that I am God* (be still in body, senses and mind and experience the Divine Being within you)*:*
> *I will be exalted among the heathen* (then I will be recognised by the previously unenlightened)*, I will be exalted in the earth* (I will be praised within Creation).
> (Psalm 46: 10)

But, as Arjuna complains to his Guru the Hindu Avatar, Krishna, in the Bhagavad Gita, this is no easy task for man's wayward mind is the product of lifetimes of inharmonious thoughts, words and deeds:

> *Verily, the mind is unsteady, tumultuous, powerful, obstinate! O Krishna, I consider the mind as difficult to master as the wind.*
> (God Talks With Arjuna, Ch. VI: 34, page 639)

Many other saints have variously described the mind as a wild beast, a drunken monkey and a thief (for stealing our peace and God-realisation from us), all concurring that the errant mind is man's greatest obstacle to God-realisation.

Nevertheless, even putting spirituality aside, everyone should be able to appreciate that the mind is our most important tool. Without it we cannot observe, sense, and react to the world around us. It sets limits on our intellectual abilities, on our emotional condition and, to a very large extent, on our mental and physical welfare. It seems a gross oversight that though we spend most of our time cramming it with information, we spend no time at all training it to operate efficiently, a task best undertaken during our formative years. Which one of us, for instance, can readily switch the mind off a nagging worry at a moment's notice or concentrate it fully on the job in hand without it wandering here, there, and everywhere? How can we possibly expect to be efficient or happy when we have so little control over this most vital tool?

What the Bible Says About Mankind.

Man is immortal Spirit, pure and of divine origin, having potentially the same qualities and powers as his heavenly Father. The way to operate safely in the world is to train the mind so that the voice of Spirit once more guides one's actions. Through using free will wrongly, man's soul has become identified with the limited mortal body and believes that it is the fearful and insecure ego.

Genesis 1: 27 God created man in His own Image as Spirit with all His qualities.
"So God created man in his own image, in the image of God created he him: male and female created he them (God created man and woman in pairs, as perfect soul mates)*."* See The Second Coming of Christ pages 1197-1204 for a full explanation of soul mates.

Genesis 2: 7 Man is a soul living in a human body.
"And the Lord God formed man of the dust of the ground, and breathed into his nostrils the breath of life; and man became a living soul."

Genesis 3: 23 The first humans lost their ability to communicate with God by becoming body-identified.
"Therefore the Lord God sent him (Adam or reason) *forth from the Garden of Eden* (from God-Consciousness) *to till the ground from whence he was taken* (to toil under the limitations of the senses arising from body-consciousness)*."*

Genesis 17: 1 God made man in His image so he IS perfect because God is the only perfection; there is none else.
"And when Abram was ninety years old and nine, the Lord appeared to Abram, and said unto him, I am the Almighty God; walk before me and be thou perfect."

Deuteronomy 18: 13 God commands mankind to be perfect for only perfection can be absorbed back into God.

"Thou shalt be perfect with the Lord thy God." See also 1 Kings 8: 61 & Psalm 101: 2.

Psalm 46: 10 God emphasises that we need to curb the 'noise' of the mind in order to find Him.

"Be still, and know that I am God (Be still in body, senses and mind and experience the Divine Being within you)*: I will be exalted among the heathen* (the unenlightened)*, I will be exalted in the earth* (I will be praised within Creation).*"*

Psalm 82: 6 God says, through David, that we are offspring of the most high.

"I have said, Ye are gods; and all of you are children of the most high."

Psalm 104: 30 David recognises that our souls are nothing else but part of God's Spirit.

"Thou sendest forth thy spirit, they (human beings) *are created: and thou renewest the face of the earth."*

Proverbs 8: 22-27 Man's soul was the first thing to come out of the One Consciousness of God.

"The Lord possessed me in the beginning of his way, before his works of old.

"I was set up from everlasting, from the beginning, or ever the earth was.

"When there were no depths, I was brought forth; when there were no fountains abounding with water.

"Before the mountains were settled, before the hills was I brought forth:

"While as yet he had not made the earth, nor the fields, nor the highest part of the dust of the world.

"When he prepared the heavens, I was there: when he set a compass upon the face of the depth."

Ecclesiastes 12: 7 The Preacher confirms that our souls return to God, who gave them to us in the first place.

"Then shall the dust return to the earth as it was (the body shall

disintegrate into its mineral constituents)*: and the spirit shall return unto God who gave it* (but the spirit shall return to its Origin)."

Isaiah 38: 14 Hezekiah complains of his lack of success in contacting the Lord because of his over-active mind.
"Like a crane or a swallow, so did I chatter: I did mourn as a dove: mine eyes fail with looking upward (Because of my overactive mind I failed to focus upward on the Christ Centre at the site of the Single Eye)*: O Lord, I am oppressed* (I am downhearted)*; undertake for me* (please help me)*."* See the section on 'The Higher Spiritual Centres' for the meaning of the Christ Centre.

Isaiah 45: 11 God acknowledges that we are His children, His sons, of His 'flesh'.
"Thus saith the Lord, the Holy One of Israel, and his (man's) *Maker, Ask me of things to come concerning my sons, and concerning the work of my hands command ye me."*

Ezekiel 28: 14 & 15 God describes the perfect way in which man was created and comments on his fall.
"Thou art the anointed cherub that covereth (that is supreme over creation)*; and I have set thee so* (I made you that way)*: thou wast upon the holy mountain of God* (initially you were united with Me, God the highest, in the holy mountain of the Crown Chakra)*: thou hast walked up and down in the midst of the stones of fire* (your consciousness has slid up and down the spiritual centres in your body).
"Thou wast perfect in thy ways from the day that thou wast created, till iniquity was found in thee (you were the perfect reflection of God until you fell under the thrall of satanic delusion)*."* For an explanation of 'holy mountain' and 'stones of fire' see the sections called 'The Higher Spiritual Centres' and 'The Tree of Life' respectively.

Apocrypha, The Wisdom of Solomon 2: 23 Man is immortal Spirit made in the image of God.
"For God created man to be immortal, and made him to be an image of his (God's) *own eternity."*

Apocrypha, The Wisdom of Solomon 9: 6 Without divine wisdom even the cleverest mind fails.
"For though a man be never so perfect among the children of men

(though he appears to be intellectually superior in knowledge and logic), *yet if wisdom be not with him, he shall be nothing regarded* (without the divine wisdom of intuition to guide him he will not succeed)."

Matthew 5: 48 Jesus tells his disciples to be perfect as God is perfect: for perfection is their true estate as souls.
"Be ye therefore perfect, even as your Father which is heaven is perfect."

Mark 10: 6 God made souls in pairs: wisdom and feeling, which, when united, make One.
"But from the beginning of the creation God made them male and female." All souls were made in pairs having no gender at that time. One of the pair possessed the 'male' characteristic of 'reason' and the other of 'feeling'. God's intention was for these offspring of His to enjoy Creation and then merge together into one whole in order to return to the Godhead. For further details see The Second Coming of Christ, pages 1197–1204 & 1207–9.

Luke 17: 21 Jesus confirms that we are made in God's image therefore He is within us.
"Neither shall they say, Lo here! or, lo there! for, behold, the kingdom of God is within you."

John 1: 12 As the plural in 'sons' suggests, our essential nature is that of a Son of God.
"But as many as received him, to them gave he power to become the sons of God (God gave worthy Truth-Seekers enlightenment, Oneness with Him through the Christ Consciousness), *even to them that believed on his name:"* See the section called 'The Word' for the meaning of 'name'.

John 4: 35 & 36 Jesus says that the soul is perfect already and all we have to do is to realise that it is so.
"Say not ye, There are yet four months, and then cometh the harvest (Don't you accept as a matter of course that a farmer has to put in the necessary work in order to reap the harvest of his efforts in due season?)*? behold, I say unto you, Lift up your eyes, and look on the fields; for they are white already to harvest* (But I tell you that it is different in the spiritual world for the soul is white, perfect already. No one has to labour to make it so).
"And he that reapeth receiveth wages (The devotee who makes the

effort to uncover the perfection of his soul gets his due reward), *and gathereth fruit unto life eternal* (and, in doing so, achieves immortality): *that both he that soweth* (God as the giver of wisdom and of spiritual gifts) *and he that reapeth* (the devotee who makes the effort) *may rejoice together* (may be happy in their final unity)."
For the meaning of 'lift up your eyes' see the section called 'Meditation'.

John 10: 34 Jesus confirms that our souls are perfect, one with God.
"Jesus answered them, Is it not written in your law, I said, Ye are gods?"

I Corinthians 3: 16 An incredulous St. Paul questions the spiritual knowledge of the Corinthians.
"Know ye not that ye are the temple of God, and that the Spirit of God dwelleth in you?" Essentially St. Paul is saying 'Don't you know that you ARE the Spirit of God and not the ego?'

I Corinthians 6: 19 St. Paul repeats the essential truth that human beings are not the ego but Spirit.
"What? know ye not that your body is the temple of the Holy Ghost which is in you, which ye have of God, and ye are not your own (Don't you know that the ego is a self-imposed delusion)*?"*

I Corinthians 15: 48 & 49 St. Paul says that man is a heavenly spirit made in the image of God.
"As is the earthy, such are they also that are earthy: and as is the heavenly, such are they also that are heavenly (Body-conscious people believe they belong to the world but spiritual people know that they belong to God).

"And as we have borne the image of the earthy, we shall also bear the image of the heavenly (Though we were once in body-consciousness and worldly, as we turn to Spirit it becomes clear to us that we are of Spirit and not just earthy bodies)."

II Corinthians 3: 18 St. Paul states that when we can see ourselves clearly we will realise that we are Spirit.
"But we all, with open face beholding as in a glass the glory of the Lord, are changed into the same image from glory to glory, even as by the Spirit of the Lord."

Christopher Mark Hanson

II Corinthians 6: 16 St. Paul says clearly that God resides in the human body and is the operator of it.

"And what agreement hath the temple of God with idols? for ye are the temple of the living God; as God hath said, I will dwell in them, and walk in them; and I will be their God, and they shall be my people."

2

The Higher Spiritual Centres.

And I turned to see the voice that spake with me. And being turned, I saw seven golden candlesticks; And in the midst of the seven golden candlesticks one like unto the Son of man, clothed with a garment down to the foot, and girt about the paps with a golden girdle.
(Revelation 1: 12 & 13)

Though the physical body of man was generally patterned after the physiological and anatomical instrumentalities that had resulted from the long process of evolution of animal species, human beings were created by God with a unique endowment possessed by no lower forms: awakened spiritual centres of life and consciousness in the spine and brain that gave them the ability to express fully the divine consciousness and powers of the soul.
(The Second Coming of Christ, page 46)

Early in the Old Testament Jerusalem and Zion are clearly being referred to as historic places. For instance, II Samuel 5: 6 & 7 records how David went up to Jerusalem and captured the fort of Zion, which was called the city of David. Being a fortress, it seems reasonable to assume that it was located on high ground either within the general boundaries or at least close to Jerusalem, possibly dominating the city to such an extent that it became a symbol of security, strength and impregnability to successive generations. But when the psalmists, prophets and saints arrived on the scene, they transformed the words Zion and Jerusalem into spiritual symbols. Within the context of their verses Jerusalem became a symbol for the human body, the Holy City that must be entered into in order to reach God; and Zion became the inner fortress of Cosmic Consciousness, the last refuge of the Truth–Seeker, the seat of God awareness.

In Isaiah, for example, in rousing words God calls His devotees to put all their strength into progressing to Cosmic Consciousness (Zion), so that they can adorn themselves with the divine qualities (beautiful garments) inherent within their purified bodies (Jerusalem, the holy city) and thus ensure that no impure thoughts will ever again invade their minds:

> *Awake, awake; put on thy strength, O Zion; put on thy beautiful garments, O Jerusalem, the holy city: for henceforth there shall no more come into thee the uncircumcised and the unclean.*
> (Isaiah 52: 1)

Even a brief glance at the large number of biblical quotations provided at the end of this section will be sufficient to convince the unbiased Truth-Seeker that, early on in the Old Testament, Jerusalem and Zion took on meanings of deep spiritual significance; as indeed did Babylon and Egypt in reference to the captivity of man's soul in the world through his unspiritual actions.

This obscurity inherent in the saintly language of the scriptures is added to by the ease with which Old Testament texts switch from prophesy, rich in symbolism, to historical fact. In addition, it is not unusual for the choice of a symbol to vary from one scriptural authority to another. Such an example occurs in the book of Revelation 3: 12 where God, through the angelic astral form of Jesus, uses the term 'New Jerusalem' for Cosmic Consciousness in place of the term 'Zion' favoured by the Old Testament prophets and psalmists.

It is abundantly clear also from content of the many biblical verses shown at the end of this section that, to the prophets and psalmists of the Old Testament, the term 'Zion' had the same connotation as 'Enlightenment', 'Self–realisation', 'Nirvana' and 'Nirvikalpa Samadhi' have to the adherents of today's major world faiths.

Biblical texts also make mention of another very important high spiritual centre in the body of man which the Old Testament prophets referred to as the 'Apple of the Eye' or the 'Eye of the Lord'; and Jesus called the 'Single Eye'. Examples are:

> *Keep me as the apple of the eye, hide me under the shadow of thy wings;*
> (Psalm 17: 8)

> *Behold, the eye of the Lord is upon them that fear him, upon them that hope in his mercy;*
> (Psalm 33: 18)

> *The light of the body is the eye: if therefore thine eye be single, thy whole body shall be full of light.*
> (Matthew 6: 22)

Saints have other terminologies for the Single Eye. Kabir, for instance, sometimes calls it the 'tenth door' because it is the gateway to the heavenly realms, the other nine being the remaining openings or portals to the 'nine-gated city' of the human body. On other occasions, he refers to it as the 'mole' because of its round appearance. And yet elsewhere this great Muslim saint describes the Single Eye as an inverted well because it gives one the impression of looking down into a round well-like aperture even though one's gaze is looking upward. This, Kabir says, is the 'well' from which the soul-bride draws the divine waters of God-perception.

> *That land has an inverted well*
> *With an opening, narrow as a thread,*
> *Through which the married soul draws water,*
> *Without a pitcher, without a rope.*
> (Kabir, 15th century Muslim saint)

Like their ancient and modern counterparts from other religious backgrounds and cultures, the prophets and saints of the Old and New Testaments have identified the location of these two high spiritual centres, albeit in their characteristic styles. Time and time again, when referring to these centres, they mention the mountains and hills:

> *The mountains shall bring peace to the people, and the little hills, by righteousness.*
> (Psalm 72: 3)

In modern terminology these locations equate to the Crown Chakra, the highest part of the human head (mountain), and the Medullar Chakra or Christ Centre, the seat of the Single Eye located in the forehead between the two 'little hills' of the eyebrows. Both these centres are important on the road to enlightenment.

Enlightened Ones commonly identify the 'geography' of the body by means of the four Cardinal or Magnetic Points: North (the head), South (the feet), West (the rear) and East (the front). The Single Eye lies in the front of the body (the east) and within it can be found the bright star of Cosmic Consciousness. For these reasons the centre of Cosmic Consciousness in the Single Eye is sometimes identified as the 'Star of the East'. Quite clearly, the wise men coming from the east to visit the baby Jesus lying in his crib in Bethlehem could not have been following a star in the eastern sky as this would have been behind them. They were in fact following intuitive guidance coming from the 'inner star' at the seat of Cosmic Consciousness.

> *Now when Jesus was born in Bethlehem of Judaea in the days of Herod the king, behold, there came wise men from the east to Jerusalem, Saying, Where is he that is born King of the Jews? for we have seen his star in the east, and are come to worship him.*
> (Matthew 2: 1 & 2)

It is by means of this Cardinal Point system that Genesis records the Lord creating mankind by 'planting' the absolutely indispensable 'garden' of spiritual centres in man's body through the medium of the Single Eye (eastward in Eden):

> *And the Lord God planted a garden eastward in Eden;
> and there he put the man whom he had formed.*
> (Genesis 2: 8)

These two high spiritual centres in man are vitally important to the spiritual aspirant for they are not only the means by which Eternal Spirit first descended into the material body but also define the route by which he must retrace his steps in order to return to his Celestial Home.

> *Yet have I set up my king* (My kingly soul) *upon my holy hill of Zion* (the Crown Chakra).
> (Psalm 2: 6)

> *And many people shall go and say, Come ye, and let us go up to the mountain of the Lord* (let our focus rise to the seat of Cosmic Consciousness in our heads), *to the house of the God of Jacob* (to the spiritual level Jacob enjoyed); *and he will teach us of his ways, and we will walk in his paths: for out of Zion shall go forth the law* (for out of the Crown Chakra, the seat of Cosmic Consciousness, comes all Divine Law), *and the word of the Lord from Jerusalem* (and the Holy Ghost or Word is heard at the Christ Centre).
> (Isaiah 2: 3)

Not long after an Enlightened Teacher has departed, and sometimes even before he has done so, the tendency for his unenlightened followers to externalise the sublime truths of the saint's message becomes apparent. In due course of time, the Universal Truth that the particular Master brought to the world takes on a new image: orthodox, dogma-bound, externalised and almost unrecognisable from its original form.

The end result of such a process is that instead of taking the eminently tougher road to the Inner Jerusalem, his followers begin to make pilgrimages to the outer Jerusalem. Instead of mourning tears of separation at the inner psychological barrier, the Wailing

Wall situated at the Single Eye, waiting in anguish for God to open the door to His 'Zion' of Cosmic Consciousness, mankind begins to yearn or weep at a physical Wailing Wall that is merely a symbol of the internal experience. Similarly, the highest spiritual centres in the mountains and hills of the human head, essential milestones on the way back to the Godhead, become mere geographic phenomena; and, ludicrously, the Star of the East is transformed into an astrological miracle. Christianity is by no means the only victim of this unfortunate trend.

What the Bible Says About the Higher Spiritual Centres in Man.

Man is not simply flesh and bone. The Creator has designed the human body so that mankind can express the highest levels of consciousness, equipping him with a Single Eye at the site of his Medullar Chakra or Christ Centre between the 'little hills' of his eyebrows into which he can peer in meditation in order to lift his consciousness to the Crown Chakra, the seat of Cosmic Consciousness located in the 'mountain' at the top of his head.

Genesis 2: 8 & 15 Man descended into his body from the higher worlds through the Christ Centre or Single Eye.

"And the Lord God planted a garden eastward in Eden; and there he put the man whom he had formed (God formed the garden of astral spiritual centres by planting it in the 'east' of the human body, through the portal of the Christ Centre)."

"And the Lord God took the man, and put him into the Garden of Eden to dress it and to keep it (Man was charged with maintaining his garden of spiritual centres so that he could continue in the God–consciousness he enjoyed when he was first created)." See the section on 'The Tree of Life' for details of the remaining spiritual centres forming the complete Garden of Eden.

Genesis 3: 23 & 24 The consciousness of mankind fell to a level below that of the Christ Centre.

"Therefore the Lord God sent him forth from the garden of Eden, to till the ground from whence he was taken (Through wrong choices mankind slipped from the divine state of Eden-consciousness to earthly body-consciousness).

"So he drove out the man; and he placed at the east of the garden of Eden Cherubims, and a flaming sword which turned every way, to keep the way of the tree of life (God created the Single Eye in the front of the forehead which, as the gateway to divine powers and awareness, reveals the subtle functions lying at the root of the human body)."

Genesis 49: 26 Jacob foresees that the consciousness of his son Joseph will be in his highest spiritual centres.

"The blessings of thy father (the blessings God has given me) *have prevailed above the blessings of my progenitors* (are greater than the earthly genetic inheritance from my ancestors) *unto the utmost bound of the everlasting hills* (thus enabling my offspring to reach the highest spiritual centres in the head)*: they shall be on the head of Joseph, and on the crown of the head of him that was separate from his brethren* (These divine blessings will enable Joseph to lift his consciousness to the highest centre in the crown of his head)."

Exodus 19: 3 Moses raises his consciousness to the Crown Chakra and talks to God.

"And Moses went up unto God (raised his spiritual consciousness)*, and the lord called unto him out of the mountain* (spoke to him from the seat of Cosmic Consciousness in the highest centre in Moses' head)*, saying, Thus shall thou say to the house of Jacob, and tell the children of Israel;"*

Deuteronomy 32: 10 God found Jacob, guided him through the world, and kept him as the 'apple of his eye'.

"He (God) *found him* (Jacob) *in a desert land, and in the waste howling wilderness* (lost in the meaningless clamour of the world)*; he led him about, he instructed him, he kept him as the apple of his eye* (God helped Jacob keep his focus at the Christ Centre in the

Single Eye through which God was able to guide him through the intuition)." See also the section on 'What is Intuition?'

Job 42: 5 Job tells God that previously he had only heard of Him but now can see Him by means of the Single Eye.
"I have heard of thee by the hearing of the ear: but now mine eye seeth thee."

Psalm 2: 6 The Lord says that His true devotee has his focus in the topmost spiritual centre in his head.
"Yet have I set up my king (My kingly soul) *upon my holy hill of Zion* (the Crown Chakra)."

Psalm 9: 11 David acknowledges that God dwells in Zion, the topmost spiritual centre in the head.
"Sing praises to the Lord, which dwelleth in Zion: declare among the people his doings." Of the very many references to Zion in Psalms see particularly Psalms 9: 14; 14: 7; 48: 11; 50: 2; 53: 6; 74: 2; 99: 2 ; 110: 2; & 125: 1.

Psalm 17: 8 David asks the Lord to help him keep his consciousness fixed on the Single Eye of wisdom.
"Keep me as the apple of the eye (Help me to keep my focus on the Single Eye of wisdom), *hide me under the shadow of thy wings* (for Your divine guidance will guide me safely through life),"

Psalm 33: 18 David acknowledges that the Lord communicates to man through man's 'Single Eye'.
"Behold, the eye of the Lord is upon them that fear him, upon them that hope in his mercy;" See also Psalm 34: 15 and 54: 7.

Psalm 68: 16 David refers to the Crown Centre as the high hill in which God dwells in the enlightened.
"Why leap ye, ye high hills? this is the hill that God desireth to dwell in; yea the Lord will dwell in it for ever."

Psalm 72: 3 David, the Psalmist, praises the Holy Mountains and Hills.
"The mountains shall bring peace to the people, and the little hills, by righteousness (The spiritual realms are entered into at the spot between the two little hills in the forehead, which is the doorway to the righteousness and permanent peace experienced in the highest

mountain at the top of the human head, the Crown Chakra, the centre of God–consciousness)." See also 'lifting up the eyes' in Psalm 123: 1.

Psalm 102: 16 & 21 God comes to the devotee when he has strengthened his focus on the highest centres through his spiritual practices.
"When the Lord shall build up Zion (When the devotee's spiritual efforts have been rewarded by God-contact in the Crown Chakra), *he* (God) *shall appear in his glory."*
"To declare the name of the Lord in Zion, and his praise in Jerusalem (the holy city of the purified human body);" See the section called 'The Word' for the meaning of the 'name of the Lord'.

Psalm 121: 1 & 2 David promises to continually struggle to keep his consciousness at the Christ Centre.
"I will lift up mine eyes unto the hills (I will keep my attention on the Christ Centre which resides between the two hills of my eyebrows), *from whence cometh my help* (from where comes the spiritual experiences which help me through life).
"My help cometh from the Lord (These experiences are manifestations of God and naught else): *which made heaven and earth."*

Psalm 126: 1 & 2 David recounts how people feel when their top spiritual centres are freed from ignorance.
"When the Lord turned again the captivity of Zion (When the Lord raised our consciousnesses up to the Crown Chakra once more and freed us from rebirth), *we were like them that dream.*
"Then was our mouth filled with laughter, and our tongue with singing: then said they among the heathen, The Lord hath done great things for them (those who were previously unbelievers will acknowledge their debt to the Lord)." See also Psalm 128: 5 & 129: 5 for similar references to Zion.

Psalm 133: 1-3 David speaks of the very important quality of unity to be found in Cosmic Consciousness.
"Behold, how good and how pleasant it is for brethren to dwell together in unity!
"It is like the precious ointment upon the head, that ran down upon the beard, even Aaron's beard: that went down to the skirts of his garments (it pervades one's whole nature);

Christopher Mark Hanson

"As the dew of Herman, and as the dew that descended upon the mountains of Zion: for there the Lord commanded the blessings, even life for evermore (The dew of Comic Energy descends from the Cosmic Consciousness in the mountain of the Crown Chakra where God's blessings, including immortality, are located)." See also Isaiah 134: 1-3; 137: 1-9; and 146: 10 for more references to Zion.

Proverbs 7: 2 The Lord advises us to obey the Divine Law of always keeping our attention on the Single Eye.

"Keep my commandments (Obey the divine laws governing creation), *and live* (and enjoy immortality); *and my law as the apple of thine eye* (and keep My divine law of having your focus concentrated at the Christ Centre in the Single Eye)."

Song of Solomon 2: 8 Solomon sings the praises of the Holy Mountains and Hills.

"The voice of my beloved! behold, he cometh leaping upon the mountains, skipping upon the hills (I see Him dancing at the Christ Centre between my eyebrows and in the Crown Chakra that is located in the top of the mountains in my head)." For more on the voice of God see section on 'The Word'.

Isaiah 1: 8 God sees the plight of the people who have lost their spiritual focus on Zion.

"And the daughter of Zion is left as a cottage in a vineyard, as a lodge in a garden of cucumbers, as a besieged city (The Cosmic Consciousness of God in man, the daughter of Zion, is at odds with the people because of their transgressions against their true spiritual nature)." God is regarded as the masculine force and the soul as the feminine one, or God as the Groom and man's soul as the Bride.

Isaiah 2: 3 When people turn from the world to God in the highest spiritual centre, He will be their guide.

"And many people shall go and say, Come ye, and let us go up to the mountain of the Lord (let our focus rise to the seat of Cosmic Consciousness in our heads), *to the house of the God of Jacob* (to the spiritual level Jacob enjoyed); *and he will teach us of his ways, and we will walk in his paths: for out of Zion shall go forth the law* (for out of the Crown Chakra, the seat of Cosmic Consciousness, comes all Divine Law), *and the word of the Lord from Jerusalem* (and the Holy Vibration is heard at the Christ Centre)." Of the very many

mentions of Zion in Isaiah see particularly Isaiah 3: 16 & 17; 4: 3-5; 10: 24; 12: 6; 14: 32; 18: 7; 28: 16; 29: 8; 31: 4; 33: 5 & 20; 35: 10; 40: 9; 49:14; 51: 3 & 16; 52: 1-8; 61: 3; & 66: 8. See the section on 'The Word' for the meaning of 'word' in the above verse.

Isaiah 38: 14 Hezekiah complains of his lack of success in contacting the Lord through the Christ Centre.

"*Like a crane or a swallow, so did I chatter: I did mourn as a dove: mine eyes fail with looking upward* (Because of my overactive mind I failed to focus upward on the Christ Centre at the site of the Single Eye)*: O Lord, I am oppressed* (I am downhearted)*; undertake for me* (please help me).*"*

Isaiah 51: 6 The Lord says that the astral heavens and the earth are unattractive compared to man's Cosmic Home.

"*Lift up your eyes to the heavens, and look upon the earth beneath* (Look up to Cosmic Consciousness through the Single Eye and compare the joys of God-communion to the attractions of the physical realms)*: for the heavens shall vanish away like smoke, and the earth shall wax old like a garment* (both the astral heavens and the physical world are temporary and their temporal joys will seem stale by comparison with Cosmic Consciousness)*, and they that dwell therein* (those that live in the physical world and only reach as far as the astral world at death) *shall die in like manner* (will be subject to death and rebirth)*: but my salvation shall be for ever, and my righteousness shall not be abolished* (but those achieving Cosmic Consciousness shall attain immortality in God).*"*

Isaiah 52: 1 Through Isaiah, the Lord calls for His children to awaken from ignorance into Cosmic Consciousness.

"*Awake, awake; put on thy strength, O Zion* (Wake up, My children, and reach Cosmic Consciousness, your only strength)*; put on thy beautiful garments* (put on your spirituality)*, O Jerusalem, the holy city* (the holy city of the body)*: for henceforth there shall no more come into thee the uncircumcised and the unclean* (for when you do so evil tendencies will trouble you no more).*"*

Isaiah 60: 14 God likens the body and the consciousness of the spiritual person to a holy city and to Zion respectively.

"*The sons also of them that afflicted thee shall come bending unto thee; and all they that despise thee shall bend themselves down at the soles of thy feet; and they shall call thee, The city of the Lord, The Zion of the Holy One of Israel."*

Isaiah 65: 7 Wrong actions are violations of the higher spiritual centres located in the head.
"Your iniquities, and the iniquities of your fathers together, saith the Lord, which have burned incense upon the mountains (the evil works of you and your fathers have violated the purity of the centre of Cosmic Consciousness in the crown of your head), *and blasphemed me upon the hills* (and are an affront to the Christ Centre between the two hills of your eyebrows)*: therefore shall I measure their former work into their bosom* (hence you will have to pay your dues to the Law of Karma).*"*

Jeremiah 3: 14 The Lord promises to lead people to the Zion of enlightenment as soon as they become ready.
"Turn, O backsliding children, saith the Lord; for I am married unto you (you are part of My Supreme Consciousness)*: and I will take you one of a city, and two of a family, and I will bring you to Zion* (as soon as you turn back inside, towards Me, I will bring you to enlightenment in your Crown Chakra):" For further references to Zion in Jeremiah see 4: 6; 8: 19; 14: 19; 30: 17; 31: 6 & 12; 50: 5; and 51: 10 & 24.

Lamentations 1: 4 Jeremiah mourns the loss of God-consciousness of the people.
"The ways of Zion do mourn, because none come to the solemn feats (The soul weeps because Cosmic Consciousness has been lost and no one comes to that level any more)*: all her gates are desolate* (no one meditates at the entrance to this holy portal of the Christ Centre trying to enter into the Single Eye)*: her priests sigh, her virgins are afflicted* (the prophets despair and the pure divine qualities are neglected), *and she is in bitterness."* For further references to Zion in Lamentations see 1: 6 & 17; 2: 1, 6 & 13; and 4: 2, 11 & 22.

Lamentations 2: 8, 15 & 18 Jeremiah calls the spiritual centres 'the daughters of Jerusalem and Zion'.
"The Lord hath purposed to destroy the wall of the daughter of Zion (The plan of the Lord is to break down the psychological barrier, the Wailing Wall, that keeps the soul in bondage)*: he hath stretched out a line* (he has set a limit to wickedness), *he hath not withdrawn his*

hand from destroying: therefore he made the wall and the rampart to lament (those wishing to reach Him must mourn or yearn at these barriers before they can gain entry); *they languished together* (they both wait for the true devotee to 'knock' in order to gain entry)."

"*All that pass by clap their hands at thee; they hiss and wag their head at the daughter of Jerusalem, saying, Is this the city that men call 'The perfection of beauty, The joy of the whole earth'* (ordinary men sneer at your loss of spirituality)?"

"*Their heart cried unto the Lord, O wall of the daughter of Zion, let tears run down like a river day and night: give thyself no rest* (meditate constantly with a heart yearning to be let into Zion); *let not the apple of thine eye cease* (do not let the light in the 'apple' of the Single Eye fade for lack of application in meditation)." This interpretation is suggesting that, just as it is the tendency for orthodoxy in religion to externalise spiritual things, the Wailing Wall in Jerusalem has become an outer replacement for the inner psychological barrier or wall before which we are supposed to weep, mourn and meditate day and night in order to reach God.

Ezekiel 10: 19 Ezekiel sees, at the Christ Centre, the astral angels with their vortices of spinning energy.

"*And the cherubims lifted up their wings, and mounted up from the earth in my sight* (I entered my Single Eye and saw the angels up there in the heavenly realms, not on earth): *when they went out, the wheels also were beside them* (I could see the chakras looking like wheels spinning), *and every one stood at the door of the east gate of the Lord's house* (all this was happening at the Christ Centre which is the gateway to God in my forehead); *and the glory of the God of Israel was over them above* (and everything was bathed in the Divine Light shining out of Cosmic Consciousness)." See the section called 'The Tree of Life' for the meaning of 'chakras' or 'wheels'.

Ezekiel 28: 14 & 15 God tells man that his consciousness descended from the Holy Mountain.

"*Thou art the anointed cherub that covereth* (You are a spiritual being, a soul, a spark of the Divine, supreme over creation); *and I have set thee so* (I, God, made you that way): *thou wast upon the holy mountain of God* (initially you were united with Me in the Holy Mountain of your Crown Chakra): *thou hast walked up and down in the midst of the stones of fire* (your consciousness has slid up and down the seven spiritual centres, the chakras, in your body).

"Thou wast perfect in thy ways from the day that thou wast created, till iniquity was found in thee (you were the perfect reflection of God until you fell under the thrall of satanic delusion)." For the meaning of 'stones of fire' see the section called 'The Tree of Life'.

Joel 2: 1 & 32 God warns the people to seek Cosmic Consciousness and be saved before ignorance descends.

"Blow ye the trumpet in Zion (Seek to hear the Holy Vibration in the highest spiritual centre in the top of your heads), *and sound an alarm in my holy mountain* (let these holy vibrations warn you that the forces of darkness are on their way to defeat you and to lay waste the land of your body and mind)*: let all the inhabitants of the land tremble: for the day of the Lord cometh, for it is nigh at hand* (the day of enlightenment is close by);"

"And it shall come to pass, that whosoever shall call on the name of the Lord shall be delivered (Whoever listens to the Holy Vibration within them shall be saved from evil)*: for in mount Zion and in Jerusalem shall be deliverance* (for deliverance lies in raising your consciousness to the Christ Centre in your foreheads and thereby to the Crown Centre of Cosmic Consciousness), *as the Lord hath said, and in the remnant whom the Lord shall call* (as the Lord has promised to those remnants of His flock who succeed in resisting the forces of evil)." For similar reference to Zion in Joel see 2: 15 & 23. See also the section called 'The Word' for the meaning of 'trumpet' and 'name of the Lord'.

Joel 3: 16 & 17 The highest spiritual centres of God are in the human head from the Christ Centre to the Crown.

"The Lord also shall roar out of Zion (the Voice or Holy Vibration of God sounds in the Crown Chakra of righteous people), *and utter his voice from Jerusalem* (and also from within the human body at the Christ Centre)*; and the heavens and the earth shall shake: but the Lord will be the hope of his people, and the strength of the children of Israel* (if you do this then you will find the Lord giving you strength and hope).

"So shall ye know that I am the Lord your God dwelling in Zion, my holy mountain: then shall Jerusalem be holy, and there shall no strangers pass through her any more (Then shall you know that God dwells in your highest spiritual centre in the crown of your head and the holy city of your body shall be purified and dark thoughts and

deeds will not be hatched there any more)." For more references to Zion see Joel 3: 21; Amos 1: 2 & 6: 1; and Obadiah 1: 17 & 21.

Micah 1: 13 The Lord warns the people to reign in their desires or else risk offending the God within.

"O thou inhabitants of Lachish, bind the chariot to the swift beast (reign in your desires): *she is the beginning of the sin to the daughter of Zion* (desire is the beginning of all other evils encompassing the soul): *for the transgressions of Israel were found in thee."*

Micah 3: 9 & 10 The Lord warns that Cosmic Consciousness and the bodily city are being polluted by sin.

"Hear this, I pray you, ye heads of the house of Jacob, and princes of the house of Israel, that abhor judgement, and pervert all equity (beware all ye who sin).

"They build up Zion with blood (Sins create a wall around the Cosmic Consciousness in man), *and Jerusalem with iniquity* (and pollute the body with corruption)."

Micah 4: 1 & 2 God assures the people that eventually everyone will merge into Zion, His Cosmic Consciousness.

"But in the last days it shall come to pass, that the mountains of the house of the Lord shall be established in the top of the mountains (In the last days of your ignorance, you will attain Cosmic Consciousness which resides in the highest spiritual centre at the top of your head), *and it shall be exalted above the hills* (this highest centre is closer to God-Realisation than the lower centre lying between the small hills of the eyebrows); *and people shall flow unto it* (everyone will eventually attain it).

"And many nations shall come, and say, Come, and let us go up to the mountain of the Lord, and to the house of the God of Jacob (Many people will be called to the spiritual path); *and he* (God) *will teach us of his ways, and we will walk in his paths: for the law shall go forth of Zion, and the word of the Lord from Jerusalem* (and we will be in harmony with God's Law descending from Cosmic Consciousness and the Word of God will issue from the Christ Centre located in the human body)." See the section on 'The Word' for the meaning of 'word' in the above verse.

Zephaniah 3: 14-17
The Lord tells of the great rejoicing to be found in Cosmic Consciousness.

"Sing, O daughter of Zion; shout, O Israel; be glad and rejoice with all the heart, O daughter of Jerusalem (for there will be great joy in the bliss of Cosmic and Christ Consciousness).

"The Lord hath taken away thy judgements (On reaching Cosmic Consciousness all past karma will be removed), *he hath cast out thine enemy* (He has removed Cosmic Satan and Individual Delusion from your consciousnesses): *the king of Israel, even the Lord, is in the midst of thee* (God-consciousness or enlightenment is within you): *thou shalt not see evil any more* (earthly temptations will no longer plague you).

"In that day it shall be said to Jerusalem, Fear thou not: and to Zion, Let not thine hand be slack (When the Consciousness of God has been reached, your spiritual centres will be in no further danger from delusion).

"The Lord thy God in the midst of thee is mighty; he will save, he will rejoice over thee with joy; he will rest in his love, he will joy over thee with singing (God rejoices in love when His lost children return back to Him)."

Zechariah 1: 14 & 17
The Lord promises to return to the two highest Holy Centres in man's head.

"So the angel that communed with me said unto me, Cry thou, saying, Thus saith the Lord of hosts; I am jealous for Jerusalem and for Zion with a great jealousy (I yearn for My children to be able to lift their consciousnesses to the Christ Centre and, even more so, for them to reach the lofty estate of the Crown Centre of Zion)."

"Cry yet, saying, Thus saith the Lord of hosts, My cities through prosperity shall yet be spread abroad (My lesser spiritual centres in the human body will prosper); *and the Lord shall yet comfort Zion, and shall yet choose Jerusalem* (and when this occurs the spiritual centres of Zion and Jerusalem will be comforted by My presence)."

The horns referred to in the verses immediately following the above verses are four of the major spiritual centres that were de-spiritualised and thus prevented man lifting up his consciousness, raising his head, to Jerusalem and Zion. For further references to Zion in Zechariah see also 2: 7 & 10; 8: 2 & 3; and 9: 9-11, which are said to be a prophesy of Jesus' coming.

Matthew 2: 1 & 2 The three wise men were guided to Jesus by the 'Star of the East': Cosmic Consciousness.

"Now when Jesus was born in Bethlehem of Judaea in the days of Herod the king, behold, there came wise men from the east to Jerusalem,

"Saying, Where is he that is born King of the Jews? for we have seen his star in the east, and are come to worship him." The wise men from the east would have had to travel west to Judea, not east, if they had been following an actual star.

Matthew 6: 22 Jesus identifies the Single Eye as an important spiritual centre.

"The light of the body is the eye: if therefore thine eye be single, thy whole body shall be full of light (God, manifesting in Creation as the Divine Light, can be seen at the point of the Christ Centre, the Single Eye located in the forehead of man)."

Matthew 17: 1 & 2 This collective vision emanated from the higher spiritual centres in their bodies.

"And after six days Jesus taketh Peter, James, and John his brother, and bringeth them up into a high mountain apart (to the highest spiritual centre in the head),

"And was transfigured before them: and his face did shine as the sun, and his raiment was white as the light."

Revelation 3: 12 God, via an angel, uses the term 'new Jerusalem' in place of Zion of the Old Testament.

"Him that overcometh will I make a pillar of the temple of my God (He that overcomes Cosmic Satan and individual delusion will attain enlightenment), *and he shall go no more out* (need incarnate no more)*: and I will write upon him the name of my God, and the name of the city of my God, which is new Jerusalem* (Cosmic Consciousness in the Crown Chakra), *which cometh down out of heaven from my God* (which comes from God beyond Creation)*: and I will write upon him my new name."* See the section on 'The Word' for the meaning of 'name' in the above verse.

Revelation 7: 2 & 3 St. John saw an angel ascending in his Single Eye which is located on the east side of the body.

"And I saw another angel ascending from the east (rising from the Christ Centre in my forehead), *having the seal of the living God* (the

power of Cosmic Consciousness) *and he cried with a loud voice to the four angels, to whom it was given to hurt the earth and the sea,* "*Saying, Hurt not the earth, neither the sea, nor the trees* (do not become hidden from man's perception), *till we have sealed the servants of our God in their foreheads* (till we have established the devotees of God in the Christ Centre in their foreheads)." The four angels are the four Primal Psychological forces that are the first-born differentiation of Spirit from which Creation evolves. Together these four psychological forces constitute the supreme unconditional love of God. In the Hindu Scriptures they are described as Eternal, Blissful, Ancient and Ever-New (God Talks With Arjuna pages 772-773). See the section on 'The Tree of Life' for the meaning of 'trees'.

Revelation 21: 2 & 3 St. John sees new Jerusalem coming down from God to reside with men.

"*And I John saw the holy city* (Cosmic Light), *new Jerusalem, coming down from God out of heaven* (Cosmic Consciousness), *prepared as a bride adorned for her husband.*

"*And I heard a great voice out of heaven saying, Behold the tabernacle of God is with men, and he will dwell with them, and they shall be his people, and God himself shall be with them, and be their God* (I heard the Voice of God, the Amen, saying that when man lifts his consciousness to the centre of Cosmic Consciousness in the Crown Chakra he will know that he is with Me and I am with him)." See the section on 'The Word' for the meaning of 'a great voice'.

3

The Tree of Life.

> ***They*** **(the wise)** *speak of an eternal ashvattha tree, with roots above and boughs beneath, whose leaves are Vedic hymns. He who understands this tree of life is a Veda-knower.*
> (God Talks With Arjuna, Ch. XV: 1, page 927)

> *And he shall be like a tree planted by the rivers of water, that bringeth forth his fruit in his season; his leaf also shall not wither; and whatsoever he doeth shall prosper.*
> (Psalm 1: 3)

Saints have often described the wonders of the human body that are hidden from the sight of ordinary people. The physical body, they tell us, is only the coarse outer manifestation of two other finer spiritual realms. Just as God made Creation out of the Causal, Astral and Physical Worlds, His macrocosmic garb, the human form is His microcosmic garb, brought into manifestation through the conjunction of man's individual causal, astral and physical bodies. As God's Cosmic Consciousness descends from the realm of ideas (causal) to the realm of energy (astral), man's magnificent and intricate body of light energy comes into being. This consists of seven major energy centres or chakras, supported by 72,000 minor energy centres, linked by a dense network of subtle nervous systems or energy 'cables.' At the final level of condensation or solidification of God's original ideations, the physical form of man becomes manifest with its intricate network of visible nerves.

Each of these three networks of thought, light and matter, is commonly referred to by the saints as a 'tree.' The reason for this can be most clearly understood from the perspective of the human body which, when upended with the hair hanging downwards like roots, and the branches of the nervous systems in the body and limbs stretching upwards, looks almost tree-like. The analogy can be carried further with the nerve branches seen as reaching up to the cosmic heavens to bring the energies of life down to the earth; and the fruit of the tree being the divine perceptions the seeker can gather from its spiritualised branches.

In the Second Coming of Christ, page 610, Paramahansa Yogananda describes in detail these three types of 'tree' (casual, astral and physical) that together comprise the 'Tree of Life' referred to in the scriptures, by saints in general, and the Bible in particular:

> *And out of the ground* (the earthy human body) *made the Lord to grow every tree that is pleasant to the sight, and good for food; the tree of life also in the midst of the garden, and the tree of knowledge of good and evil.*
> (Genesis 2: 9)

Many different kinds of tree are used in this analogy, depending on the culture of the author concerned. In scriptures originating in Middle East, as indeed the biblical books were, the fig tree and the vine often feature:

> *Return, we beseech thee, O God of hosts: look down from heaven, and behold, and visit this vine; And the vineyard which thy right hand hath planted, and the branch that thou madest strong for thyself.*
> (Psalm 80: 14 & 15)

Quite clearly the 'trees' comprising the Tree of Life are essential to the existence of human kind, to the way in which we gain our perceptions of the world, and to our spiritual development. In this the 'tree of knowledge of good and evil' plays an essential role as unspiritual thoughts, words and deeds remove the perpetrator even further from the Godhead, while 'good' thoughts and actions lead to spiritual progress.

> *Even so every good tree bringeth forth good fruit; but a corrupt tree bringeth forth evil fruit.*
> (Matthew 7: 17)

In defining the difference between good and evil actions Jesus is reported as saying:

> *And whosoever speaketh a word against the Son of man, it shall be forgiven him: but whosoever speaketh against the Holy Ghost, it shall not be forgiven him, neither in this world, neither in the world to come.*
> (Matthew 12: 32)

By this Jesus did not mean that any evil thoughts, words or actions directed at an ordinary man (the Son of man) could be forgiven but not those directed at God (as the Holy Ghost). The real meaning of this saying is that any evil done by man to man will not cause the evildoers permanent separation from God, though it will prolong it of course. But, since the Holy Ghost is the way back to God (See the section headed 'The Word'), man cannot return to his celestial home while he continues to ignore this God-given Way, whether he be in the physical body (this world) or after death in the astral world (the world to come).

For this reason Jesus continues his saying by encouraging man to make up his mind whether he wants to return Home or not, for God will not receive a prodigal son into His Kingdom if his Tree of Life cannot yield the fruits of divine perceptions.

> *Either make the tree good, and his fruit good; or make the tree corrupt, and his fruit corrupt: for the tree is known by his fruit.*
> (Matthew 12: 33)

This point is also made at the end of the Bible in the book of Revelation, where God emphasises the importance of the Tree of Life to man's spiritual quest by pointing out that those who lead spiritual lives (obey the laws of right behaviour, God's commandments) will be given the opportunity to spiritualise their Tree of Life. This they can do, God says through the ascended Jesus, by passing through the 'gates' of the Single Eye into the 'holy city' within the body.

> *Blessed are they that do his commandments, that they may have right to the tree of life, and may enter in through the gates into the city.*
> (Revelation 22: 14,)

It follows that whether one is a Christian or from any other faith, the Way back to God is by spiritualising one's Tree of Life, the major centres of which are the seven main energy concentrations of life force called chakras. These are not physical centres but astral and causal in nature and are spaced up the spine. The two highest chakras, the Crown Chakra and the Christ Centre or Single Eye between the eyebrows, have been discussed in the last section. The other five chakras are located at the throat (Cervical Chakra), the heart (Dorsal Chakra), the navel (Lumbar Chakra), midway between the navel and the genitals (Sacral Chakra), and at the base of the spine (Coccygeal Chakra). Each astral chakra consists of a particular group of energies responsible for the operation and manifestation of certain functions of the human body and properties of man's life and consciousness. The Coccygeal Chakra for instance underpins all matter in the body and governs the elimination process, while the Christ Centre or Medullar Chakra is the gateway to God. Furthermore each chakra emits a characteristic astral sound, a sub-sound of the mighty Aum resounding at the Christ Centre or Single Eye. These are in descending order: the roar of a distant ocean, the sound of a gong or conch, the playing of a lyre of harp, the sound of a flute and the humming of a bee.

The details of the workings of the various chakras are beyond the scope of this book. It is enough to record here that these centres exist and have to be freed from materialistic tendencies and spiritualised before man's three bodies (physical, astral and causal) are refined sufficiently for him to be admitted to the higher spiritual realms. These centres are alluded to in both Old and New Testaments including the book of Revelation where they are called the seven 'churches':

> *He that hath an ear, let him hear what the Spirit saith unto the churches; To him that overcometh will I give to eat of the tree of life, which is in the midst of the paradise of God* (the human body).
> (Revelation 2: 7)

These inner spiritual wonders are often likened in saintly literature, including the Holy Bible, to a flower garden growing amazing blooms of divine experiences. In the poem below by one of India's most renown lovers of God, Mira, the Indian warrior-princess talks of the rare blooms that grow in the human body under the care of the divine honeybee (The Word) and the accompanying Divine Light. The Word and Light are described later, in the section called 'What is Knowledge?'.

> *In your body are gardens with rare blooms,*
> *But a honeybee alone will seek their fragrance.*
> *Within your body burns a flame*
> *In resounding waves of brilliant Light.*
> (Mira, 16th century Indian saint)

What the Bible Says About The Tree of Life.

The life and consciousness of man is expressed through seven main spiritual centres and 72,000 minor ones. This is the miraculous garden through which man walks and talks with his Creator.

Genesis 2: 9 God put the Tree of Life in the centre of man's body.
"And out of the ground made the Lord to grow every tree that is

pleasant to the sight, and good for food; the tree of life also in the midst of the garden, and the tree of knowledge of good and evil (The Lord formed in the body of man the trees of consciousness, life force and the physical nervous system, which collectively make up the main Tree of Life essential for man to harvest or taste the fruits of his good and evil actions on earth)."

Genesis 3: 8 Adam and Eve could not contact God directly after their Trees of Life had become corrupted.
"And they (Adam and Eve) *heard the voice of the Lord God walking in the garden in the cool of the day: and Adam and his wife hid themselves from the presence of the Lord God among the trees of the garden."* For the meaning of the 'Voice of God' see the section on 'The Word'.

Psalm 1: 3 The Tree of Life of the man who meditates on the Law of God will be purified so that he can attain enlightenment.
"And he shall be like a tree planted by the rivers of water (like a Tree of Life planted in the divine current of Cosmic Consciousness), *that bringeth forth his fruit in his season* (brings enlightenment in due course); *his leaf also shall not wither* (the leaves of divine revelations growing from his Tree of Life shall also endure); *and whatsoever he doeth shall prosper."* See the section on 'Enlightenment'.

Psalm 52: 8 David says that his spiritual 'olive' Tree of Life has been enlivened through God.
"But I am like a green olive tree in the house of God: I trust in the mercy of God for ever and ever."

Psalm 80: 7, 8, 14 & 15 David uses the vine as a symbol for the Tree of Life.
"Turn us again (May Your power O Lord draw our attention inwards to You once again), *O God of hosts, and cause thy face to shine* (so that Your divine Light shines within us once more); *and we shall be saved.*
"Thou hast brought a vine out of Egypt (You have put the subtle Tree of Life in each one of us which saves us from ignorance of body-consciousness): *thou hast cast out the heathen, and planted it* (You cast out the darkness of ignorance when You planted the Tree

of Life in the human body and whenever You return through man's spiritual efforts the Tree becomes pure)."

"*Return, we beseech thee, O God of hosts: look down from heaven, and behold, and visit this vine* (Come down again from Cosmic Consciousness and spiritualise this Tree);

"*And the vineyard which thy right hand hath planted, and the branch that thou madest strong for thyself* (and redeem the 'vines' of all Your children in their 'vineyards' and redeem mankind which is nought but a branch of Your Cosmic Self)." Here is another example of Egypt being used as a metaphor for the darkness of ignorance which holds man captive in the cycle of death and rebirth.

Proverbs 3: 18 & 23 Wisdom rises spontaneously from a perfected Tree of Life.

"*She is a tree of life to them that lay hold upon her* (She, wisdom, arises out of a perfected Tree of Life): *and happy is every one that retaineth her* (and happy are those who attain and retain wisdom)."

"*Then shalt thou walk in thy way safely, and thy foot shall not stumble.*"

Proverbs 11: 30 Enlightenment comes when the Tree of Life is perfected.

"*The fruit of righteousness is a tree of life* (Enlightenment comes when our Tree of Life and consciousness is pure): *and he that winneth souls is wise* (the Master who snatches souls out of the clutches of worldly temptations achieves it by Divine Wisdom)."

Ezekiel 28: 14 & 15 God describes how man's consciousness has moved up and down the seven chakras.

"*Thou art the anointed cherub that covereth* (You are the soul, supreme over creation); *and I have set thee so* (I made you that way): *thou wast upon the holy mountain of God* (initially you were united with Me in the Holy Mountain of your Crown Chakra): *thou hast walked up and down in the midst of the stones of fire* (your consciousness has slid up and down the seven spiritual centres, chakras, in your body).

"*Thou wast perfect in thy ways from the day that thou wast created, till iniquity was found in thee* (You were the perfect reflection of God until you fell under the thrall of satanic delusion)."

Micah 4: 3 & 4 The Lord says that when man turns to Him he will be secure in his spiritualised Tree of Life.

"And he (God) *shall judge among many people, and rebuke strong nations afar off* (through His Law of Karma); *and they shall beat their swords into plowshares, and their spears into pruninghooks: nation shall not lift up a sword against nation, neither shall they learn war any more* (and a time of non-violence and spirituality shall come to the earth).

"But they shall sit every man under his vine and under his fig tree (The minds and actions of men will be in harmony with their spiritualised Trees of Life); *and none shall make them afraid: for the mouth of the Lord of hosts hath spoken it* (and they will not fear death or any such earthly calamity for they will realise that they are spirit and not flesh)." See the section called 'The Word' for the meaning of 'the mouth of God'.

Matthew 3: 10 John the Baptist berates the priesthood for having cut themselves off from their Trees of Life.

"And now also the axe is laid unto the root of the trees: therefore every tree which bringeth not forth good fruit is hewn down, and cast into the fire (All hypocrites will lose contact with their subtle spiritual centres and will become the victims of the fires of their own desires)."

Matthew 7: 17 Jesus confirms the results of man having spiritual and unspiritual Trees of Life.

"Even so every good tree (person with a spiritualised Tree of Life) *bringeth forth good fruit* (performs spiritual actions); *but a corrupt tree* (a spiritually ignorant person whose Tree of Life has become corrupted) *bringeth forth evil fruit* (out of his own choice performs evil actions)."

Matthew 12: 32 & 33 An unspiritual Tree of Life yields bad actions but a spiritual one yields good actions.

"And whosoever speaketh a word against the Son of man (Whoever unjustly condemns an ordinary person), *it shall be forgiven him* (he will be forgiven eventually): *but whosoever speaketh against the Holy Ghost, it shall not be forgiven him, neither in this world, neither in the world to come* (Since being in total harmony with God-the-

Holy Ghost is the only way to reach enlightenment, a person who persists in violating this great force of spiritual harmony cannot possibly become One with the Godhead while they continue to do so).

"Either make the tree good, and his fruit good (Either spiritualise the composite Tree of Life and benefit accordingly); *or make the tree corrupt, and his fruit corrupt* (or ruin your Tree of Life by bad actions and suffer accordingly): *for the tree is known by his fruit* (a good person has a spiritualised Tree of Life and performs good actions and vice versa)."* See the section called 'The Word' for the meaning of 'the Holy Ghost'.

Revelation 1: 12-14 St. John describes the seven spiritual centres 'growing' in the Tree of Life of man.

"And I turned to see the voice that spake with me. And being turned, I saw seven golden candlesticks (the seven spiritual centres that underpin the physical body of man);

"And in the midst of the seven golden candlesticks one like unto the Son of man (the astral form of the angel resembling a human being), *clothed with a garment down to the foot, and girt about the paps with a golden girdle.*

"His head and his hairs were white like wool, as white as snow; and his eyes were as a flame of fire;"

Revelation 1: 19 & 20 The astral angel explains the significance of the seven stars and the candlesticks.

"Write the things which thou hast seen, and the things which are, and the things which shall be hereafter;

"The mystery of the seven stars which thou sawest in my right hand, and the seven golden candlesticks, The seven stars are the angels of the seven churches (The seven stars are the Cosmic Energy enlivening the seven centres of the astral energy vortices shaped like candlesticks); *and the seven candlesticks which thou sawest are the seven churches* (the seven candlesticks are the Holy Edifices through which the Divine Light manifests as life)."*

Revelation 2: 7 Those who overcome the pull of the world shall reap the benefits flowing from their Trees of Life.

"He that hath an ear, let him hear what the Spirit said unto the

churches (hear what God has to say about the seven subtle spiritual centres in man); *To him that overcometh will I give to eat of the tree of life* (I will give divine perceptions to the person who overcomes the delusions of this world through his Tree of Life), *which is in the midst of the paradise of God* (which is in the middle of the human body and which I, God, created to enable man to express the 'paradise' of God-union)."

Revelation 7: 2-4 Man cannot return to the Godhead until his entire Tree of Life is spiritualised.

"And I saw another angel ascending from the east (from the realm of Christ Consciousness), *having the seal of the living God* (having the power of Cosmic Consciousness): *and he cried with a loud voice to the four angels, to whom it was given to hurt the earth and the sea,*

"Saying, Hurt not the earth (the physical body), *neither the sea* (the astral body of fluid light energy), *nor the trees* (Trees of Life), *till we have sealed the servants of our God* (till the true devotees of God have their consciousnesses established) *in their foreheads* (in their Single Eyes).

"And I heard the number of them which were sealed: and there were sealed an hundred and forty and four thousand of all the tribes of the children of Israel." There are 72, 000 minor energy centres (Nadis) in a human being's Tree of Life, each one of which has a positive and negative pole, making 144, 000 energy centres which must be spiritualised or saved before man can become enlightened.

Revelation 14: 1 St. John sees God-the-Son amidst the Tree of Life.

"And I looked, and, lo, a Lamb (I saw the Lamb of Primal Purity, the Christ Consciousness) *stood on the mount Sion* (ensconced in Cosmic Consciousness in the Crown Chakra), *and with him an hundred forty and four thousand, having his Father's name written on their foreheads."* God supplies Cosmic Energy to the human body through the Christ Consciousness and the 144,000 minor centres, the Nadis, comprising the Tree of Life and consciousness in man. The Nadis have to be purified in the stream of the Cosmic Aum or Amen for man to become enlightened. See the section called 'The Word' for the meaning of 'his Father's name'.

Revelation 22: 1 & 2 St. John sees his purified Tree of Life with all its subtle branches carrying energy to the body.

"And he (the angel) *shewed me a pure river of water of life* (spiritual

energy flowing out of God to maintain the human body), *clear as crystal, proceeding out of the throne of God and of the Lamb* (out of Cosmic and Christ Consciousness).

"In the midst of the street of it (in the middle of this energy stream), *and on either side of the river, was there the tree of life, which bare twelve manner of fruits, and yielded her fruit every month* (The Tree of Life was purified by the clear stream of Cosmic Consciousness and yielded the fruits of Divine Realisation in the appropriate way and time): *and the leaves of the tree were for the healing of the nations* (and the spiritual gifts 'hanging' from the Tree are there for the purpose of spiritualising all people)."

Revelation 22: 14 St. John is told that whoever follows Divine Law will reach God through their pure Tree of Life.

"Blessed are they that do his commandments (that follow Divine Law), *that they may have right to the tree of life* (that they will have earned the right to a spiritualised Tree of Life), *and may enter in through the gates into the city* (and may then reach God-union through the 'gates' of the centres of Christ and Cosmic Consciousness)."

4

What is Intuition?

> **Wisdom is the principal thing; therefore get wisdom:**
> **and with all thy getting get understanding.**
> (Proverbs 4: 7)

> *As a donkey is tied to another donkey,*
> *So are men tethered to their predilections.*
> *He who sees with his soul's eye*
> *Is the truly realised one.*
> *Biased with one view or another,*
> *All the rest dwell in delusion.*
> (Kabir, 15th century Muslim Saint)

Before the expulsion of man from the Garden of Eden, the state of God-consciousness, he enjoyed direct contact with his Source. Through his highly spiritualised Tree of Life, the archetypal man, Adam, could see God clearly in vision and could converse directly with Him in audible words.

> And *the Lord God called unto Adam, and said unto him, Where art thou? And he said, I heard thy voice in the garden* (among my spiritual centres)*, and I was afraid, because I was naked* (had become body-conscious)*; and I hid myself.*
> (Genesis 3: 9 & 10)

But after the 'Fall', as man began to listen more and more to the dictates of his ego, the gulf between man and God increased such that, by the time of the prophet Samuel, this direct contact had been lost to most men.

> *And the child Samuel ministered unto the Lord before Eli. And the word of the Lord was precious in those days; there was no open vision."*
> (I Samuel 3: 1)

Thereafter mankind needed the prophets, the Self-Realised saints, to act as intermediaries between God and man.

> *And there came a man of God unto Eli, and said unto him, Thus saith the Lord, Did I plainly appear unto the house of thy father, when they were in Egypt in Pharaoh's house?*
> (I Samuel 2: 27)

Today, modern man is responding most of the time to the dictates of his own ego, which makes its demands through the medium of his mind. Consequently the gulf between himself and God-consciousness is vast. But God has not left us entirely bereft. His guidance is always there if we but look for it. Our problem though is that in almost everyone the ego voice is so loud that it drowns out another much quieter voice that is continuously trying to reach us from the centre of silence within. This is the voice of God, the voice of our soul, which speaks to us from the inner silence of the stilled mind.

> *Thus saith the Lord, thy Redeemer, the Holy One of Israel; I am the Lord thy God which teacheth thee to profit, which leadeth thee by the way that thou shouldest go.*
> (Isaiah 48: 17)

This divine guidance, when we can hear it, is infallible. It is the wisdom of God referred to by all saints, including Jesus and the Old Testament prophets, as explained by St. Paul:

> *Howbeit we speak wisdom among them that are perfect: yet not the wisdom of this world, nor of the princes of this world that come to nought: But we speak wisdom of God in a mystery, even the hidden wisdom, which God ordained before the world unto our glory: Which none of the princes of this world knew: for had they known it, they would not have crucified the Lord of glory.*
> (I Corinthians 2: 6–8)

Whether we are aware of it or not, we all experience flashes of intuition. Such experiences come to us as moments when we know with absolute clarity what we should do in a particular situation, even though the divine guidance runs contrary to what our ego wants us to do.

> *For my thoughts are not your thoughts, neither are your ways my ways, saith the Lord. For as the heavens are higher than the earth, so are my ways higher than your ways, and my thoughts than your thoughts.*
> (Isaiah 55: 8 & 9)

Those who have been fortunate enough to spend time in the presence of an Enlightened Teacher can confirm that he/she does not act indiscriminately or rashly. Such Great Ones perform all actions in perfect harmony with Divine Will, which involves doing the right thing, at the right time, in the right way.

> *To every thing there is a season, and a time to every purpose under the heaven:*
> (Ecclesiastes 3: 1)

When actions are in perfect accord with the Will of God, they attract no karmic effect. Such actions become what the saints refer to as 'Action-less Actions.' Thus, in order to avoid accruing karma, the aim of every spiritual seeker is to increase this intuitive contact with God.

> *In all thy ways acknowledge him, and he shall direct thy paths.*
> (Proverbs 3: 6)

A person with a well–developed intuition will be able to distinguish more easily between the demands of the ego-voice in the mind and that of the quiet voice of the soul. And when the intuition is perfectly developed, the ego-voice will have receded completely into the background.

A wise person is very different from an intelligent one. Intuition 'knows' with infallible precision what to do, when to do it, and how it should be done. It is the Great Synthesiser. No matter how complicated the issue, it 'knows' the result. The function of the intellect is to follow this infallible guidance and work out the details of how to put it into practice. Thus when intellect operates under the guidance of the intuition, the result is perfect. On the other hand, when intellect is influenced by ego, the normal state of the mind of man, though the logic based on the set of evidence available may appear faultless, the end conclusion is almost always erroneous.

Even today, Masters fully united with God have the ability to 'walk and talk' with their Creator through direct vision. During daily activity, while conversing with or teaching their disciples, it is not unusual for them to slip into Christ or Cosmic Consciousness and speak directly with the voice of God. There are many instances recorded throughout the Old and New Testaments of Enlightened Ones doing just that.

> *I, even I, am he that comforteth you: who art thou, that thou shouldest be afraid of a man that shall die, and of the son of man which shall be made as grass?*
> (Isaiah 51:12)

> *Jesus saith unto him, I am the way, the truth, and the life: no man cometh unto the Father, but by me.*
> (John 14: 6)

In view of the imagery and other literary tools used by the saints of all times, today's Enlightened Teachers warn that any of the world's scriptures, including the Bible, can be understood only through the intuition. More often than not, Divine Truths are distorted into untruth when filtered through the faulty screen of the ego-mind.

Although it is vital to develop and practise intuitive guidance, spiritual seekers should be aware of the grave danger of assuming that they have perfected the art when they have not. It is as well to remember that the ego principle was the cause of man's original fall from Grace in the early days of Creation: the Garden of Eden. Ego was the first step in man's separation from his Maker and it is always the last thing to go. Ego is not tamed completely until one is enlightened; and enlightenment is by no means just a matter of **belief**. It is **experienced**. It is won through a process of rigorous spiritual discipline under the guidance of a spiritually qualified teacher, an Enlightened One.

What the Bible Says About Intuition.

The man who depends solely upon his reasoning power is a lost soul. A vastly higher level of guidance exists which man ignores at his peril. Logic and intellect are simply not enough. One must be able to access the wisdom of the intuition: the silent voice of God who resides within the human body as Soul.

Genesis 1: 1 to 3: 24 This story of how mankind lost its ability to 'walk and talk' freely with God is purely allegorical. The Garden of Eden was a high spiritual state. Adam represents the 'male' characteristics of the soul: justice and wisdom. Eve is the female aspect of the soul: compassion, creativity and emotion. The 'Fall' represents the loss of ability of mankind to freely converse with God through his intuitive all-seeing faculty. It occurred as a result of the wisdom of man (Adam) being overcome by his feelings (Eve tendencies). When that happened the first barrier was drawn between mankind and God. By successive steps of violating God-uniting laws, mankind eventually lost the ability to go into the Silence within himself and commune there with his Maker.

Genesis 3: 9 & 10 Adam heard God's voice talking to him among the 'garden' of his spiritual centres.

"And the Lord God called unto Adam, and said unto him, Where art thou?

"And he said, I heard thy voice in the garden (among the spiritual centres in my body), *and I was afraid, because I was naked* (I had become body-conscious and afraid); *and I hid myself."*

Genesis 7: 1 Unlike most of mankind at that time the righteous Noah could still talk directly with God.

"And the Lord said unto Noah, Come thou and all thy house into the ark; for thee have I seen righteous before me in this generation."

Exodus 3: 1 to 4: 17 In this episode of the burning bush the detail of the conversation suggests that God spoke directly to Moses in the form of an audible voice. Since Moses was an enlightened soul, the 'voice' may have been formed out of the Word (See the section on 'The Word'), or may have come to him in an ecstatic vision. On other occasions, however, it is likely that God 'spoke' to Moses through the prophet's well-developed intuition. By this stage in man's sojourn on earth, ordinary man had separated himself so thoroughly from his inner Self, God within, that he was unable to contact his intuition. God contact had become the preserve of the prophets. See also I Samuel 3: 1 quoted below.

Exodus 19: 3 & 5 Moses hears the voice of God 'talking' to him in a state of inner ecstatic communication.

"And Moses went up unto God (raised his spiritual consciousness), *and the lord called unto him out of the mountain* (intimated his wishes through the silent voice of God within, the seat of which is the highest centre in the head of man: the Holy Mountain of Cosmic Consciousness), *saying, Thus shall thou say to the house of Jacob, and tell the children of Israel;"*

"Now therefore, if ye will obey my voice indeed, and keep my covenant, then ye shall be a peculiar treasure unto me above all people (if you obey My voice of intuition which speaks from the Silence within you, you will be a rare one among the people of the earth): *for all the earth is mine:"*

Deuteronomy 32: 10 God found Jacob in the desert of the world and guided him through his intuition.

"He (God) *found him* (Jacob) *in a desert land, and in the waste howling wilderness* (lost in the meaningless clamour of the world); *he led him about, he instructed him* (God guided Jacob through the voice of intuitive wisdom), *he kept him as the apple of his eye* (and helped Jacob keep his focus at the Christ Centre)."

I Samuel 2: 27 God speaks to Eli through the agency of an Enlightened One's intuition.
"And there came a man of God unto Eli, and said unto him, Thus saith the Lord, Did I plainly appear unto the house of thy father, when they were in Egypt in Pharaoh's house?"

I Samuel 3: 1 By the time Samuel was born, God rarely spoke in direct vision even to the prophets.
"And the child Samuel ministered unto the Lord before Eli. And the word of the Lord was precious in those days; there was no open vision."

Psalm 46: 10 God emphasises that we need to curb the 'noise' of the mind in order to find Him.
"Be still, and know that I am God (Be still in body, senses and mind and experience the Divine Being within you)*: I will be exalted among the heathen* (even the ignorant will eventually come to know Me)*, I will be exalted in the earth* (I will be praised within Creation)*."*

Proverbs 3: 5 Have faith in the Lord's silent voice within you and do not rely on the urgings of your ego.
"Trust in the Lord with all thine heart; and lean not unto thine own understanding."

Proverbs 3: 6 When you practise listening to the intuition it will lead you perfectly in everything you do.
"In all thy ways acknowledge him (God)*, and he shall direct thy paths* (and He will guide you through the silent voice of intuition)*."*

Proverbs 4: 7 Wisdom is intuitive knowledge of what to do, when to do it, and how it should be done.
"Wisdom is the principal thing; therefore get wisdom: and with all thy getting get understanding."

Ecclesiastes 3: 1 The intuition leads man to do the right thing at the right time.
"To every thing there is a season, and a time to every purpose under the heaven:"

Isaiah 48: 17 The Lord announces that He is the silent voice within that is constantly guiding us back to Him.

"Thus saith the Lord, thy Redeemer, the Holy One of Israel; I am the Lord thy God which teacheth thee to profit, which leadeth thee by the way that thou shouldest go."

Isaiah 51:12 Isaiah, the Enlightened One, speaks with the voice of God.

"I, even I, am he that comforteth you: who art thou, that thou shouldest be afraid of a man that shall die, and of the son of man which shall be made as grass?" For Masters to speak with the voice of God is a phenomenon considerably more common than generally recognised.

Isaiah 55: 8 & 9 It is difficult to understand God except through direct perception: the intuition.

"For my thoughts are not your thoughts, neither are your ways my ways, saith the Lord (Spiritual ways of thinking differ considerably from those of materially inclined mankind).

"For as the heavens are higher than the earth, so are my ways higher than your ways, and my thoughts than your thoughts (Just as the heavenly realms are more subtle than gross earthly vibrations, spiritual thoughts differ from the thoughts of body-conscious man)."

Micah 4: 2 The Lord advises man to lift his consciousnesses and listen to intuitive guidance.

"And many nations shall come, and say, Come, and let us go up to the mountain of the Lord (let us raise our consciousnesses up to the higher spiritual centres in the mountain of the head), *and to the house of the God of Jacob* (where Cosmic Consciousness, that Jacob enjoyed, resides); *and he will teach us of his ways, and we will walk in his paths* (and God shall guide us through our intuition): *for the law shall go forth of Zion* (for Cosmic Consciousness and its laws of harmony descend from God into the Crown Chakra of man), *and the word of the Lord from Jerusalem* (and the Word descends from the Christ Centre)." See the section on 'The Word' for the meaning of 'word'.

Apocrypha, Ecclesiasticus 1: 5 Intuition is the voice of God issuing from the bosom of the Holy Word.

"The word of God most high is the fountain of wisdom; and her

ways are everlasting commandments (wisdom as received through the silent voice of God within, intuition, should be followed to the letter)." See the section on 'The Word' for the meaning of 'word'.

Apocrypha, Ecclesiasticus 4: 26 We must be humble enough to confess our sins and follow the intuition.

"*Be not ashamed to confess thy sins, and force not the course of the river* (do not go against the constant stream of God's advice coming through the intuition)."

Matthew 4: 18-22 Jesus' disciples intuitively recognised their Master and immediately followed him.

"*And Jesus, walking by the sea of Galilee, saw two brethren, Simon called Peter, and Andrew his brother, casting a net into the sea: for they were fishers.*

"*And he saith unto them, Follow me, and I will make you fishers of men.*

"*And they straightway left their nets, and followed him.*

"*And going on from thence, he saw other two brethren, James the son of Zebedee, and John his brother, in a ship with Zebedee their father, mending their nets; and he called them.*

"*And they immediately left the ship and their father, and followed him.*" See also Mark 1: 16-20. These verses as well as others in the New Testament tell how Jesus' disciples so readily gave up their normal lives to follow him. This is because they had been his disciples in former lives and recognised him at a deep intuitive level.

Matthew 16: 15-17 Peter identifies, by means of his intuition, Jesus as the one with the Christ Consciousness.

"*He saith unto them, But whom say ye that I am?*

"*And Simon Peter answered and said, Thou art the Christ, the Son of the living God.*

"*And Jesus answered and said unto him, Blessed art thou, Simon Barjona: for flesh and blood hath not revealed it unto thee, but my Father which is in heaven.*"

Mark 6: 2 Jesus spoke his words of wisdom from the power of intuition, the silent voice of God within him.

"*And when the Sabbath day was come, he* (Jesus) *began to teach in the synagogue: and many hearing him were astonished saying,*

From whence hath this man these things? and what wisdom is this which is given unto him, that even such mighty works are wrought by his hands?" Ordinary men get fleeting glimpses of intuitive understanding. By contrast Masters like Jesus live constantly in the Silence from which pure undistorted wisdom flows from the intuition.

John 8: 28 Jesus affirms that he does not follow his own ego but God's voice though his intuition.

"Then Jesus said unto them, When ye have lifted up the Son of man (when you have spiritualised your consciousness), *then shall ye know that I am he, and that I do nothing of myself; but as my Father hath taught me, I speak these things* (then you will know that I do not speak from the ego but through the silent voice of God within me: my intuition)."

John 14: 6 An example of Jesus speaking directly with the Voice of the Christ Consciousness which is the fount of God's intuitive guidance.

"Jesus saith unto him, I am the way, the truth, and the life: no man cometh unto the Father, but by me." The Christ Consciousness is the gateway all must pass through to unite with the Godhead.

I Corinthians 2: 6-8 St. Paul explains the difference between the wisdom of intuition and worldly cleverness.

"Howbeit we speak wisdom among them that are perfect: yet not the wisdom of this world, nor of the princes of this world that come to nought (the wisdom we speak is not the same as that of earthly men nor of the intellectual elite):

"But we speak wisdom of God in a mystery, even the hidden wisdom (our wisdom comes from the secret place of Silence within), *which God ordained before the world unto our glory* (which is a facet of our souls which God made before He made the material creation):

"Which none of the princes of this world knew: for had they known it, they would not have crucified the Lord of glory (If the leaders of this world had known of this source of God's guidance and followed it, they would not have crucified Jesus but followed his teachings instead)."

I Corinthians 2: 12 & 13 The voice of spirit inside us is the intuitive guidance given by the Grace of the Holy Ghost.

"Now we have received, not the spirit of the world, but the spirit

which is of God; that we might know the things that are freely given to us of God.

"Which things also we speak, not in the words which man's wisdom teacheth, but which the Holy Ghost teacheth; comparing spiritual things with spiritual."

I John 2: 27 **St. John tells his initiates to trust in their intuition which has come about through their initiation.**

"But the anointing which ye hath received of him abideth in you (The initiation you have received from me by the grace of the crucified Jesus is a lasting thing)*, and ye not that any man teach you* (and no one has to teach you anything else because the Knowledge you have received is complete in itself)*: but as the same anointing teacheth you of all things, and is truth, and is no lie, and even as it hath taught you, ye shall abide in him* (and the same initiation or anointing will bring you into contact with your intuition and bring all things to you in due course provide you keep faith with the Master's teachings)*."*
See the section on 'Initiation into the Path' for the meaning of 'baptism' and 'anointing'.

Part 4.

Starting on the Journey.

1

Paths to God.

And we have known and believed the love that God hath to us. God is love; and he that dwelleth in love dwelleth in God, and God in him.
(I John 4: 16)

*Love is God's cast,
Love is God's nature,
Love is God's form,
And God's colour,
O Dadu, is love.*
(Dadu, 16th century Indian saint)

The Perennial Philosophy recognises three main paths to union with the Godhead: Discriminative Wisdom, Service and Devotion.

The path of union with God through Discriminative Wisdom is called Jnana Yoga. It involves the practitioner focusing his attention at the site of the Single Eye, the Christ or Krishna Centre, and experiencing the 'Pure Awareness' free from conceptual constructs that is his real Self. One of the greatest exemplars of this path in recent times was the southern Indian saint Ramana Maharshi, who taught his followers to ask themselves the question *"Who am I?"* This practice does not involve any repetition of the question in the form of words but consists in following the initial thought to its Source. Every time the mind wanders away from concentrating on its Source, the practitioner draws it back to its focus via the thought. In due course of time the meditator begins to realise that he is not the 'I' he thought he was. This is exemplified in the quotation by Ramana Maharishi referred to earlier when discussing non-duality.

> *If the first person, "I", exists, then the second and third persons, "you" and "he", will also exist. By enquiring into the nature of the "I", the "I" perishes. With it "you" and "he" also perish. The resultant state, which shines as Absolute Being, is one's own natural state, the Self.*
>
> (From Forty Verses on Reality by Sri Ramana Maharshi)

The basis of Ramana Maharshi's teachings is that the mind and ego are products of our wrong associations and imagination and have no reality. Once the practitioner begins to look inside himself for the 'I ', the ego 'I' disappears and he finds himself 'face to face' with his real self: Pure Awareness or Absolute Being.

For the beginner, the path of Discriminative Wisdom is recognised as the most difficult of the three paths to God-union as it leads directly to the formless God, as opposed to the step-by-step methods from form to the formless employed in the other two paths. Only those who have progressed far along the spiritual path, in this or former lifetimes, are able to use their intellect to good effect and 'punch through' the remaining veils of ignorance to discover their true identity.

For many, Mother Teresa represents the best modern exemplar of the path of union with God through Service or Karma Yoga as it is known in the East. This path suits the devotee who has a giving nature. All those in the nurturing professions, who are consciously serving the God-in-man, such as doctors, teachers, nurses and carers, are on this Godward path. Even those who are in business, not to fill their own coffers but motivated by the urge to provide needful service to communities, also qualify. Among the enlightened saints of India, Shivananda stands out as one of the greatest exponents of the Path of Service. This great 20th century saint, a qualified medical doctor, spent most of his working life giving free medical treatment to the poor. On retiring, he set up an ashram at Rishikesh in the foothills of the Himalayan Mountains and led many worthy disciples to enlightenment.

Jesus also extolled the virtues of the Path of Divine Service in the wonderfully colourful imagery of God as the King of souls calling all compassionate servers of mankind to join Him in His kingdom.

> *Then shall the King say unto them on his right hand, Come, ye blessed of my Father, inherit the kingdom prepared for you from the foundation of the world: For I was an hungred, and ye gave me meat: I was thirsty, and ye gave me drink: I was a stranger, and ye took me in: Naked, and ye clothed me: I was sick, and ye visited me: I was in prison, and ye came unto me. Then shall the righteous answer him, saying, Lord, when saw we thee an hungred, and fed thee? or thirsty, and gave thee drink? When saw we thee a stranger, and took thee in? or naked, and clothed thee? Or when saw we thee sick, or in prison, and came unto thee? And the King shall answer and say unto them, Verily I say unto you, Inasmuch as ye have done it unto one of the least of these my brethren, ye have done it unto me.*
> (Matthew 25: 34-40)

Of the three paths of union, that of Devotion or Bhakti Yoga is said to be the easiest way for it is the closest to God's heart. God Himself is love and that is the very good reason why Jesus extolled love as the greatest law. Of all the divine lovers of all time in the Christian world, Solomon must rate among the greatest.

> *By night on my bed I sought him whom my soul loveth: I sought him, but found him not. I will rise now, and go about the city in the streets, and in the broad ways I will seek him whom my soul loveth: I sought him, but I found him not.*
> (Song of Solomon 3: 1 & 2)

The Songs of Solomon are mostly misunderstood and they certainly do not represent the cooing of a gay man for his lover as is sometimes claimed by cynical westerners. Rather, they are the outpourings of a devotee deeply in love with his Maker, his 'Beloved'.

The theme of the lover yearning to be united to his Beloved, in language often highly sensual in nature, emerges time and time again throughout the literature of the saints, among whom are Kabir, Rumi, Yogananda, Sai Baba and many others.

> *Your charm lured me*
> *to the edge of madness.*
> *I lost my composure.*
> *Humbled, I was sent away.*
> *Then, You touched my heart,*
> *transformed and shaped me*
> *into any form You fancied.*
> (Rumi, 13th century Sufi)

Rumi says that love is the flame that burns up everything except the Beloved and within such a flame all worldly temptations pale into insignificance. At the end of the 'Path' or 'Way', only the Loved One remains.

In trying to illustrate the depth of eternal love binding God and mankind together, saints of all ages have resorted to the analogy of the marriage between the bride and the groom. In this analogy the soul is usually the bride and God is the groom. When they are parted, both bride and groom yearn to be united once more and, when they are together, they have eyes for each other alone.

Saint Arjan Dev, the fifth of the Sikh Gurus, says that, for the soul-bride, life without the divine Husband is worthless. But even when the soul-bride is smeared with the dust of bad karmas, the act of marriage with the Divine Groom cleanses her until she, the soul, shines forth in all her original glory.

> *Without my Husband I will throw all fineries into the*
> *fire; even if I am smeared with dust, I will shine in glory*
> *if you, beloved Husband, are with me.*
> (Guru Arjan Dev, Sikh saint, 1563-1606)

Jesus also quite clearly favoured this analogy of love between the bride and groom. In his Parable of the Ten Virgins, Matthew 25: 1-13, the virgins represent those pure, karma-free souls ready to unite with God, the Bridegroom. The story tells of how five souls were wise and kept the lamps of their minds full of the oil of devotion and the wicks of their Single Eyes aflame with divine love; whereas the remaining five let their lamps go out and were not ready to go to the wedding when the divine Bridegroom came for them. Fuller details of this allegory, and others, are given in the quotations at the end of this section.

> *Then shall the kingdom of heaven be likened unto ten virgins, which took their lamps, and went forth to meet the bridegroom.*
> (Matthew 25: 1)

Yet again, Jesus employed the wedding analogy in the Parable of Marriage of the King's Son, Matthew 22: 1-14. Here, God, in the persona of the king, sent out His messengers of divine vibration (servants) to invite those souls most karmically worthy of union with Him to meet His Son, the Enlightened Master.

> *The kingdom of heaven is like unto a certain king, which made a marriage for his son, And sent forth his servants to call them that were bidden to the wedding: and they would not come.*
> (Matthew 22: 2 & 3)

But the chosen guests declined the invitation because they were still wrapped up in worldly actions. And they continued to ignore the divine servants even when God sent out stronger vibrations to them describing (metaphorically) the wonderful things available to the devotee who is fortunate enough to meet one of God's Sons.

> *Again, he sent forth other servants, saying, Tell them which are bidden, Behold, I have prepared my dinner: my oxen and my fatlings are killed, and all things are*

> *ready: come unto the marriage.*
> (Matthew 22: 4)

When the preferred ones refused to attend for the second time, God sent out His vibrations of invitation to others, less worthy in terms of the quality and quantity of their karmas. For a detailed explanation of the entire parable see 'The Second Coming of Christ,' pages 1274-1276.

But the kind of love that is common currency in the world is very different from the love talked about by the saints. Human love is very 'conditional.' It is tainted with self-interest. As Kabir points out, we should love God because He is the only lover who remains faithful to us throughout our many lives and to whom we return at the very end of all our earthly incarnations. If we do not embrace the Lord, the 'multicoloured love' of the world will continue to stain us with its conditionality 'all the more'.

> *Love him who maintains your love to the very end;* (because) *the multicoloured love of the world will stain you all the more.*
> (Kabir, 15th century Muslim saint)

Human love is said to be 'conditional' because we 'love' certain people whom we regard as our own, who fulfil our needs, and we drop them or 'fall out of love' when that bargaining position or trade-off falls into disuse. This is contrary to the love between God, Master and Disciple. Divine love is unconditional. It cannot be expressed as 'I love you' or even as 'I love'. It is simply 'love', a natural feeling that lies at the root of the soul and is without strings of any kind. It is akin to the love the ideal mother feels for her child whom she forgives no matter what that child does. This is the love that Jesus felt for his disciples and, actually, for all mankind.

> *A new commandment I give unto you, That ye love one another; as I have loved you, that ye also love one another. By this shall all men know that ye are my*

disciples, if ye have love one to another.
(John 13: 34 & 35)

There is, in reality, little difference other than emphasis between the three paths of Discriminative Wisdom, Devotion and Service. All lead to the same point and all employ meditation as the basic tool for achieving the ultimate goal of divine union or yoga. Most of today's Enlightened Ones advocate spiritual disciplines that are a combination of the three and can thus accommodate the natural leanings of any of their devotees; and all, without exception, advise their students to put God first, before absolutely everything else.

> *But seek ye first the kingdom of God, and his righteousness; and all these things* (in worldly life) *shall be added unto you.*
> (Matthew 6: 33)

What the Bible Says About The Paths to God.

God provides different paths for different types of personalities to follow. The three basic paths are Discriminative Wisdom or Self-Enquiry, Service and Devotion. All lead to God and the one who has attained union with his Lord gains the qualities of each in equal measure. In today's high-tempo world the Masters commonly combine the three paths into one so that all ranges of personalities can benefit from the same teaching.

Exodus 20: 5 Union with God requires whole-hearted devotion.
"Thou shalt not bow down thyself to them, nor serve them: for I the Lord thy God am a jealous God (a God who demands complete devotion to the exclusion of the worship of material things)*"*

Psalm 18: 1 David recognises the link between the love of God and the power in man.
"I will love thee, O Lord, my strength."

Christopher Mark Hanson

Psalm 25: 6 David experiences God as eternally loving and kind.
"Remember, O Lord, thy tender mercies, and thy lovingkindnesses; for they have been ever of old."

Psalm 36: 7 Because God is almighty, loving and kind, we can put our trust in Him.
"How excellent is thy lovingkindness, O God! therefore the children of men put their trust under the shadow of thy wings."

Psalm 48: 9 David again identifies God's quality of loving kindness lying within the temple of our bodies.
"We have thought of thy lovingkindness, O God, in the midst of thy temple."

Proverbs 8: 17 The God of love promises that we shall unite with Him in this life if we seek Him from youth.
"I love them that love me; and those that seek me early shall find me."

Proverbs 8: 22, 23 & 30 Solomon, as Wisdom personified, expresses his union with God as one of 'possession'.
"The Lord possessed me in the beginning of his way, before his works of old.
"I was set up from everlasting, from the beginning, or ever the earth was."
"Then I was by him, as one brought up with him: and I was daily his delight, rejoicing always before him;"

Ecclesiastes 3: 15 The past has gone and the future is not yet come. Only the NOW is important.
"That which hath been is now (our present is determined by our past actions)*, and that which is to be hath already been* (our future experiences are an inescapable product of our past and present actions)*; and God requireth that which is past* (only how we deal with the NOW, which is a product of our past actions, is important to God)*."*

Song of Solomon 1: 2 Solomon sings of his desire for God's love, expressing it in worldly terms.
"Let him (God) *kiss me with the kisses of his mouth: for thy* (God's)

love is better than wine." The saints refer to the back entrance to the Christ Centre as the 'mouth of God'.

Song of Solomon 1: 15 Solomon sings of God as a lover longing for his Beloved.
"Behold, thou art fair, my love: behold, thou art fair; thou hast doves eyes." The Masters liken the 'Eye of God' that appears at the site of the Single Eye or Christ Centre to that of the eyes of a dove. For further details on the Single Eye refer back to the section on 'The Higher Spiritual Centres'.

Song of Solomon 2: 8 Solomon hears the voice of his Beloved descending from his higher spiritual centres.
"The voice of my beloved! behold, he (God) *cometh leaping upon the mountains, skipping upon the hills."*

Song of Solomon 3: 1 & 2 Solomon sings of his anguish when searching inside his body for God, his lover.
"By night on my bed I sought him whom my soul loveth: I sought him, but found him not.
"I will rise now, and go about the city in the streets (I will cast my consciousness into the interior of this bodily city)*, and in the broad ways I will seek him whom my soul loveth: I sought him but I found him not* (I looked for Him in the external world but did not find Him there)*."*

Song of Solomon 5: 8 The true lover of God yearns to be united with Him as a lover yearns for the beloved.
"I charge you, O daughters of Jerusalem (all who are contained in a bodily city), *if ye find my beloved, that ye tell him, that I am sick of* (with) *love."*

Song of Solomon 7: 10 Solomon describes the mutual pull of love between God and His devotee.
"I am my beloved's, and his desire is toward me."

Isaiah 61: 10 Isaiah describes the relationship of love between God and His devoted lovers.
"I will greatly rejoice in the Lord, my soul shall be joyful in my God; for he hath clothed me with the garments of salvation (given me freedom from the cycle of birth, death, rebirth)*, he hath covered*

Christopher Mark Hanson

me with the robe of righteousness, as a bridegroom decketh himself with ornaments, and as a bride adorneth herself with jewels."

Isaiah 62: 5 Isaiah confirms the lover/beloved relationship between God and His children.
"For as a young man marrieth a virgin, so shall thy sons marry thee: and as the bridegroom rejoiceth over the bride, so shall thy God rejoice over thee." For more analogies of the bride and groom see Matthew 9: 15; John 3: 29; and Revelation 18: 23 & 21: 2.

Malachi 1: 2 God loves His children even when they are not aware of it. God's love is unconditional.
"I have loved you, saith the Lord, Yet ye say, Wherein hast thou loved us....?"

Apocrypha, The Wisdom of Solomon 8: 4 The soul of man loves God's works.
"For she (the wisdom of the soul) *is privy to the mysteries of the knowledge of God, and a lover of his works."*

Matthew 6: 33 Put God first and all else will fall into place.
"But seek ye first the kingdom of God, and his righteousness; and all these things (material necessities, as opposed to uncontrolled desires) *shall be added unto you."*

Matthew 22: 2-4 Though God 'calls' His children to meet His Son, the Master, many refuse to come.
"The kingdom of heaven is like unto a certain king, which made a marriage for his son (The Path to enlightenment starts with God preparing His children, through the Law of Karma, to meet His Divine Son, the Master),
"And sent forth his servants to call them that were bidden to the wedding: and they would not come (In preparation for the joyous occasion, He sends out His heavenly messengers, the divine vibrations, inviting them to the marriage of their souls with God; but they refuse, being too tied up in worldly concerns).
"Again, he sent forth other servants, saying, Tell them which are bidden, Behold, I have prepared my dinner: my oxen and my fatlings

are killed, and all things are ready: come unto the marriage (I have prepared many divine perceptions for those who attend).*"*

Matthew 22: 37-40   Jesus succinctly describes the everlasting union of love between God and humanity.

"Jesus said unto him (the lawyer), *Thou shalt love the Lord thy God with all thy heart, and with all thy soul, and with all thy mind.*
"This is the first and great commandment.
"And the second is like unto it, Thou shalt love thy neighbour as thyself.
"On these two commandments hang all the law and the prophets."
These laws of universal and all-embracing love between God and His children, and between man and man, fulfil all divine law. When these two laws are followed all human behaviour becomes spiritualised. See also Leviticus 19:18; Deuteronomy 6: 5; Mark 12: 29-31; and Luke 10: 27.

Matthew 25: 1-13   Through this lengthy parable of the Ten Virgins Jesus warns devotees to be always thinking about God as the time of His arrival in our consciousness is unpredictable. Those virgins who always keep the lamps of their attention full of the oil of devotion and the wicks of their Single Eyes aflame with divine light are the wise ones. The others who allow their devotion to lapse are foolish. God, the bridegroom, will take only the wise ones into His bedchamber of Cosmic Consciousness.

Matthew 25: 34-40   In wonderful imagery, Jesus spells out the importance of serving the God in man.

"Then shall the King say unto them on his right hand, Come, ye blessed of my Father, inherit the kingdom prepared for you from the foundation of the world:
"For I was an hungred, and ye gave me meat: I was thirsty, and ye gave me drink: I was a stranger, and ye took me in:
"Naked, and ye clothed me: I was sick, and ye visited me: I was in prison, and ye came unto me.
"Then shall the righteous answer him, saying, Lord, when saw we thee an hungred, and fed thee? or thirsty, and gave thee drink?
"When saw we thee a stranger, and took thee in? or naked, and clothed thee?
"Or when saw we thee sick, or in prison, and came unto thee?
"And the King shall answer and say unto them, Verily I say unto you, Inasmuch as ye have done it unto one of the least of these my brethren, ye have done it unto me."

John 3: 16 & 17 God made the world out of love so that we would return back to Him out of love.

"For God so loved the world, that he gave his only begotten Son (God made the world out of love and imbued it with the Christ Consciousness, His only beloved offspring, part of His own consciousness), *that whosoever believeth in him should not perish, but have everlasting life* (that whoever seeks Him shall realise the immortality of their souls).

"For God sent not his Son into the world to condemn the world (God did not create the world through His Son, the Christ Consciousness, to entrap mankind); *but that the world through him might be saved* (but that His children might return back to Him via the gateway of the Christ Consciousness)."

John 3: 35 God is love and therefore the world is made out of love. Love pervades all things.

"The Father (Cosmic Consciousness) *loveth the Son* (the Christ Consciousness, His 'offspring'), *and hath given all things into his hand* (the Son is the guiding intelligence of God within Creation)."

John 13: 34 & 35 Jesus spells out the union of love between a Master and his disciples, for God is Love.

"A new commandment I give unto you, That ye love one another; as I have loved you, that ye also love one another.

"By this shall all men know that ye are my disciples, if ye have love one to another."

John 14: 15 Jesus talks of the principle that out of love alone the disciple should follow the spiritual path.

"If ye love me (the Master and the Christ Consciousness), *keep my commandments* (follow the spiritual instructions and meditation techniques I have given you)." See later for the sections on 'What is Knowledge?' and 'Meditation'.

John 14: 21 Jesus teaches the principle of union with God through love.

"He that hath my commandments (has been given my teachings), *and keepeth them* (practises them), *he it is that loveth me* (will automatically come to love the Master and the Christ Consciousness in that Master): *and he that loveth me shall be loved of my Father,*

and I will love him (the earnest devotee), *and will manifest myself to him* (will bring him into oneness with the Christ and Cosmic Consciousnesses that are in me)." See John 15: 19-11 for a similar statement.

John 14: 23 A poignant meeting between the Master and his betrayer. Was this Judas' last chance in this incarnation?
"Jesus answered and said unto him (Judas), *If a man love me* (loves the Master with the Christ Consciousness), *he will keep my words* (will follow the spiritual discipline I have given him)*: and my Father will love him, and we* (the Cosmic and Christ Consciousness) *will come unto him, and make our abode with him* (and he will become one with God through the Christ Consciousness)."

John 15: 13 The Master takes on his disciples' karmic load out of unconditional love.
"Greater love hath no man than this, that a man lay down his life for his friends (There is no greater love on earth than the love a Master shows by allowing himself to be crucified as a ransom to the Law of Karma to pay off the karmic burdens of his disciples)." See the section called 'The Functions of Enlightened Ones' for details of the Master's role in taking on the karmas of his disciples.

John 17: 26 Jesus records for posterity that initiation into the Holy Name brings the union of love.
"And I have declared unto them thy name, and will declare it: that the love wherewith thou hast loved me may be in them, and I in them." See the sections called 'The Word' and 'Initiation into the Path' for the meaning of 'have declared unto them thy name'.

Galatians 5: 22 & 23 St. Paul mentions love as the first fruit of Spirit.
"But the fruit of the Spirit is love, joy, peace, longsuffering, gentleness, goodness, faith,
"Meekness and temperance: against such there is no law (being Godly qualities these are free of any karmic implications)."

Ephesians 5: 1 & 2 The Christ Consciousness is love and we should emulate it as Jesus did.
"Be ye therefore followers of God, as dear children;
"And walk in love, as Christ (Jesus the Christed One) *also hath loved us, and hath given himself for us an offering and a sacrifice to God for a sweet smelling savour* (and has allowed himself to be

crucified so that we, his disciples, may become pure)." See the section called 'The Functions of Enlightened Ones' for the meaning of 'an offering and a sacrifice to God'.

I John 4: 16 St. John says that God is love and when we begin to love unconditionally we become united to God.

"And we have known and believed the love that God hath to us. God is love; and he that dwelleth in love dwelleth in God, and God in him."

2

Qualities of the Truth-Seeker.

As the hart panteth after the water brooks, so panteth my soul after thee, O God. My soul thirsteth for God, for the living God: when shall I come and appear before God?
            (Psalm 42: 1 & 2)

> *Will someone bring me the news*
> *That my Lord is coming;*
> *Yes, news of His coming*
> *That my heart ever longs for.*
> (Mira, 16th century Indian saint)

The above quotations from the book of Psalms and from Mira, the Indian warrior princess, identify the major requirement of any Truth-Seeker. A true devotee wants to unite with God as keenly as a deer dying of thirst in a desert wants water. This is the first and foremost requirement.

As to the other main requirements of a seeker after Truth, there is no better or more comprehensive exposition in biblical teachings than at the beginning of Jesus' Sermon on the Mount, Matthew 5: 3-12, in the verses known as the Beatitudes.

In the opening verse of this sermon, Jesus points out that people who are ready (blessed) to enter the path leading to the kingdom of God are 'poor in spirit'; which means that they are sufficiently unattached to material possessions (poor in material desires) to have spiritual inclinations.

Blessed are the poor in spirit: for their's is the kingdom of heaven.

This realisation is followed automatically by a yearning that is akin to mourning the death of a loved one. Those yearning for that spiritual 'something' missing from their lives will be comforted with divine realisations and, ultimately, union with God.

Blessed are they that mourn: for they shall be comforted.

The Truth-Seeker is also blessed if he/she is meek, that is, has a non-violent nature. Such people will inherit happiness on earth as well as in heavenly realms.

Blessed are the meek: for they shall inherit the earth.

A further important quality of the spiritual aspirant is that of behaving in conformity with divine laws such as those laid down in the scriptures of world religions. Jesus uses the word 'hunger' to describe the driving desire of the devotee to live in harmony with God's Will. Those who think, speak and act righteously will be 'filled' that is they will find their lives complete.

Blessed are they which do hunger and thirst after righteousness: for they shall be filled.

The fifth Beatitude addresses the issue of mercy. Those who hold no grievances but readily forgive others no matter how many times they are offended ('seventy times seven' – meaning without end – see Matthew 18: 21 & 22) shall, through the Law of Karma, also receive mercy.

Blessed are the merciful: for they shall obtain mercy.

Devotees who have all the above qualities and who follow the spiritual discipline given to them by an Enlightened One will automatically have pure hearts and be blessed with the opportunity to experience God at first hand (in meditation and by other divine means).

Blessed are the pure in heart: for they shall see God.

And those who find the peace of God welling up within them as their real nature, will be blessed with the realisation that they are none other than sparks shed by the Great Light: children of the Most High.

Blessed are the peacemakers: for they shall be called the children of God.

In his teachings Jesus frequently mentions another vital quality: faith. To begin on the spiritual path the devotee must have a certain amount of faith. This may not be as great at first as that of the Roman centurion, whose faith in Jesus was remarkable considering his position as one of the conquering class

The centurion answered and said, Lord, I am not worthy that thou shouldest come under my roof: but speak the word only, and my servant shall be healed......When Jesus heard it, he marvelled, and said to them that followed, Verily I say unto you, I have not found so great faith, no, not in Israel.
(Matthew 8: 8 & 10*)*

but it should be at least sufficient to enable the devotee to enter the path with enough conviction to believe in the truths spoken and demonstrated by the Enlightened Ones.

Now faith is the substance of things hope for, the evidence of things not seen.
(Hebrews 11: 1)

Humility is another desirable quality. The spiritual quality of humility, though referred to many times by the Masters, including the

Old and New Testament prophets and saints, is often misunderstood. It means much more than meekness, which is associated with a non-violent personality. The word 'humility' comes from the Latin 'humus' meaning earth; but this does not imply earthiness or a down-to-earth person who employs commonsense. It is necessary to dig even deeper than that to unearth its spiritual meaning. A humble person, in actuality, is someone who realises that though the body may come from the earth, the essential nature of a person is neither of the earth nor is it earthbound. It is Spirit. Thus, a humble person is someone who is not body-identified and therefore is without ego and its bed-fellow: pride.

> *Pride goeth before destruction, and an haughty spirit before a fall. Better it is to be of an humble spirit with the lowly, than to divide the spoil with the proud.*
> (Proverbs 16: 18 & 19)

The best exemplars of this quality of humility are children.

> *Whosoever therefore shall humble himself as this little child, the same is greatest in the kingdom of heaven.*
> (Matthew 18: 4)

Humility is one of the most sought-after spiritual qualities as it is a negation of ego, the very principle that caused man's 'Fall' from Divine Grace in the Garden of Eden. The Masters consider the quality of humility so important that they take every opportunity to demonstrate it to their devotees, as Jesus did when he washed the feet of his disciples.

> *After that he poureth water into a bason* (basin)*, and began to wash the disciples' feet, and to wipe them with the towel wherewith he was girded.*
> (John 13: 5)

It goes without saying that the devotee who wishes to make progress on the spiritual path has to have made some inroads into curbing the ego-instigated cycle of desires, pride and anger.

Of course there are many good people in the world who have no interest in spiritual matters at all and would not recognise an Enlightened One even if they knew him socially. Yet there may be others who, while not exactly leading good lives, might be stimulated to pursue the spiritual path by even a cursory encounter with a Master. Thus goodness in itself is insufficient to lead one to the spiritual path. It appears that a degree of receptivity to spiritual teachings is vital.

Whereas ordinary folk flocked to the Master because they wanted to be healed and see at first hand the miracles he was renowned for performing, Jesus' disciples clearly had a keen receptivity to their Master's teachings and understood the subtle meanings behind his words.

> *And he said, Unto you* (my disciples) *it is given to know the mysteries of the kingdom of God: but to others in parables; that seeing they may not see, and hearing they might not understand.*
> (Luke 8: 10)

Naturally, all disciples or devotees of the Masters are eternally grateful to the God-essence lying within themselves for having blessed them with the insight to understand spiritual things, as St. Paul clearly was:

> *Giving thanks unto the Father, which hath made us meet* (fit) *to be partakers of the inheritance of the saints in light.*
> (Colossians 1: 12)

The Masters also recognise that, no matter how karmically suited for the spiritual path a devotee might be, he may still be so fast 'asleep' in ignorance that he may need to be woken up.

Wherefore he saith, Awake thou that sleepest, and arise from the dead, and Christ shall give thee light.
(Ephesians 5: 14)

To people who have no interest in spiritual matters, Enlightened Teachers have a stark message. They say that those who believe this world is real and that they are independent actors in it are living in a fantasy, a dream of their own making. The world is impermanent, ever-changing. It cannot possibly fulfil its promise of permanent happiness. That is just another illusion. Permanent happiness and peace lie elsewhere and sooner or later the Laws of Karma and Reincarnation will force everyone to search for their real Source. Why prolong the anguish by continuing to look in all the wrong places? Find an Enlightened One who can show you the way.

What the Bible Says About the Qualities of the Spiritual Aspirant.

The fitness of any man to enter onto the spiritual path is judged by God through his Masters. The principal qualities are a non-violent personality (meekness), humility (egolessness), and an unquenchable thirst to unite with the Creator.

Psalm 8: 2 David acknowledges the power of a childlike, ego-less, humility which alone can overcome karma.

"*Out of the mouth of babes and sucklings has thou ordained strength because of thine enemies* (You have given only the innocent and humble the strength to overcome their ego–filled tendencies), *that thou mightest still the enemy* (calm the mind) *and the avenger* (and keep the Law of Karma at bay)."

Psalm 27: 11 David humbly prays to God for help in overcoming the Truth-Seeker's inner 'enemies'.

"*Teach me thy way, O Lord, and lead me in a plain path* (the inward path), *because of mine enemies* (because my real enemies, the ones opposing my spiritual progress, are the inner ones of desires, anger, pride, greed etc.)."

Psalm 42: 1 & 2 The Divine Seeker thirsts to return to the Godhead.
"As the hart panteth after the water brooks, so panteth my soul after thee, O God.
"My soul thirsteth for God, for the living God: when shall I come and appear before God?"

Proverbs 3: 7 Avoid the trap of falling into the clutches of your own ego as this false voice will lead you astray.
"Be not wise in thine own eyes (Those who think wisdom comes from themselves are fooling themselves)*: fear the Lord* (fear the Lord's Law of Karma)*, and depart from evil."*

Proverbs 15: 33 Solomon remarks that humility is more important than one's personal reputation.
"The fear of the Lord is the instruction of wisdom; and before honour is humility."

Proverbs 16: 18 & 19 The ego causes us to fall in spirituality and it is better therefore to be humble.
"Pride goeth before destruction (Pride leads to our spiritual downfall)*, and an haughty spirit before a fall* (and so does a haughty attitude).
"Better it is to be of an humble spirit with the lowly, than to divide the spoil with the proud (It is better to be humble and mix with egoless people than to keep the company of the proud)."

Proverbs 22: 4 By egolessness and fear of karma man gains all God's gifts.
"By humility (egolessness) *and the fear of the Lord* (fear of the Lord's Law of Karma) *are riches, and honour, and life* (lead to spiritual riches, honour of the soul, and immortality in God)."

Proverbs 29: 20 The Truth–Seeker should be moderate and thoughtful in his speech.
"Seest thou a man that is hasty in his words? there is more hope of a fool than of him."

Proverbs 29: 22 & 23 The Truth-Seeker should avoid anger and pride.
"An angry man stirreth up strife, and a furious man aboundeth in transgression.
"A man's pride shall bring him low: but honour shall uphold the humble in spirit (the humble person, who is without ego, shall be honoured by men as well as by God)."

Ecclesiastes 8: 1 The Preacher points out the benefit of true wisdom to the Truth-Seeker.
"Who is as the wise man? and who knoweth the interpretation of a thing? a man's wisdom maketh his face to shine, and the boldness of his face shall be changed (arrogance will disappear from his nature)."

Song of Solomon 3: 1 & 2 Solomon expresses the deep unconditional love felt by the devotee for his Maker.
"By night on my bed I sought him whom my soul loveth: I sought him, but found him not.
"I will rise now, and go about the city in the streets (I will search for God within the city of my body, in the streets and ways of my inner perceptions), *and in the broad ways I will seek him whom my soul loveth: I sought him, but I found him not* (I looked for Him in the external world but could not find Him there)."

Isaiah 29: 19 The non–violent and non–acquisitive will reach the highest spiritual state.
"The meek (non–violent) *also shall increase their joy in the Lord, and the poor among men* (those who do not covet material things above the spiritual) *shall rejoice in the Holy One of Israel."*

Isaiah 57: 15 Those turning to God in humility will dwell with God: will unite with Cosmic Consciousness.
"For thus saith the high and lofty One that inhabiteth eternity (the Absolute Godhead), *whose name is Holy; I dwell in the high and holy place* (I dwell as Cosmic Consciousness in your Crown Chakra), *with him also that is of a contrite and humble spirit* (which is attained by the ones who have chosen to turn to God in all humility), *to revive the spirit of the humble, and to revive the heart*

of the contrite ones (to encourage the ones who are still struggling to cast off their egos)."

Jeremiah 1: 6 & 9 The truly humble speak with the voice of God.
"Then said I, Ah, Lord God! behold I cannot speak: for I am a child."
"Then the Lord put forth his hand, and touched my mouth. And the Lord said unto me, Behold, I have put my words in thy mouth."

Apocrypha, Ecclesiasticus 4: 26 We must be humble enough to confess our sins and follow the intuition.
"Be not ashamed to confess thy sins, and force not the course of the river" (do not go against the constant stream of God's advice coming through the intuition)."

Matthew 5: 3-12 Jesus lists the qualities needed by those who become disciples of Enlightened Ones.
"Blessed are the poor in spirit: for their's is the kingdom of heaven" (Blest are they who are sufficiently unattached to their material possessions to realise that their lives lack a spiritual dimension, for this is the start of the Path to God–Realisation).
"Blessed are they that mourn: for they shall be comforted" (Blest are they that yearn to be reconnected to God in the same way that one mourns the loss of a dear relative or lover, for they shall win the greater love of God).
"Blessed are the meek: for they shall inherit the earth" (Blest are the non–violent and humble people for they will inherit happiness on earth as well as in heavenly realms).
"Blessed are they which do hunger and thirst after righteousness: for they shall be filled" (Blest are they who long after spiritual truths and to act rightly, for their needs shall be satisfied by God–directed events).
"Blessed are the merciful: for they shall obtain mercy" (Blest are those who forgive the transgressions of others, for they will see like for like returned through karmic law).
"Blessed are the pure in heart: for they shall see God" (Blest are those who have purified themselves by spiritual practice for they shall be united to God).

"Blessed are the peacemakers: for they shall be called the children of God (Blest are those who spread their own inner peace out into the world, for they are manifesting an important facet of their Father's nature).

"Blessed are they which are persecuted for righteousness' sake: for their's is the kingdom of heaven (Blest are those who are not discouraged from the spiritual path by well-meaning friends and relatives who do not want them to change).

"Blessed are ye, when men shall revile you, and persecute you, and shall say all manner of evil against you falsely, for my sake (Blest are you when you persist on the Path in spite of resentments of worldly people who fear the obvious comparison of goodness to their own lack of moral character).

"Rejoice, and be exceedingly glad: for great is your reward in heaven: for so persecuted they the prophets which were before you (Rejoice for you will experience the extreme joy of God-contact in meditation and enjoy freedom in the glorious subtle astral heavens, or in unity with the Father, when you leave this body at earthly death)."

Matthew 5: 14 & 16 Jesus points out that the good disciple serves God through setting a good example.

"Ye (my disciples) *are the light of the world. A city that is set on a hill cannot be hid."*

"Let your light so shine before men, that they may see your good works, and glorify your Father which is in heaven."

Matthew 5: 21-24 Jesus teaches the importance of forgiveness.

"Ye have heard that it was said by them of old time, Thou shalt not kill; and whosoever shall kill shall be in danger of the judgment (the Law of Karma):

"But I say unto you, That whosoever is angry with his brother without a cause shall be in danger of the judgment: and whosoever shall say to his brother, Raca, shall be in danger of the council: but whosoever shall say, Thou fool, shall be in danger of hell fire.

"Therefore if thou bring thy gift to the altar, and there rememberest that thy brother hath ought against thee;

"Leave there thy gift before the altar, and go thy way; first be reconciled to thy brother, and then come and offer thy gift." No one can effectively worship at the inner altar of God and penetrate his consciousness into the Single Eye if he harbours any ill will against another human being.

Matthew 6: 19-21 Put not your trust in the temporary things of the world but in the One who created it.

"Lay not up for yourselves treasures upon earth, where moth and rust doth corrupt, and where thieves break through and steal:

"But lay up for yourselves treasures in heaven, where neither moth nor rust doth corrupt, and where thieves do not break through nor steal:

"For where your treasure is, there will your heart be also."

Matthew 8: 8 & 10 Jesus' disciples receive a lesson in faith and humility from an unexpected source.

"The centurion answered and said, Lord, I am not worthy that thou shouldest come under my roof: but speak the word only and my servant shall be healed."

"When Jesus heard it, he marvelled, and said to them that followed, Verily I say unto you, I have not found so great faith, no, not in Israel."

Matthew 18: 4 Jesus says the most spiritual people are those who are ego-less like little children.

"Whosoever therefore shall humble himself as this little child, the same is greatest in the kingdom of heaven." See also Luke 18-17.

Matthew 20: 1-16 Jesus' Parable of the Labourers teaches that every person gets exactly the same reward on having reached Cosmic Consciousness after labouring in the vineyard of life. This equality in powers and perceptions also applies to all Enlightened Teachers. No Enlightened Being is higher or lower than another; to think or claim so is simply an illusion held by overzealous and unenlightened followers.

Matthew 23: 12 God is without ego and those who are like Him are candidates for Enlightenment.

"And whosoever shall exalt himself shall be abased (The proud and arrogant shall keep on returning to this gross manifestation: earth)*; and he that shall humble himself shall be exalted* (the ego-less shall rise to the highest spiritual level).*"*

Matthew 25: 1 Jesus warns his disciples to keep the lamps of their devotion ever burning.

"Then shall the kingdom of heaven be likened unto ten virgins (pure souls), *which took their lamps* (the light of their Single Eyes), *and went forth to meet the bridegroom* (God).*"*

Mark 10: 15 An important quality of the Truth-Seeker is to have an open, pure and absorbent mind.

"Verily I say unto you, Whosoever shall not receive the kingdom of God as a little child, he shall not enter therein." Our preconceived ideas must be shed when we enter the spiritual path for God cannot appear to someone whose mind is hedged in by dogmas, prejudices and concepts. Don't always be telling God what He is. Allow Him to tell you Himself.

Luke 8: 10 Truth-Seekers need to be receptive to their Master's teachings.

"And he (Jesus) *said, Unto you* (my disciples) *it is given to know the mysteries of the kingdom of God: but to others in parables; that seeing they might not see, and hearing they might not understand."* In this teaching Jesus points out to his disciples that not everyone can or wants to understand spiritual teachings, in which case simple allegories will do.

Luke 9: 59-62 These verses relate in quick succession how Jesus taught two would-be disciples that they must renounce worldly desires and concerns in order to gain union with the Godhead. The stories should not be interpreted as Jesus having a callous attitude to the problems of others. He was merely using the events to press home his teaching of non-attachment for he of all people knew that, if you want God, it is essential to put Him first in every thought, word and deed. See also Luke 12: 22-31.

Luke 18: 18-25 In these verses Jesus stresses the importance of the devotee being unattached to riches. Enlightened Ones teach that it is not the possession of riches per se that is the problem. It is our attachment to them that causes us to reincarnate time and again until we have seen through the illusion that wealth brings security and permanent happiness.

Luke 18: 28-30 Jesus teaches of the importance of non-attachment to the things of this world.

"Then Peter said, Lo, we have left all, and followed thee.

"And he (Jesus) *said unto them, Verily I say unto you, There is no man that hath left house, or parents, or brethren, or wife, or children, for the kingdom of God's sake,*

"Who shall not receive manifold more in this present time, and in the world to come life everlasting (By giving up your unhealthy attachments to worldly things your consciousnesses will broaden to realise that you can count all the human family among your dearest

relations and you shall want for nothing in this life and beyond it.)."

John 4: 23 Truth-Seekers should give up ritualistic worship and seek God as the Spirit living inside themselves.
"But the hour cometh, and now is, when the true worshipper shall worship the Father in Spirit and in truth (It is time for you to give up worshipping God in mere meaningless ritual and ceremonies)*: for the Father seeketh such to worship him."*

John 13: 5 Jesus demonstrates the importance of humility by washing the feet of his disciples.
"After that he (Jesus) *poureth water into a bason* (basin)*, and began to wash the disciples' feet, and to wipe them with the towel wherewith he was girded."*

John 13: 34 & 35 The Truth Seeker needs to develop unconditional love.
"A new commandment I give unto you, That ye love one another; as I have loved you, that ye also love one another.
"By this shall all men know that ye are my disciples, if ye have love one to another."

Ephesians 5: 14 St. Paul issues the clarion call of God to those still asleep in ignorance: Wake up! Wake up!
"Wherefore he (God) *saith, Awake thou that sleepest* (Awake you people who are asleep in ignorance)*, and arise from the dead* (arise from your ignorance: spiritual death)*, and Christ shall give thee light* (you shall attain the light of the Christ Consciousness)*."*

Colossians 1: 12 St. Paul says that Truth-Seekers should be thankful to God for making them fit for the Path.
"Giving thanks unto the Father, which hath made us meet (fit) *to be partakers of the inheritance of the saints in light* (to inherit the Divine Light as the saints of all times before us have done)*:"* See the section on 'The Divine Light' for the meaning of 'the saints in light'.

I Timothy 6: 17-19 St. Paul advises Truth-Seekers not to be attached to their riches and to do good works.
"Charge them that are rich in this world, that they be not highminded,

nor trust in uncertain riches, but in the living God, who giveth us richly all things to enjoy;

"That they do good, that they be rich in good works, ready to distribute, willing to communicate (Use your riches to help others);

"Laying up in store for themselves a good foundation against the time to come, that they may lay hold on eternal life (and you will be rewarded justly through the Law of Karma)."

Hebrews 11: 1-3 St. Paul advises devotees to have faith as it leads to understanding God's works.

"Now faith is the substance of things hope for, the evidence of things not seen (Faith is a subtle quality of the soul yearning to unite with its Creator).

"For by it the elders obtained a good report (By faith the saints reached their goal).

"Through faith we understand that the worlds were framed by the word of God, so that things which are seen were not made of things which do appear (Through faith we begin to understand that the material world was made from the unseen God as the Word and not from any other cause)." There is a considerable difference between belief and faith. Belief comes from the mind. Faith comes from the soul and is a 'knowing' not a mere 'belief' in something. A person with great faith is close to discovering his/her soul and the Maker of it. See the section on 'The Word' for the meaning of 'the worlds were framed by the word of God'.

Hebrews 11: 7 Noah's faith in his inner promptings from the Lord was sufficient to spur him into action.

"By faith, Noah, being warned of God of things not seen as yet, moved with fear, prepared an ark to the saving of his house: by the which he condemned the world, and became heir of the righteousness which is by faith."

3

How to Identify False Teachers.

> *Beware of false prophets, which come to you in sheep's clothing, but inwardly they are ravening wolves. Ye shall know them by their fruits. Do men gather grapes of thorns, or figs of thistles?*
> (Matthew 7: 15 & 16)

> *What is the test of a Perfect Master? This Divine Knowledge. If this Knowledge gives you peace, he who gave it to you is a Perfect Master. If it does not give you peace, then he is not a Perfect Master.*
> (The Master K.B.N)

Not long after a Master has left the body, and sometimes even before he has done so, false prophets emerge and try to step into his shoes to live off the fame that the ever-humble Master never sought in the first place. These unscrupulous, ego-driven, people have no regard for God's inescapable laws. They little realise that their duplicity will inevitably incur the full wrath of karmic law, for no sin is graver than that of deliberately leading God's children away from their True Paths.

> *For there shall arise false Christs, and false prophets, and shall shew great signs and wonders; insomuch that, if it were possible, they shall deceive the very elect.*
> (Matthew 24: 24)

The most dangerous of these false prophets are the ones who claim to know the Way but do not. They may know the letter of the scriptures but have not experienced God themselves and therefore cannot lead anyone to Him. Throughout his long life Saint Kabir was plagued by such people.

> *Though devoid of mercy*
> *And blind to other's suffering,*
> *You claim to be a high soul.*
> *You read and recite scriptures*
> *And mislead the world.*
> *Says Kabir: Some claim divine descent,*
> *But, themselves deluded,*
> *Delude also the world.*
> (Kabir, 15th century Muslim saint)

Jesus and many other saints of all ages have suffered at the hands of the ignorant, including those holding high clerical office and their equally 'blind' fellow theologians.

> *And he spake a parable unto them, Can the blind lead the blind? shall they not both fall into the ditch?*
> (Luke 6: 39)

So the question arises 'How can an earnest Truth-Seeker avoid being duped by the charlatans of this world?' Jesus gives sound guidance on this matter too:

> *Beware of false prophets, which come to you in sheep's clothing, but inwardly they are ravening wolves. Ye shall know them by their fruits. Do men gather grapes of thorns, or figs of thistles?*
> (Matthew 7: 15 & 16)

The above quotation from Matthew explains in a nutshell how to identify false prophets from those who have been ordained by God to lead others back to Him. As Jesus indicates, the best way to identify a false teacher is by the 'fruits' he or she bears. Even a little time spent observing a false prophet will reveal his true intent to be self-interest. False prophets seek name, fame and fortune. They love the adoration and flattery of the masses.

> *But all their works they do for to be seen of men: they make broad their phylacteries, and enlarge the borders of their garments, And love the uppermost rooms at feasts, and the chief seats in the synagogues. And greeting in the markets, and to be called of men, Rabbi, Rabbi.*
> (Matthew 23: 5-7)

Many of today's false prophets almost invariably demand money for their services. They may have other agenda too and begin to 'prey' on the most vulnerable of their flock.

Another trademark of false prophets is that they love to cut off the heads of others to make themselves appear taller. In pursuit of this tactic they often make statements to the effect that someone else's Master is false or that True Masters do not exist at all. This was the point St. John was making when he advised:

> *Hereby know ye the Spirit of God: Every spirit that confesseth that Jesus Christ is come in the flesh is of God: And every spirit that confesseth not that Jesus Christ is come in the flesh is not of God: and this is that spirit of antichrist, whereof ye have heard that it should come; and even now already is it in the world.*
> (I John 4: 2 & 3)

No genuine Master criticises another Master. In fact they all support each other because they share the same purpose and serve the same God. Preferring to let their 'works' speak for them, they do not normally call themselves 'Masters'. Neither do they advertise their spiritual accomplishments for they realise that the power they have is not their's but comes from God through the Christ Consciousness.

> *But be not ye called Rabbi: for one is your Master, even*

> *Christ; and all ye are brethren.*
> (Matthew 23: 8)

In the following verse Saint John also hints that the ultimate test of whether a spiritual teacher is genuine or not is by 'trying the spirits', that is by the spiritual quality of intuition. What is the silent voice of God saying within you?

> *Beloved, believe not every spirit, but try the spirits whether they be of God: because many false prophets have gone out into the world.*
> (I John 4: 1)

But, beware! It is difficult to 'try the spirits' in the early stages of spiritual progress when the ego's voice is louder than the inner voice of God. When one is starting out on the spiritual path it is wise to study a Master carefully. Find out all you can about his life and teachings and the quality of his more advanced disciples. In Tibet, it was customary for the disciple to first observe the Master for several years before approaching him. The Master would then study the disciple for a further period of several years (on probation) before accepting him. Unfortunately this tried and trusted method does not suit the hectic pace of modern living and has been largely disbanded. Today's devotees may have only days in which to make up their minds. Extra caution is required but information is more readily available through modern technology.

Though false teachers will always be with us, it is completely wrong to believe that Jesus was a one-off event, never to be repeated. God has provided for all His children at all times and throughout all races and cultures. The works and words of some of the saints from non-Christian backgrounds have been recorded in this book; and the Old Testament is bulging with the records of God-knowing saints such as Isaiah, Jeremiah, Elijah and Elisha. In addition, the New Testament bears record that John the Baptist was 'sent by God'. It is on record too, that all Jesus' disciples, except Judas, became 'free' while living and went on to teach, initiate others, and perform miracles in their Master's Name (See the section on The Word for the meaning of

Name). It is also worth remembering that all those revered ones who appear in the Christian Bible were of eastern origin.

Indeed, the Master-disciple relationship is as old as mankind itself. In the Orient, there is a very pertinent saying:

When the disciple is ready, the Master appears.

Whenever and wherever the need is acute, God sends His messengers to earth to lead His lost children back to Him. Our part is to have developed sufficient spiritual savvy to be able to recognise the particular Enlightened One that God has specifically chosen for us.

What the Bible Says About False Teachers.

There have always been people willing to mislead others for their own gain. They can be identified by their 'fruits' for they attract the gullible, enlighten no one and are destined to suffer greatly through God's Law of Karma.

Isaiah 9: 15 & 16 Isaiah speaks of the fruits of evil that spring from false prophets.
"The ancient and honourable (God), *he is the head; and the prophet that teacheth lies, he is the tail* (the false prophet is at the bottom of the spiritual ladder).
"For the leaders of this people (the false prophets) *cause them to err; and they that are led of them are destroyed* (the spiritual life of those who follow false prophets is ruined)."

Jeremiah 6: 13 The Lord says that false prophets can be detected by their desires and false dealings.
"For from the least of them even unto the greatest of them every one is given to covetousness; and from the prophet even unto the priest every one dealeth falsely."

Matthew 7: 15-17 & 20 A teaching too often used to justify Christian exclusiveness.
"Beware of false prophets, which come to you in sheep's clothing (pretending to be spiritual but wanting wealth and to gather a large band of followers around them), *but inwardly they are ravening wolves* (are full of ego and self interest).
"Ye shall know them by their fruits (You shall be able to detect them by their actions, the type of followers they attract, and by their lack of real spirituality). *Do men gather grapes of thorns, or figs of thistles?* (Thistles and thorns cannot yield good fruit).
"Even, so every good tree bringeth forth good fruit; but a corrupt tree bringeth forth evil fruit."
"Wherefore by their fruits ye shall know them (You will be able to identify them by their false teachings, their dubious motives, and their self-interested actions)."

Matthew 23: 1-39 This entire chapter is devoted to Jesus haranguing the Scribes and Pharisees for their hypocritical attitudes, love of pomp and ceremony and for leading the people astray. Note that he advises his disciples not to call themselves Rabbis or Masters as the Pharisees do because the true Master lies within them. The true Master, as all Masters attest, is the voice of intuitive God-wisdom coming from the soul.

Matthew 24: 24 Being able to perform miracles etc is not necessarily the hallmark of an Enlightened Teacher.
"For there shall arise false Christs, and false prophets, and shall shew great signs and wonders; insomuch that, if it were possible, they shall deceive the very elect (shall fool even those who have made good spiritual progress)."

Mark 9: 38-40 Jesus acknowledges that those who are able to use the power of 'The Word' are of God.
"And John answered him, saying, Master, we saw one casting out devils in thy name (by the power of the Word you have shown us), *and he followeth not us* (he is not one of our group)*: and we forbad him* (we told him to stop), *because he followeth not us.*
"And Jesus said, Forbid him not: for there is no man which shall do a miracle in my name, that can lightly speak evil of me (Do not stand in his way for the power to heal by the Holy Ghost is not confined to one person but is available to all who have truly attained the level of the Christ Consciousness).

"For he that is not against us is on our part." See the section on 'The Word' for the meaning of 'thy name'.

Luke 6: 39 Jesus says that teachers who have not travelled the Path to God themselves cannot lead others there.

"And he spake a parable unto them, Can the blind lead the blind? shall they not both fall into the ditch?" A Perfect Master speaks with the voice of authority born of direct experience of God

John 10: 11-15 Jesus likens the Master to a 'Good Shepherd' who is prepared to lay down his life for his sheep (his chosen disciples) compared to the false teacher (the hireling who is seeking fame and fortune) who flees as soon as the wolves arrive at the door. See The Second Coming of Christ page 1017 for further details.

John 12: 44-46 Jesus offers us a test for identifying false teachers: they look for crowds of adoring followers.

"Jesus cried and said, He that believeth on me, believeth not on me, but on him that sent me (When you are attracted to me and my teachings, actually you are not believing in me but in the God that is shining from within me).

"And he that seeth me seeth him that sent me (You think that you are attracted to my human personality but that is only an illusion because you are so addicted to what you can see rather than to the unseen Spirit that is in me and in you too).

"I am come a light into the world, that whosoever believeth on me should not abide in darkness (the real Master is one who can show you the Light of God).*"* See the sections on 'The Functions of Enlightened Ones' and 'The Divine Light' for the meaning of 'I am come a light into the world'.

II Peter 2: 1 & 3 A trademark of a false prophet is that he wants to make money out of the gullible.

"But there were false prophets also among the people, even as there shall be false teachers among you, who privily (soon) *shall bring in damnable heresies, even denying the Lord that bought them, and bring upon themselves swift destruction."*

"And through covetousness shall they with feigned words make merchandise of you: whose judgement now of a long time lingereth not, and their damnation slumbereth not (The people who want money and other material things from you have no judgement and are always looking for opportunities to profit from their evil ways).*"*

I John 4: 1-3 St. John warns against those false prophets who deny the historic fact of Jesus' life.

"Beloved, believe not every spirit, but try the spirits whether they be of God (Don't believe everything that you hear. Use your intuition to test the truth)*: because many false prophets have gone out into the world.*

"Hereby know ye the Spirit of God: Every spirit that confesseth that Jesus Christ is come in the flesh is of God (Those who know that God's Christ Consciousness was manifested in the body of Jesus is of the Truth)*:*

"And every spirit that confesseth not that Jesus Christ is come in the flesh is not of God: and this is that spirit of antichrist, whereof ye have heard that it should come; and even now is already in the world (Everyone who denies the spiritual greatness of Jesus is a false prophet and against God). *"* This also applies to all people who deny or reject any of God's chosen messengers or instruments, including those who say that they believe in Jesus yet criticise the saints and prophets of other religions or the leaders of the various genuine non-aligned spiritual paths.

4

The Nature of Enlightened Ones.

If ye had known me, ye should have known my Father also: and from henceforth ye know him, and have seen him.
(John 14: 7)

I am as you see me, an ordinary human being with the same two eyes, two ears, two legs, two arms and all the faculties you have. The only slight difference is that I have experienced this Knowledge. It is just beautiful! It is fantastic! It is Bliss!
(The Master K.B.N)

How is it possible for words to reflect even a small portion of the Light of the saints? Though once ordinary men, the Masters have conquered the three worlds. They are indeed 'kings' of the Physical, Astral and Causal Worlds, embedded firmly in God-consciousness. Free of the Laws of Karma and Reincarnation they carry out all actions in absolute harmony with Divine Will and come to earth only at God's bidding. In Essence they are pure Spirit, at one with their Maker

I and my Father are one.
(John 10: 30)

and when you know the Master then you know God.

> *If ye had known me, ye should have known my Father also: and from henceforth ye know him, and have seen him.*
>
> (John 14: 7)

How can the limited human mind grasp such monumental facts?

> *The heaven for height, and the earth for depth, and the heart of kings* (kingly souls) *is unsearchable.*
>
> (Proverbs 25: 3)

The nature of Enlightened Ones can be properly understood only by clearly distinguishing between their bodily forms and spiritual status. The Hindu Avatar of the Bhagavad Gita, was born with the family name 'Yadava' but was awarded the title 'Krishna' when it was recognised that he had attained the spiritual level of Krishna Consciousness. In Christian terms this is oneness with the Christ Consciousness, the Only Begotten Son of God. Similarly, the Christian Avatar became known as 'Jesus the Christ'. Jesus was the name given to him at birth and 'Christ' was the title conferred upon him later in recognition of his spiritual status: the one with the Christ Consciousness. Throughout his ministry Jesus was at pains to draw attention to this distinction, calling himself the Son of man when referring to his bodily form and personality, and as the Son of God when drawing attention to the Christ Consciousness that was within him.

To Jesus this distinction between family origin and spiritual attainment was so important that he derided the Pharisees, the intellectual elite of his time, for not understanding the difference. The Pharisees believed that the body of the Messiah and the Christ Consciousness within that body were one and the same. But Jesus quoted to them Psalm 110: 1 when pointing out to them that what David was actually saying in that Psalm proved that there was a definite difference between the body and the level of consciousness within it. Both Jesus and the Pharisees accepted that the Messiah would come from the house of David but, as Jesus pointed out to them, David would under no circumstances have referred to a son of his as his 'Lord'. Rather, while in a state of divine communion, David was referring to the connection between the Lord God (Cosmic Consciousness) and David's Lord (the Christ Consciousness): a permanent and irreversible connection that will remain all-powerful (sit on the right hand) for as long as the Cosmos and its inherent Satanic Force exists

> *While the Pharisees were gathered together, Jesus asked them, Saying, What think ye of Christ? whose son is he? They say unto him, The son of David. He saith unto them, How then doth David in spirit call him Lord, saying, The Lord said unto my Lord, Sit thou on my right hand, till I make thine enemies thy footstool? If David then called him Lord, how is he his son? And no man was able to answer him a word, neither durst any man from that day forth ask him any more questions.*
> (Matthew 22: 41-46)

From the devotee's point of view this distinction is very important. Enlightened Ones do not encourage their devotees to become fixated on, or worship, the Master's bodily form. They teach that the real Master is God who resides within His devotees waiting to guide them, through their blossoming intuition, back to Him.

> *God hath granted me to speak as I would, and to conceive as is meet* (fitting) *for the things that are given me: because it is he* (God) *that leadeth unto wisdom, and directeth the wise.*
> (Apocrypha, The Wisdom of Solomon 7: 15)

Far from courting worship for himself, the Master is the humblest of the humble. He takes every opportunity to point out to his disciples that he is the servant of God and of all people:

> *But so shall it not be among you: but whosoever will be great among you, shall be your minister: And whosoever*

> *of you will be the chiefest, shall be the servant of all.*
> (Mark 10: 43 & 44)

and he is at pains to point out that any powers or abilities he may show from time to time come from God alone.

> *I* (Jesus) *can of mine own self do nothing: as I hear, I judge: and my judgement is just; because I seek not mine own will, but the will of the Father which hath sent me.*
> (John 5: 30)

Another marked characteristic of a Master is that he speaks with the authority born of direct experience and not from mere theory or from information passed on to him by his worldly father.

> *I* (Jesus) *speak that which I have seen with my Father* (God)*: and ye do that which ye have seen with your* (earthly) *father.*
> (John 8: 38)

As a result of this direct experience and Oneness with the Almighty a Master speaks with infallible wisdom. The voice of Truth is easily recognised by those who love Truth.

> *And they* (the disciples) *were astonished at his doctrine: for he taught them as one that had authority, and not as the scribes.*
> (Mark 1: 22)

Being united to Divine Will, which is not static or inflexible but changes from moment to moment according to the circumstances, a Master is completely fluid in thought, word and deed. This quality makes it very difficult for ordinary beings to understand the nature of such a person, a fact best illustrated by the verses from Isaiah quoted previously in the section called 'What is Intuition?'

> *For my thoughts are not your thoughts, neither are your*

ways my ways, saith the Lord. For as the heavens are higher than the earth, so are my ways higher than your ways, and my thoughts than your thoughts.
(Isaiah 55: 8 & 9)

But, more importantly, this unity with God ensures that the Masters share all those mighty divine qualities of the Creator discussed in the section called 'God the Father'. In short, from time to time, when necessary, the Masters display God's powers of omniscience, omnipresence and omnipotence. Jesus demonstrated the power of omniscience by foreknowledge of his pending crucifixion. The fact that he knew of Lazarus' death, even though it was taking place far away from where he was, was proof that his consciousness was omnipresent. And his miracles and resurrection firmly established his omnipotence over all nature. These qualities are also among the hallmarks of every True Master.

What the Bible Says About God's Chosen Masters.

The Masters are servants of the Lord and share all God's divine qualities. Their words and deeds are often misunderstood because they are guided by God through the Christ Consciousness rather than by the conventions of society or by logic alone. They often attract the animosity of evil and materially-minded people because their teachings threaten the supremacy of selfishness and the values of those who lead hedonistic lifestyles.

Psalm 50: 5 Enlightened Teachers have made a Covenant of unity with God.
"Gather my Saints together unto me; those that have made a covenant with me by sacrifice (I, God, draw to me all those who have achieved unity with Me by giving up and overcoming the temptations of the world)."

Psalm 110: 1 This Psalm was quoted by Jesus to prove that his body was different from the Christ Consciousness.

"The Lord said unto my Lord, Sit thou at my right hand, until I make thine enemies thy footstool." See also Matthew 22: 41-46 below.

Proverbs 11: 30 Masters who save souls perform the greatest service to God.

"The fruit of righteousness is a tree of life (The result of following a spiritual path is a purified Tree of Life)*: and he that winneth souls is wise* (The Master who snatches souls out of the clutches of worldly temptations achieves it by Divine Wisdom)*."*

Proverbs 25: 3 Enlightened Ones do not think, speak, and act like ordinary human beings for they obey Divine Will.

"The heaven for height, and the earth for depth, and the heart of kings (kingly souls) *is unsearchable* (unfathomable)*."*

Isaiah 11: 2 Enlightened Teachers are united to God and share all His divine qualities.

"And the spirit of the Lord shall rest upon him (the Master)*, the spirit of wisdom and understanding, the spirit of council and might, the spirit of knowledge and of the fear of the Lord* (fear of the Lord's Law of Karma)*;"*

Isaiah 50: 4 Enlightened Ones live in the consciousness of the Holy Ghost and it guides them in all things.

"The Lord hath given me (the spiritual teacher) *the tongue of the learned, that I should know how to speak a word in season to him that is weary: he* (God the Holy Ghost Vibration) *wakeneth morning by morning, he wakeneth my ear to hear as the learned* (with divine wisdom)*."* See the section on 'The Word' for the meaning of 'a word in season'.

Isaiah 52: 7 & 8 Through Isaiah God tells us that His Masters are one with Him and with each other.

"How beautiful upon the mountains (upon the high spiritual centres in the human head) *are the feet of him that bringeth good tidings* (is the 'light tread' of the Christ Consciousness, the forerunner of the state of Cosmic Consciousness: Zion)*, that publisheth peace; that bringeth good tidings of good, that publisheth salvation; that saith unto Zion, Thy God reigneth!*

"Thy watchmen (the Enlightened Ones of the world and their disciples) *shall lift up the voice* (shall issue forth the Sound Vibration)*; with the voice together shall they sing* (all Masters are in tune with the Holy Ghost Vibration and among themselves)*: for they shall see eye to eye, when the Lord shall bring again Zion* (for those who are united to God shall speak together with the Voice of God)."

Isaiah 55: 8 & 9 Masters, like God, follow Divine Law and think and act unlike ordinary people.
"For my thoughts are not your thoughts, neither are your ways my ways, saith the Lord.
"For as the heavens are higher than the earth, so are my ways higher than your ways, and my thoughts than your thoughts."

Malachi 2: 6 & 7 God describes the qualities of Levi, a true Priest of God.
"The law of truth was in his mouth, and iniquity was not found in his lips: he walked with me in peace and equity, and did turn many away from iniquity (did save the souls of many people).
"For the priest's lips should keep knowledge (The true 'Priest' should know God and be able to lead people to God)*, and they should seek the law at his mouth* (and priests should seek the Truth from the Holy Ghost that issues from the Mouth of God)*: for he is the messenger of the Lord of hosts."* See the sections on 'What is Knowledge?' and 'The Word' for the meanings of the 'should keep knowledge' and 'mouth of God' respectively.

Apocrypha, The Wisdom of Solomon 7: 15 Enlightened Ones follow God's commands.
"God hath granted me to speak as I would, and to conceive as is meet (to think and speak as is fitting) *for the things that are given me* (the things that come into my mind are from God)*: because it is he* (God) *that leadeth unto wisdom, and directeth the wise* (for it is the Lord that sends His wisdom in the form of intuition into the minds of the Enlightened Ones)."

Apocrypha, The Wisdom of Solomon 7: 27 Masters are embodiments of divine wisdom.
"And being but one (part of the unity of the Godhead)*, she* (wisdom) *can do all things* (is omnipotent)*: and remaining in herself, she maketh all things new: and in all ages entering into holy souls* (in

all ages wisdom enters into Enlightened Ones), *she maketh them friends of God* (makes them One with God), *and prophets* (wisdom makes men into Masters)." This is an unambiguous statement to the effect that God sends His Masters to earth whenever they are needed and transforms ordinary men into enlightened prophets too.

Apocrypha, The Wisdom of Solomon 18: 1 The Light, the Sound and the Masters are all One.
"Nevertheless thy saints had a very great light (All the Enlightened Ones live in God's Divine Light), *whose voice they hearing, and not seeing their shape* (they all hear the sound of the invisible Holy Ghost Vibration), *because they also had not suffered the same things, they counted them happy."* See the sections on 'The Word' and 'The Divine Light' for further explanations.

Apocrypha, Ecclesiasticus 1: 10 God gives wisdom according to the spiritual level of men.
"She (wisdom) *is with all flesh* (mankind) *according to his gift* (according to their ability to receive), *and he* (God) *hath given her* (wisdom) *to them that love him* (to Enlightened Ones)."

Apocrypha, Ecclesiasticus 4: 14 The Masters, loving God and being full of divine wisdom, serve Him.
"They that serve her (wisdom) *shall minister to the Holy One* (shall serve God as He wishes): *and them that love her* (wisdom) *the Lord doth love."*

Matthew 8: 26 Enlightened Ones, being one with God, have power over all nature.
"And he saith unto them (to his disciples who were in the boat with him), *Why are ye fearful, O ye of little faith? Then he arose, and rebuked the winds and the sea* (used the power of the Word through his voice to order the storm to subside); *and there was a great calm."* See the sections on 'The Word' and the 'I Am He' for the power of the Master's voice.

Matthew 11: 27 Jesus spells out the Father-Son relationship between God and the Masters.
"All things are delivered unto me of my Father (God gives me power over all things): *and no man knoweth the Son, but the Father* (No ordinary person has experienced Christ Consciousness except God); *neither knoweth any man the Father, save the Son, and he to*

whomsoever the Son will reveal him (and no ordinary person knows God except a Master who is united to the Christ Consciousness and those fortunate ones who have been initiated by a Master)." See the section on 'Initiation into the Path'.

Matthew 22: 41-46 Jesus is at pains to point out the difference between his body and his spirit.

"While the Pharisees were gathered together, Jesus asked them,
"Saying, What think ye of Christ? whose son is he? They say unto him, The son of David.
"He saith unto them, How then doth David in spirit call him Lord, saying,
"The Lord said unto my Lord, Sit thou on my right hand, till I make thine enemies thy footstool?
"If David then called him Lord, how is he his son?
"And no man was able to answer him a word, neither durst any man from that day forth ask him any more questions." Jesus points out that David was referring to the spiritual level of 'God the Son' as his Lord and not to any offspring or descendent of his.

Matthew 26: 34 The Master once again shows his power of omniscience.

"Jesus said unto him (to Peter), *Verily I say unto thee, That this night, before the cock crow, thou shalt deny me thrice."*

Mark 1: 22 The teachings of the Enlightened Ones are powerful because they are the Truth in Word form.

"And they (the disciples) *were astonished at his doctrine* (teachings)*: for he taught them as one that had authority* (like someone who was relating personal experience and not theoretical information or theology), *and not as the scribes."*

Mark 2: 5 & 10 Enlightened Ones have the power to ameliorate or even remove bad karma.

"When Jesus saw their faith (the faith of those carrying the sick man), *he said unto the sick of the palsy, Son, thy sins be forgiven thee."*

"But (I do this miracle of healing) *that ye may know that the Son of man* (the embodied Master) *hath power on earth to forgive sins."*
See the section on 'The Functions of Enlightened Ones' for details of the power of Masters over the Law of Karma.

Mark 5: 30 Enlightened Ones have full control over the life force within them.

"And Jesus, immediately knowing in himself that virtue (spiritual life force) *had gone out of him, turned him about in the press* (in the crowd), *and said, Who touched my clothes?"* See also Luke 8: 43-48.

Mark 10: 43 & 44 Jesus teaches the importance of being humble, without ego, a distinctive trait of Masters.

"But so shall it not be among you: but whosoever will be great among you, shall be your minister (The most spiritual one among you will be the one who is sufficiently without ego to serve the others):

"And whosoever of you will be the chiefest, shall be the servant of all (The one who wants to be the top of the roost will find himself the lowest on the spiritual ladder)."

Mark 12: 1-9 In the Parable of the Vineyard Jesus describes how the Masters of all ages must tolerate the ignorance and abuse of worldly people. It describes how the one with the Christ Consciousness who comes to redeem mankind is killed by grasping worldly people. The owner of the vineyard is God. The vineyard is the world. The harvest is the reward of spiritual life. The servants of God are His lesser prophets who come to warn of the consequences of not following God's laws. The son of the owner of the vineyard is the Enlightened Master, the one with the Christ Consciousness, the Son of God.

Mark 12: 35-37 In his discourse in the temple Jesus is at pains to point out that the Christ is not a person, a descendent of David, but a spiritual power: the Christ Consciousness or Only Begotten Son of the Father in Creation. Throughout the New Testament, Jesus constantly distinguishes between his human aspect, the Son of man, and the Christ Consciousness within him, the Son of God. See also Matthew 22: 41-46

Mark 14: 61 & 62 Jesus confirms that he is the Messiah capable of leading others to God.

"...Again the high priest asked him, and said unto him, Art though the Christ, the Son of the Blessed (Are you the one with the Christ Consciousness)?

"And Jesus said, I am: and ye shall see the Son of man sitting on the right hand of power, and coming in the clouds of heaven (and the proof of who I am is that you will see those I have initiated and who have made sufficient spiritual progress, becoming enlightened too)."

Luke 1: 41 The soul of John the Baptist senses the presence of his beloved disciple, the soul to be called Jesus.

"And it came to pass, that when Elizabeth (pregnant with the baby

that was to become John the Baptist) *heard the salutation of Mary* (pregnant with the baby Jesus), *the babe leapt in her womb* (John's soul, ever awake in God, recognised instantly the mother of the baby Jesus, the same Jesus that, as Elisha, had been his disciple in their previous lifetime when John had been the prophet Elijah); *and Elizabeth was filled with the Holy Ghost:"* For further details see The Second Coming of Christ, pages 39-42.

Luke 2: 47 & 49 Even as a youth Jesus spoke with the power of the Word & Divine Wisdom behind him.

"And all that heard him (the child Jesus) *were astonished at his understanding and answers."*

"And he said unto them (his parents), *How is it that ye sought me? wist ye not that I must be about my Father's business* (Don't you understand that I must do God's work? For that is why I came into the world in the first place)?" See the sections on 'The Word' and the 'I Am He' for the power of the Master's voice.

John 1: 6 Jesus and all Masters incarnate at the express wish of the Creator and John the Baptist was no different.

"There was a man sent from God whose name was John (John the Baptist)."

John 1: 14 The Holy Ghost is in Creation as the form of the Master and as the solid universe itself.

"And the word (the Holy Ghost) *was made flesh* (into matter) *and dwelt among us* (exists in the midst of us as the body of man, especially the Master, and as the universe) *and we beheld his glory* (we marvelled at God's creation), *the glory of the only begotten of the Father* (the glory of the Christ Consciousness, God-in-creation), *full of grace and truth."* See the section on 'The Word' for the meaning of 'and the word was made flesh'.

John 1: 26 & 27 The outgoing Master always highly praises his successor.

"John answered them saying, I baptise with water: but there standeth one among you, whom ye know not (Jesus, my spiritual successor, stands among you but you do not recognise his spiritual stature);

"He it is, who coming after me is preferred before me (My God-allocated task is to herald the coming of Jesus who has been chosen

to play a more important role on the present stage of life than I), *whose shoe's latchet I am not worthy to unloose."*

John 1: 33 & 34 The Master, John the Baptist, identifies Jesus as his rightful successor.
"And I knew him not (I could not recognise the spiritual stature of Jesus with my physical eyes); *but he* (God) *that sent me to baptize with water, the same said unto me, Unto whom thou shalt see the Spirit descending, and remaining on him* (The one whose Spiritual Eye opens permanently when you initiate him), *the same is he which baptizeth with the Holy Ghost* (is the one who is the awaited Messiah).
"And I saw, and bare record that this is the Son of God (that this is the Master destined to give the Christ Consciousness to ardent Truth-Seekers)."

John 2: 19 Jesus shows the quality of Omniscience in foretelling of his resurrection: his Omnipotence.
"Jesus answered and said unto them (those demanding proof of his spiritual status), *Destroy this temple* (Destroy my body, the temple of God), *and in three days* (in three stages: physical, causal and astral), *I will raise it up* (I will resurrect it)."

John 3: 1 & 2 Through the miracles, Nicodemus identified Jesus as an Enlightened One sent from God.
"There was a man of the Pharisees, named Nicodemus, a ruler of the Jews:
"The same came to Jesus by night, and said unto him, Rabbi, we know that thou art a teacher come from God: for no man can do these miracles that thou doest, except God be with him." World Teachers such as Jesus, Krishna and Sathya Sai Baba may choose to perform miracles in front of the public but other Enlightened Ones only do so for specific purposes, usually to increase the faith of their chosen disciples.

John 3: 34 John the Baptist explains that the power of an Enlightened One is from God and unlimited.
"For he whom God hath sent speaketh the words of God: for God giveth not the Spirit by measure unto him (for God gives the Master wisdom and power without limit)."

John 5: 19 & 20 The Master carries out the Will of God, not his own will.
"Then answered Jesus and said unto them, Verily, verily, I say unto you, The Son (the Enlightened One with the Christ Consciousness) *can do nothing of himself, but what he seeth the Father do* (can only do the will of God)*: for what things soever he doeth, these also doeth the Son likewise* (and like unto God his power is unlimited).
"For the Father loveth the Son, and showeth him all things that himself doeth: and he will shew him greater works than these, that ye may marvel (and you will see me, the God–chosen Master, perform even greater miracles than the ones I have done so far)*."*

John 5: 21 & 22 Enlightened Ones have power over death through the Law of Causation: Karma
"For as the Father raiseth up the dead, and quickeneth them (puts life force back into their bodies)*; even so the Son quickeneth whom he will* (Just as God can bring people to life, so also can His Chosen Masters who have the Christ Consciousness).
"For the Father judgeth no man (God does not judge man directly; it is His Law of Karma that judges)*, but hath committed all judgement unto the Son* (karma works through the Christ Consciousness)*:"*

John 5: 27-29 The Master has power over the Law of Karma through his oneness with the Holy Ghost.
"And (God) *hath given him* (the Master) *authority to execute judgement also* (authority to exercise power over karma)*, because he is the Son of man* (because, although he was once an ordinary mortal, Son of man, he has achieved Christ Consciousness).
"Marvel not at this: for the hour is coming, in which all that are in the graves shall hear his voice (All that are spiritually dead, but worthy of initiation, shall respond to the Holy Vibration in the Master, God's Voice),
"And shall come forth (emerge from spiritual death)*; they that have done good* (the ones with enough good karma), *unto the resurrection of life* (will be born again into the spiritual life)*; and they that have done evil, unto the resurrection of damnation* (and they that have done evil will have to wait until they have accrued enough good karmas to become disciples of a Master)*."* See the section on 'The Functions of Enlightened Ones' for the power of Masters over karmic law and the section on 'The Word' for the meaning of 'shall hear his voice'.

John 5: 30 The Master confirms that Enlightened Ones like himself simply do the Will of God.

"*I* (Jesus) *can of mine own self* (of my human ego) *do nothing: as I hear* (I listen to my God-given intuition)*, I judge: and my judgement is just; because I seek not mine own will, but the will of the Father which hath sent me* (and my judgement is perfect because it is the judgement of God and not from my human ego)*.*"

John 5: 45 & 46 Masters always face widespread disbelief even from those who claim to be experts.

"*Do not think that I* (Jesus) *will accuse you* (my critics) *to the Father: there is one that accuseth you, even Moses, in whom ye trust* (Moses will be your accuser because you pretend to revere him but you do not follow his teachings).

"*For had ye believed Moses, ye would have believed me: for he wrote of me* (Had you been sufficiently developed spiritually to recognise a Master and his teachings, you would have believed both Moses and myself)*.*"

John 6: 54 A contentious teaching in the language of the Masters that drove many of Jesus' disciples away.

"*Whosover eateth my flesh* (He who unites with the Christ Conscious that is within me)*, and drinketh my blood* (and imbibes the divine life energy that courses through my veins)*, hath eternal life* (will become enlightened)*; and I will raise him up at the last day* (will lead him at death to the spiritual level in the heavens that he has earned during his sojourn on earth)*.*"

John 7: 16 & 17 Enlightened beings, like Jesus, never claim ownership of God's teachings.

"*Jesus answered them* (the people in the temple)*, and said, My doctrine is not mine, but his that sent me* (God's).

"*If any man will do his* (God's) *will, he shall know of the doctrine* (he will understand the spiritual teachings brought by the Enlightened Ones)*, whether it be of God, or whether I speak of myself* (the developing intuition of the devotee will inform him of the validity of the teachings: whether they come from my ego or from God)*.*"

John 7: 27 Enlightened Teachers are invariably exposed to the doubting minds of the masses.

"Howbeit we know this man whence he is (He is the same Jesus that we have known since he was a child)*: but when Christ cometh, no man knoweth whence he is* (but when the real Messiah comes his origins will be shrouded in mystery).*"* See also John 7: 40-43.

John 8: 12 Jesus speaks from the level of his oneness with the Christ Consciousness.

"Then spake Jesus again unto them, saying, I am the light of the world (I am one with God's creative light)*: he that followeth me shall not walk in darkness* (shall not live in ignorance), *but shall have the light of life* (but will be blessed with spiritual understanding).*"* See the section on 'The Divine Light' for the meanings of 'I am the light of the world' and 'the light of life'.

John 8: 38 Enlightened Ones speak from experience and not from theory obtained from books.

"I speak that which I have seen (experienced) *with my Father* (out of my oneness with God)*: and ye do that which ye have seen with your father* (but you copy your earthly father, your parent).*"*

John 8: 58 The Master Jesus speaks from his oneness with the Christ and Cosmic Consciousness.

"Jesus said unto them, Verily, verily, I say unto you, Before Abraham was, I am (I know from my oneness with God that I existed as spirit even before the person you know as Abraham was born on earth).*"* See also the section on 'I Am He'.

John 9: 5 While the Master is in the world he can pass on the Divine Light and Knowledge to earnest seekers.

"As long as I (Jesus) *am in the world, I am the light of the world* (while I am incarnate on earth I can give others the Divine Light of the Christ Consciousness, something that I cannot do after I have left this body).*"* See the section on 'The Divine Light' for the meaning of 'I am the light of the world'.

John 10: 30 In this simple verse Jesus sums up the relationship between all Enlightened Ones and God.

"I and my Father are one (The Enlightened Ones are in complete unity with the Godhead and can exactly express the Divine Will).*"*

John 12: 44-46 Jesus talks of the unity between the Enlightened One and God.
"Jesus cried (in a loud voice) *and said, He that believeth on me* (he that believes in the one with the Christ Consciousness), *believeth not on me* (does not worship my personality or the Jesus form), *but on him* (God) *that sent me.*

"And he that seeth me (sees God in creation as the Christ Consciousness) *seeth him that sent me* (sees Absolute God beyond creation).

"I am come a light into the world (the bearer of the Divine Light of God), *that whosoever believeth on me* (on my teachings and the Christ Consciousness in me) *should not abide in darkness* (will be free of spiritual ignorance)." See the section on 'The Divine Light' for the meaning of 'I am come a light into the world'.

John 13: 4 & 5 Always the most humble of men, the Master washes his disciples' feet.
"He (Jesus) *riseth from supper, and laid aside his garments; and took a towel, and girded himself.*

"After that he poureth water into a bason (basin), *and began to wash the disciples' feet, and to wipe them with the towel wherewith he was girded."*

John 13: 33-35 Jesus spells out the union of love between a Master and his disciples.
"Little children (My beloved disciples, fledglings in spiritual matters), *yet a little while I am with you. Ye shall seek me: and I said unto the Jews, Whither I go, ye cannot come* (I am ascending to Cosmic Consciousness which is as yet out of your reach); *so now I say unto you.*

"A new commandment I give unto you, That ye love one another; as I have loved you, that ye also love one another.

"By this shall all men know that ye are my disciples, if ye have love one to another."

John 14: 6 Jesus, from his level of oneness with the Christ Consciousness, confirms it to be the Way to God.
"Jesus saith unto him, I (the Christ Consciousness) *am the way, the truth, and the life: no man cometh unto the Father, but by me* (no man can get to Cosmic Consciousness, God beyond Creation, other than through the Christ Consciousness, God within Creation)." Refer

The Truth Seeker's Guide to the Bible

back to the section on 'The Higher Spiritual Centres' for the Christ Consciousness as the Way to God.

John 14: 7 Enlightened Ones are embodiments of the Christ Consciousness and are thus one with God.

"If ye had known me (If you, Thomas, had previously had enough faith you would have known the Christ Consciousness in me), *ye should have known my Father also* (and you would have automatically known God the Father beyond Creation): *and from henceforth ye know him* (but because you now have sufficient faith in me), *and have seen him* (you can recognised me as the embodiment of God as the Christ Consciousness)."

John 15: 16 By means of the Holy Vibration the Master draws his chosen disciples to his side.

"Ye have not chosen me, but I have chosen you, and ordained you (have initiated you on to the spiritual path), *that ye should go and bring forth fruit* (obtain the qualities of God: wisdom, joy, compassion etc), *and that your fruit should remain* (will not fade away with time): *that whatsoever ye shall ask of the Father in my name* (through the power of the Holy Ghost Vibration), *he* (God) *may give it you."* See the sections on 'The Word' and 'Initiation into the Path' for the meanings of 'in my name' and 'initiation' respectively.

John 20: 17 The Master has power over bodily death through the power of Cosmic Consciousness.

"Jesus sayeth unto her (to Mary), *Touch me not; for I am not yet ascended to my Father* (I have not yet raised myself through the three stages, physical, astral and causal, necessary to be one with Cosmic Consciousness): *but go to my brethren* (to my disciples), *and say unto them, I ascend unto my Father, and your Father* (I am going into Cosmic Consciousness); *and to my God, and your God."*

Acts 5: 1-11 The story of the man and his wife falling dead at Peter's feet when they had lied over the price of the land they had sold and donated to the early church, was not the result of anything that St. Peter did. The event illustrates the fate of evil when it directly confronts the high spiritual force emanating from an Enlightened One, in this case Peter. All eleven disciples of Jesus became enlightened under his care and became images of their own Master: Jesus. See also the story of Elisha, the children, and the bear, II Kings 2: 23 & 24.

Colossians 1: 12-15 St. Paul's words describe the essential nature of the Master as a Son of God.

"Giving thanks unto the Father, which hath made us meet to be partakers of the inheritance of the saints in light (has made us fit to become like His saints):

"Who hath delivered us from the power of darkness, and hath translated us into the kingdom of his dear Son (Who has saved us from the darkness of ignorance and lifted us up spiritually to be of the same Christ Consciousness as our Master, Jesus):

"In whom we have redemption through his blood, even the forgiveness of sins (Who has redeemed us by carrying our karmic debts by allowing himself to be crucified):

"Who is the image of the invisible God, the firstborn of every creature (Whose perfected soul is the image of God, the Christ Consciousness, which is the origin of the life and consciousness as soul in every living creature)."* See the section on 'The Functions of Enlightened Ones' for details of the power of Masters over the Law of Karma.

Hebrews 2: 9 & 16 St. Paul reveals an interesting aspect of a Master and Karma.

"But we see Jesus, who was made a little lower than the angels for the suffering of death (But, as we saw, Jesus, unlike the angels, had to take on the worldly karma of his disciples in order to liberate them and fulfil his destiny of crucifixion), *crowned with glory and honour; that he by the grace of God should taste death for every man."*

"For verily he took not on him the nature of angels; but he took on him the seed of Abraham (Although Jesus was a Master sent from God, he had to take on a karmic burden, like every man who has ever come into this world or else he would have been too pure to even enter into the physical world)."*

I John 1: 1-3 St. John praises God and eulogises his Master as a Son of God.

"That which was from the beginning (God's Cosmic Light), *which we have heard* (as the Word), *which we have seen with our eyes* (the Word in form as the Master), *which we have looked upon, and our hands have handled, of the Word of life;*

"For the life (the Light as the life of men) *was manifested, and we have seen it, and bear witness, and shew unto you that eternal life,*

which was with the Father (which originates from God beyond Creation), *and was manifest unto us* (shown to us by the Master at initiation.);

"That which we have seen and heard declare we unto you, (the Light and Word the Master showed to us we are now able to give to you) *that ye may also have fellowship with us* (that you can be disciples of God like us)*: and truly our fellowship is with the Father, and with his Son Jesus Christ* (Truly our fellowship is with God and the Christ Consciousness that was in Jesus our Master, the fully fledged Son of God)." See the sections on 'The Functions of Enlightened Ones', 'The Word' and 'The Divine Light' for further details.

5

The Functions of Enlightened Ones.

> *To open the blind eyes, to bring out the prisoners from the prison, and them that sit in darkness out of the prison house.*
> (Isaiah 42: 7)
>
> *O Arjuna! whenever virtue declines and vice predominates, I incarnate as an Avatar. In visible form I appear from age to age to protect the virtuous and to destroy evildoing in order to re-establish righteousness.*
> (God Talks With Arjuna, Ch. IV: 7-8, page 439)

The Perennial Philosophy tells us that we have very many ordinary teachers during our numerous lifetimes on earth. Though we can learn much from observing the actions of birds and insects or plants and people, our very first and most important teacher is the Law of Karma at whose knee we learn to behave through the unbroken chain of cause and effect. Then, having been fine-tuned by karmic law and having begun to look for some meaning to our lives, the Lord starts to answer our questions through books, world religions and through minor spiritual teachers. Finally, when we begin truly to yearn for Him and Him alone, He appears in the form of an Enlightened One who has suffered as we have suffered and who knows the way Home.

> *The Spirit of the Lord God is upon me: because the Lord hath anointed me to preach good tidings unto the meek; he hath sent me to bind up the broken hearted, to*

proclaim liberty to the captives, and the opening of the prison to them that are bound.
(Isaiah 61: 1)

The biblical record shows the nation of Israel to have been blessed with an impressive list of Enlightened Ones beginning with Moses and by no means ending with Jesus. Isaiah, Elisha, Elijah and Malachi are but a few of many Enlightened Ones appearing throughout the Old Testament. As God confirmed to one of these elite Masters, Jeremiah:

Before I formed thee in the belly I knew thee; and before thou camest forth out of the womb I sanctified thee, and ordained thee a prophet unto the nations.
(Jeremiah 1: 5)

The Supreme Power never, ever, cuts His children off from the Truth and knows all too well the folly of relying on unenlightened men to keep the Holy Teachings pure. For this reason He sends His saints to earth in different guises throughout time to renew the Truth.

Not all of God's Enlightened Ones have the same mission. Some move behind the scenes intent only on raising the level of spiritual vibrations of the world by the power of their presence. Others come with the purpose of leading small groups of earnest Truth-Seekers back to God. Yet others appear as World Teachers with the objective of significantly lifting the spiritual understanding of all humanity and, sometimes, to alleviate the effects of some pending world disaster brought about by man's collective karma. Krishna, Jesus, Buddha, Mohammed, Guru Nanak, Yogananda and Sathya Sai Baba are among the notable World Teachers appearing within the recorded history of our times.

The most important function of a World Teacher is to remind suffering humanity of the Truth that previous Great Ones have brought which has since become polluted by the earthly desires and ambitions of influential people both within and outside the clergy. Thus we see Jesus assuring the people of his time that he had not come to criticise the Law of Moses but to bring back the true teachings that Moses had previously brought to the Middle East.

> *Think not that I am come to destroy the law, or the prophets: I come not to destroy, but to fulfil.*
> (Matthew 5:17)

All Enlightened Teachers who come on earth to renew the Truth do so at the risk of being maltreated by ignorant people. As always, it is the orthodox and fundamentalist branches of the various religions — those fearful souls with entrenched concepts, dogmas and fragile faith, but very little real wisdom — that are the worst offenders. And so it has been, is, and always will be as mankind sinks and rises through the cycles of manifestation. Ask a Master and he will tell you that persecution is written into his job description.

> *Blessed are ye, when men shall revile you, and persecute you, and shall say all manner of evil against you falsely, for my sake. Rejoice, and be exceedingly glad: for great is your reward in heaven: for so persecuted they the prophets which were before you.*
> (Matthew 5: 11 & 12)

Jesus came not only as a World Teacher but also to lead a few chosen Truth-Seekers back to God. These are the ones God has 'marked' as karmically fit to begin the journey back to Him. Nevertheless, the power of satanic delusion is strong, and even advanced devotees may need to be woken up from their sleep of ignorance. In the following verses Isaiah is calling to potentially receptive souls (the captive daughters of Cosmic Consciousness or Zion) to shake off the dust of karma and become free spirits, true children of God.

> *Shake thyself from the dust; arise, and sit down, O Jerusalem: loose thyself from the bands of thy neck, O captive daughter of Zion. For thus saith the Lord,*

Ye have sold yourselves for nought; and ye shall be redeemed without money.
(Isaiah 52: 2 & 3)

Once their prospective disciples have been woken up sufficiently, the Master introduces them to the Knowledge (described later) and lifts at least part of their karmic burden (iniquities) so that they can experience what the Master has to give them.

He shall see of the travail of his soul, and shall be satisfied: by his knowledge shall my righteous servant justify many; for he shall bear their iniquities.
(Isaiah 53: 11)

A Master cannot just shrug off these accrued karmas. The Law of Karma has to be satisfied and that means the Master must suffer in the place of his devotees. Jesus was aware that the karmic burden he was carrying for his disciples and for all those he had healed of their sicknesses was so grave that it would lead to his crucifixion.

Even as the Son of man came not to be ministered unto, but to minister, and to give his life a ransom for many.
(Matthew 20: 28)

But a Master does not do this without purpose. It is a necessary step to fulfilling his principal function of leading his disciples back to Zion, to the Godhead.

And the ransomed of the Lord shall return, and come to Zion with songs and everlasting joy upon their heads: they shall obtain joy and gladness, and sorrow and sighing shall flee away.
(Isaiah 35: 10)

Once he has left the body, the Master can do much less to help either his disciples or suffering humanity. This is the meaning of the following verses where Jesus warns his disciples that the Light of the

Master will be with them for only a short time. They should make the most of him (walk in the light) while they have the chance.

> *Then Jesus said unto them, Yet a little while is the light with you. Walk while ye have the light, lest darkness come upon you: for he that walketh in darkness knoweth not whither he goeth. While ye have the light, believe in the light, that ye may be children of the light....*
> (John 12: 35 & 36)

But, even then, the Master does not leave his disciples completely comfortless. Very often he passes on the Mastership to one of his disciples who has become enlightened under his care. This conforms to the ancient tradition of the Master-disciple relationship as the touching scene between Jesus and Peter recorded in the following verses attests, wherein Jesus subtly empowers Peter to become the next Master in his place.

> *So when they had dined, Jesus saith to Simon Peter, Simon, son of Jonas, lovest thou me more than these? He saith unto him, Yea, Lord; thou knowest that I love thee. He saith unto him, Feed my lambs. He saith to him again the second time, Simon, son of Jonas, lovest thou me? He saith unto him, Yea, Lord; thou knowest that I love thee. He saith unto him, Feed my sheep. He saith unto him the third time, Simon, son of Jonas, lovest thou me? Peter was grieved because he said unto him the third time, Lovest thou me? And he said unto him, Lord, thou knowest all things; thou knowest that I love thee. Jesus saith unto him, Feed my sheep.*
> (John 21: 15-17)

Masters are the original alchemists. By their God-given powers they can transmute the lead of humanity into the pure gold of soul. They can transform ordinary men firstly into Sons of God and then into God Himself. As Mawlana Rumi puts it: to know "I am God" is the science of true religion. In the following passage Jesus assures his disciples James and John that they will become Masters like him: 'be baptised with the baptism that I am baptized with' – the Baptism of Cosmic Consciousness.

> *But Jesus said unto them* (James and John), *Ye know not what ye ask: can ye drink of the cup that I drink of? And be baptized with the baptism that I am baptized with? And they said unto him, We can. And Jesus said unto them, Ye shall indeed drink of the cup that I drink of; and with the baptism that I am baptized withal shall ye be baptized.*
> (Mark 10: 38 & 39)

What the Bible Says About the Functions of Masters.

God's chosen Masters come to earth at the Lord's behest to lead His children back to Him through the 'straight and narrow way': the universal Path by which man's soul descended into matter and by which he must return when he is ready to unite once more with his ever-loving Father. The Master's assistance is essential in this process.

Deuteronomy 32: 3 Moses as the first Master of Israel speaks of his work to initiate others into the Name.
"Because I will publish the name of the Lord (Because I initiate people into the Holy Ghost Vibration), *ascribe ye greatness unto our God* (worship God and not me).*"* See section on 'The Word' for the meaning of the 'Holy Ghost Vibration'.

Psalm 22: 22 David similarly sees his task as one of spreading the knowledge of God.
"I will declare thy name unto my brethren (Lord, I will teach people about Your Name and give to those who are ready Thy Holy Vibration)*: in the midst of the congregation will I praise thee."* See the section of 'The Word' for the meaning of 'name'.

Psalm 25: 8 David gives an assurance that God will lead us to Him, which He does through His Enlightened Ones.

"Good and upright is the Lord: therefore will he teach sinners in the way (God will, through His Masters, bring His erring children to the Spiritual Path or Way).*"*

Isaiah 30: 20 & 21 God's Messengers bring the Holy Vibration to lead us back to Him.

"And though the Lord give you the bread of adversity, and the water of affliction (And though God brings you adversity through the Law of Karma), *yet shall not thy teachers be removed into a corner any more* (yet God's Spiritual Teachers will always be with you), *but thine eyes shall see thy teachers* (and the particular Teacher or Enlightened One that God has chosen for you will appear before you in body form):

"And thine ears shall hear a word (You will be given the ability by your Master to hear the Holy Ghost Vibration) *behind thee* (inside yourself: in the opposite direction to the usual outward way), *saying* (guiding you), *This is the way, walk ye in it, when ye turn to the right hand, and when ye turn to the left* (It will be calling you back to the Holy Father from whom the Holy Vibration comes. Let it guide you in everything that you do)." See the section on 'The Word' for the meaning of 'a word'.

Isaiah 33: 5 & 6 Isaiah praises the Lord as the Source of the wisdom and Knowledge brought by the Masters.

"The Lord is exalted; for he dwelleth on high: he hath filled Zion with judgement and righteousness (for He dwelleth in the high spiritual centres in man and is perfect).

"And wisdom and knowledge shall be the stability of thy times (and wise people will grow strong in the Knowledge of how to unite with the Godhead), *and strength of salvation* (and in the process of liberation): *the fear of the Lord is his treasure* (the Law of Karma is the friend of all just men)." See also the section on 'What is Knowledge?'.

Isaiah 35: 10 The Master leads his disciples to eternal joy in Cosmic Consciousness.

"And the ransomed (those held against the will of their souls by the world) *of the Lord shall return, and come to Zion* (shall return to Cosmic Consciousness in God) *with songs and everlasting joy*

upon their heads: they shall obtain joy and gladness, and sorrow and sighing shall flee away."

Isaiah 42: 7 The work of the Master Jesus, and all Enlightened Teachers, is described by Isaiah.
"*To open the blind eyes* (To make people 'see' the Truth), *to bring out the prisoners from the prison* (to release the captives from the prison of their locked-up minds), *and them that sit in darkness out of the prison house* (and to release souls living in ignorance from the bondage of this world)."

Isaiah 52: 2 & 3 Isaiah, the Enlightened One, encourages the receptive to free themselves from captivity.
"*Shake thyself from the dust* (Escape from the evil of the world); *arise, and sit down, O Jerusalem* (lift your consciousnesses in meditation): *loose thyself from the bands of thy neck* (free yourself from karmic ties that keep you returning to the world like slaves), *O captive daughter of Zion* (O people imprisoned by your own ignorance and not claiming your high spiritual estate).
"*For thus saith the Lord, Ye have sold yourselves for nought* (You have sold your souls for nothing worthwhile, for nothing worthwhile exists in the world to which you have become attached); *and ye shall be redeemed without money* (and the Path of redemption will cost you nothing and you will realise that you have, in reality, had to give up nothing to attain enlightenment)."

Isaiah 53: 11 Enlightened Ones come for the specific purpose of leading erring humanity back to God.
"*He* (The Enlightened One) *shall see of the travail of his soul, and shall be satisfied* (shall understand what his own soul has suffered through lifetimes of bondage to the world): *by his knowledge shall my righteous servant* (by his spiritual power the Enlightened Teacher) *justify many* (will lead many back to God); *for he shall bear their iniquities* (for he will carry their karmic burdens to enable them to do so)."

Isaiah 61: 1-3 An important description of the functions of the Enlightened Teacher.
"*The Spirit of the Lord God is upon me* (the Enlightened Teacher):

because the Lord hath anointed me (chosen me) *to preach good tidings unto the meek* (to teach Knowledge to the non-violent); *he hath sent me to bind up the broken hearted* (He has sent me to heal those yearning for God), *to proclaim liberty to the captives* (to show men how to free themselves from the prison of satanic delusion), *and the opening of the prison to them that are bound* (and to give them the means of escaping from their captivity).

"*To proclaim the acceptable year of the Lord* (To teach what is acceptable to the Lord), *and the day of vengeance of our God* (and to inform devotees of the workings of the Law of Karma); *to comfort all that mourn* (to bring God-union to all those who yearn for it);

"*To appoint unto them that mourn in Zion* (To call to me those that weep for the Cosmic Consciousness they have lost), *to give unto them beauty for ashes, the oil of joy for mourning, the garment of praise for the spirit of heaviness, that they* (the earnest Truth-Seekers) *might be called the trees of righteousness, the planting of the Lord, that he might be glorified* (through their example)." For the meaning of 'the trees of righteousness' see the earlier section on 'The Tree of Life' and for the meaning of 'knowledge' see the section called 'What is Knowledge?'.

Isaiah 62: 1 Isaiah, the Enlightened Teacher, vows never to give up until all good people are also enlightened.

"*For Zion's sake will I not hold my peace* (I will continue to lead good souls to union with God i.e. Zion), *and for Jerusalem's sake I will not rest, until the righteousness thereof go forth as brightness, and the salvation thereof as a lamp that burneth* (and I will not rest until those God has chosen for me to lead have entered the inner citadel of Spirit i.e. Jerusalem)."

Jeremiah 1: 5 An Enlightened One comes down to earth at God's behest to lead mankind back to Him.

"*Before I* (the Lord) *formed thee* (Jeremiah) *in the belly I knew thee* (you had become one with Me); *and before thou camest forth out of the womb I sanctified thee* (before you were born in this life I had already purified you), *and ordained thee a prophet* (selected you to be an Enlightened Teacher) *unto the nations.*"

Jeremiah 3: 14 & 15 The Lord promises the people to send 'pastors' that will guide them back to Him.

"*Turn, O backsliding children, saith the Lord* (Turn back towards Me, you errant children of Mine)*; for I am married unto you* (for we are united together in Spirit)*: and I will take you one of a city, and two of a family, and I will bring you to Zion* (and when you turn back inside, towards Me, I will bring you Enlightenment)*:*

"*And I will give you pastors according to mine heart, which shall feed you with knowledge and understanding* (I will bring you Enlightened Teachers who can lead you back to Me)."

Apocrypha, The Wisdom of Solomon 2: 14-16 The Master comes to purify our minds.

"*He* (the Enlightened One) *was made to reprove our thoughts* (was brought to earth to point out to us where we are going wrong).

"*He is grievous unto us even to behold* (He is difficult to understand)*: for his life is not like other men's, his ways are of another fashion.*

"*... he pronounceth the end of the just to be blessed* (he tells us that the reward of following God's Will is to be united to God), *and maketh his boast that God is his father* (and proves by his actions and teachings that he is 'One with the Father')."

Matthew 5: 11 & 12 To be persecuted by the ignorant is part of a Master's job description.

"*Blessed are ye, when men shall revile you, and persecute you, and shall say all manner of evil against you falsely, for my sake.*

"*Rejoice, and be exceedingly glad: for great is your reward in heaven: for so persecuted they the prophets which were before you.*"

Matthew 5:17 Enlightened Teachers come to remind us of the Truth, the Perennial Philosophy.

"*Think not that I am come to destroy the law* (of Moses), *or the prophets* (or to discredit the Enlightened Ones of the past)*: I come not to destroy, but to fulfil* (I come to remind you of the true teachings which mankind has forgotten)." Not long after an Enlightened One has left the earth, unenlightened and misguided followers begin to distort their Master's universal message and create yet another exclusive religion.

Matthew 8: 16 & 17 The Masters heal through the Word but take the karma onto themselves.

"When the even was come, they brought unto him (Jesus) *many that were possessed with devils: and he cast out the spirits with his word* (he cast out the evil spirits in them by the power of the Holy Ghost Vibration in him), *and healed all that were sick:*

"That it might be fulfilled which was spoken by Esaias (Isaiah) *the prophet, saying, Himself took our infirmities, and bare our sicknesses* (he took on our karmas and suffered the consequences)." See the section on 'The Word' for the meaning of 'his word' in the above verses.

Matthew 10: 34 The teachings of Enlightened Ones cause divisions between believers and non–believers.

"Think not that I am come to send peace on earth: I came not to send peace, but a sword."

Matthew 11: 28-30 Enlightened Ones carry the karmic burdens of their disciples to enable them to progress.

"Come unto me, all ye that labour and are heavily laden (Come to me all you who are loaded with light–extinguishing karma), *and I will give you rest* (I will give you relief by lifting it).

"Take my yoke upon you (adopt my spiritual discipline), *and learn of me* (learn what I have to teach you); *for I am meek* (non–violent) *and lowly* (without ego) *in heart: and ye shall find rest unto your souls* (and you will discover the peace of your souls).

"For my yoke is easy (My spiritual discipline is easy by comparison to the karmic burden you are carrying), *and my burden is light* (I can carry your karma without it affecting me unduly)."

Matthew 14: 19-33 By performing the miracles of multiplying food and walking on the water, Jesus increased the faith of his disciples in him. Enlightened Ones occasionally perform such miracles for this purpose.

Matthew 16: 19 The Master Jesus gives Knowledge to the worthy disciple.

"And I (Jesus your Master) *will give unto thee* (Peter my disciple) *the keys of the kingdom of heaven* (the methods of contacting God)..."
See also the section on 'What is Knowledge?'.

Matthew 16: 27 & 28 The Master assures his disciples that they will achieve Cosmic Consciousness: God-union.

"*For the Son of man* (the striving devotee) *shall come in the glory of his Father with his angels* (shall become one with the glory of God, Cosmic Consciousness)*; and then he shall reward every man according to his works* (and the devotee will see that God rewards everyone according to his effort).

"*Verily I say unto you, There be some standing here, which shall not taste of death, till they see the Son of man coming in his kingdom* (Some of you will achieve enlightenment before you undergo the experience of bodily death).*"*

Matthew 20: 28 Jesus, the Master, came to lead his disciples back to God.

"*Even as the Son of man came not to be ministered unto, but to minister* (I came not to be taught, but to teach)*, and to give his life a ransom for many* (and, by the workings of karmic law, to give my life in exchange for the sins I have lifted from the shoulders of my disciples and many others).*"*

Matthew 26: 26-28 Jesus refers again to the karmic debts his crucifixion will pay off.

"*And as they were eating, Jesus took the bread, and blessed it, and break it, and gave it to the disciples, and said, Take, eat; this is my body* (this bread is symbolic of my teachings).

"*And he took the cup, and gave thanks, and gave it to them, saying, Drink ye all of it;*

"*For this is my blood of the new testament* (Drink deeply for this wine is symbolic of the spiritual life I want you to continue living as you have done while I have been with you on earth)*, which is shed for many for the remission of sins* (also my body will be broken and my blood will be shed as a sacrifice to the Law of Karma so that many will be free of the accumulated effects of their bad deeds).*"*

Mark 3: 14 & 15 Enlightened Ones initiate their disciples into the Spiritual Path.

"*And he ordained* (initiated into the Spiritual Path) *twelve, that they should be with him* (so that their souls should be in harmony with his soul)*, and that he might send them forth to preach,*

Christopher Mark Hanson

"And to have power to heal the sicknesses, and to cast out devils." Masters are able to pass their powers on to their disciples if they so wish. See the section on 'Initiation into the Path' for the meaning of 'ordained'.

Mark 10: 38 & 39 Jesus assures two of his disciples that he will indeed lead them to enlightenment.

"But Jesus said unto them (James and John), *Ye know not what ye ask: can ye drink of the cup that I drink of* (can you carry out the tasks required of a Master)*? and be baptized with the baptism that I am baptized with* (and be united to Cosmic Consciousness)*?*

"And they said unto him, We can. And Jesus said unto them, Ye shall indeed drink of the cup that I drink of; and with the baptism that I am baptized withal shall ye be baptized (You shall indeed become like me, Masters in your own right)*."*

Luke 1: 76, 77 & 79 The father of John the Baptist foresees the Divine Mission of his baby son.

"And thou, child, shalt be called the prophet of the highest (you shall be an Enlightened One of God)*: for thou shalt go before the face of the Lord to prepare his ways* (for you will carry out God's Will on earth)*;*

"To give knowledge of salvation unto his people by the remission of their sins (You will give the Knowledge of Enlightenment and carry the karmic burden of those given into your care by God)*."*

"To give light to them that sit in darkness and in the shadow of death, to guide our feet into the way of peace (You will give the Divine Light of liberation to those that live in the darkness of ignorance and lead them to enjoy the peace of God-union)*."* John the Baptist was destined to play the role of Jesus' Master and, on his own account, to lead men back to God. Christendom does not yet acknowledge the greatness of this man who was the prophet Elijah in his previous lifetime –see Matthew 17: 12 & 13.

John 1: 6 & 7 The Masters come on earth to bring the Light (enlightenment) to earnest seekers.

"There was a man sent from God, whose name was John (John the Baptist).

"The same came for a witness, to bear witness of the Light, that all men through him might believe." See also the section on 'The Divine Light'.

John 1: 12 & 13 The purpose of a Master, as God's instrument, is to make worthy disciples into Masters.

"But as many as received him (made the effort to experience God as Divine Light within themselves), *to them gave he power to become the sons of God* (God gave those worthy seekers enlightenment, Oneness with Him through the Christ Consciousness brought by the Master), *even to them that believed on his name* (even to those who reached the Christ Consciousness through meditating on the Holy Ghost):

"Which were born, not of blood, nor of the will of the flesh, nor of the will of man, but of God (which have been initiated by their Master into the Spiritual Path)." See also the sections on 'The Word', 'The Divine Light' and 'Initiation into the Path'.

John 3: 2 Miracles attract people to the teachings & Nicodemus recognised that Jesus was a Master sent by God.

"The same (a Pharisee called Nicodemus) *came to Jesus by night* (to avoid detection from other Pharisees), *and said unto him, Rabbi, we know that thou art a teacher come from God: for no man can do these miracles that thou doest, except God be with him."*

John 3: 3 An important part of an Enlightened Teacher's task is to lead worthy people like Nicodemus to God.

"Jesus answered and said unto him (Nicodemus), *Verily, verily, I say unto thee, Except a man be born again* (unless he has his eye of intuitional wisdom re-opened as it was 'in the beginning'), *he cannot see the kingdom of God* (he will not be able to perceive the manifestations of God evident in meditation)."

John 3: 28 & 30 John the Baptist reveals his role as a Master in God's scheme.

"Ye (My disciples and questioners) *yourselves bear me witness, that I said, I am not the Christ* (I am not the Messiah that was promised by the prophets of old), *but that I am sent before him* (but I was sent to do the groundwork ready for the Messiah's ministry)."

"He (Jesus) *must increase* (must flourish), *but I must decrease* (fade out of the picture now that my work of publicising his presence is done)." Part of the reason why John the Baptist played down his role as a Master was because his task was to initiate a select band of disciples whereas Jesus was a World Teacher.

John 9: 39 Masters come to dispel ignorance and once the Truth is known ignorance is no excuse.

"And Jesus said, For judgment I am come into this world, that they which see not (those that are spiritually ignorant) *might see* (might understand spiritual things); *and that they which see* (the ones who think they know the truth but see only matter, not spirit) *might be made blind* (might be exposed as ignorant)."

John 10: 7-10 In this parable of the shepherd and his sheep, Jesus portrays the Master as the Good Shepherd who knows his sheep (his disciples) and who has the qualification of being able to enter the door of the Christ Centre and lead his disciples through it to safety. See pages 1015-1017 of 'The Second Coming of Christ' for further details.

John 10: 16 & 28 Jesus tells of how the current Master must look after the departed Master's flock.

"And other sheep I have (those of the departed Master, John the Baptist), *which are not of this fold* (not directly mine): *them also I must bring* (take care of), *and they shall hear my voice* (be drawn to me through the Holy Word); *and there shall be one fold, and one shepherd".*

"And I give unto them eternal life; and they shall never perish (I have promised God not to let them slip back into ignorance now that their own Master has departed), *neither shall any man* (false prophet) *pluck them out of my hand* (take them away from me)." See the section on 'The Word' for the meaning of 'my voice'.

John 12: 26 Jesus makes the same promise made by all Enlightened Teachers to their devotees.

"If any man serve me (those who follow my spiritual instructions), *let him follow me* (practise them); *and where I am* (where I go to in the spiritual realms after bodily death), *there shall also my servant be* (my devotees or disciples will come to me there): *if any man serve me, him will my Father honour* (anyone who faithfully follows the spiritual discipline I have given him will be enlightened by God)."

John 12: 35 & 36 Jesus explains that the Master can only help directly while he is on earth, in body form.

"Then Jesus said unto them, Yet a little while is the light (as the Master) *with you. Walk* (make spiritual progress) *while ye have the light* (while the Master is with you), *lest darkness* (spiritual

ignorance) *come upon you: for he that walketh in darkness* (in ignorance) *knoweth not whither he goeth* (does not know the real nature of the world and why he is in it).
"While ye have the light (in the form of the Master), *believe in the light, that ye may be children of the light...."* See also the section on 'The Divine Light'.

John 14: 2 & 3 The Enlightened One assures his disciples that he will look after them even after they have died.
"In my Father's house are many mansions (In the heavenly realms are many different levels of vibration designed to accommodate people of low, moderate or high spiritual attainment): *if it were not so, I would have told you. I go to prepare a place for you* (It is my task as your Master to prepare such a place for you, my disciples).
"And if I go and prepare a place for you, I will come again, and receive you unto myself (Even though after my crucifixion I will have left this earthly realm, through the Christ Consciousness in me I will draw you to me at the time of your death); *that where I am* (in the heavenly realms), *there ye may be also."*

John 14: 6 The Enlightened Teacher helps his disciples to attain unity with God through the Christ Consciousness.
"Jesus saith unto him (Thomas), *I am the way, the truth, and the life* (I am one with the Christ Consciousness, the fountain of life): *no man cometh unto the Father, but by me* (not one of you can attain God-union without first having attained Christ Consciousness, the gateway to God)."* Here Jesus is speaking with the voice of the Christ Consciousness. He is not inferring that no one can get to God except through his human personality: Jesus. See also Krishna in the Bhagavad Gita and the Old Testament prophets for examples of Enlightened Ones speaking with the voice of God.

John 14: 12 & 13 The function of a Teacher is to transform his disciples into Enlightened Beings, like himself.
"Verily, verily, I say unto you, He that believeth on me, the works that I do shall he do also: and greater works than these shall he do; because I go unto my Father (You will attain the power to teach and perform miracles through the Holy Ghost Comforter that I am going to send you after I have risen to the level of Cosmic Consciousness).

"And whatever ye shall ask in my name (Whatever you ask through the power of the Holy Ghost), *that I will do* (I will give you), *that the Father may be glorified in the Son* (that ordinary people may believe in God because of the deeds you, my disciples, have done)." See the section on 'The Word' for the meaning of 'my name' and 'Comforter'.

John 15: 13 The Master takes on his disciples' karmic load out of unconditional love.
"Greater love hath no man than this, that a man lay down his life for his friends (There is no greater love on earth than the love a Master shows by allowing himself to be crucified as a ransom to the Law of Karma to pay off the karmic debts of his disciples)."

John 16: 7 The Master must at some time remove his outward form from the sight of his disciples.
"Nevertheless I tell you the truth; It is expedient for you that I go away (It is in your spiritual interest that I remove my physical form from your sight)*: for if I go not away* (if I don't leave you), *the Comforter will not come unto you* (you will remain fixated on my outer physical form instead of finding the Holy Ghost within you)*; but if I depart, I will send him unto you* (you will be more likely to contact God as the Holy Ghost Vibration within yourselves after I have departed this earth)." No True or Perfect Master wants his disciples to become attached to his physical form and personality. If the Master sees that this is happening he will either remove his presence from the disciple or send the disciple away. A Perfect Master wants his disciples to focus their attention on the Spirit residing within themselves.

John 17: 1 & 2 The Enlightened Teacher leads his disciples to God that they may become enlightened too.
"These words spake Jesus, and lifted up his eyes unto heaven (lifted his eyes to the Christ Centre, the 'Single Eye' of intuitive wisdom), *and said, Father, the hour is come* (my time on earth is running out)*; glorify thy Son* (glorify the Christ Consciousness in me), *that thy Son may also glorify thee* (that I may glorify You by my resurrection)*:
"As thou hast given him power over all flesh* (You have given the Christ Consciousness, Your Son, power over death), *that he should give eternal life* (that, through the agency of the Master, the Christ Consciousness can give freedom from the dream of death) *to as many as thou hast given him* (to the disciples who You have given to me to lead to enlightenment)."

John 17: 6, 11 & 12 The Master describes his spiritual duty to lead his Chosen Ones back to God.

"I have manifested thy name (the Holy Vibration) *unto the men which thou gavest me out of the world* (the ones You chose to be my disciples)*: thine they were* (their souls are part of Your Cosmic Consciousness)*, and thou gavest them me* (You have asked me to look after them on Your behalf)*; and they have kept thy word* (they have kept in harmony with the Holy Vibration through meditation)*."*

"And now I am no more in the world (I am gradually withdrawing my consciousness from the world of matter)*, but these are in the world, and I come to thee* (and I am coming to the level of Cosmic Consciousness when I leave this body)*. Holy Father, keep through thine own name those whom thou hast given me, that they may be one, as we are* (Since they will not have my outer form to rely on any more, help them to keep in unity with Thee, as I am, through the Holy Vibration).

"While I was with them in the world, I kept them in thy name (While I was in this body called Jesus my task was to keep them connected to the Holy Ghost Vibration)*: those that thou gavest me I have kept* (and I have done so)*, and none of them is lost, but the son of perdition* (except Judas)*; that the scripture might be fulfilled* (so that the prophesies made by past Enlightened Ones will be shown to be true)*."* See the section on 'The Word' for the meaning of 'thy name'.

John 17: 22-24 Jesus again describes the purpose of all Enlightened Ones: to lead their disciples to God.

"And the glory which thou (My God) *gavest me* (Jesus) *I have given them* (my disciples)*; that they may be one* (united together in the Godhead)*, even as we are one* (even as You and I are united)*:*

"I in them, and thou in me, that they may be made perfect in one (that they may be perfect in unity with You as I am)*; and that the world may know that thou hast sent me* (so that people will understand that I was sent by You)*, and hast loved them, as thou hast loved me* (and that You have loved them as You have loved me).

"Father, I will that they also, whom thou hast given me (my disciples)*, be with me where I am* (be united with me in the great 'I am', the Christ Consciousness)*; that they may behold my glory* (that they may enjoy the same spiritual experience of the Godhead that I have),

which thou hast given me: for thou lovest me before the foundation of the world (for You loved me as Your spiritual child before You even created this material world).*"* See the section on 'I Am He' for the spiritual significance of 'I am'.

John 18: 37 Jesus clearly states his mission, and that of all Enlightened Teachers, to Pilate.

"...To this end was I born, and for this cause came I into the world, that I should bear witness unto the truth (My function as a Master is to tell people of what I know from firsthand experience of the Godhead and how to reunite with that Supreme Power). *Every one that is of the truth* (All those who are sufficiently spiritually developed to see beyond the superficial) *heareth my voice* (understands my teachings and intuitively feels the Holy Word vibrating within my body and speech).*"* See the section on 'The Word' for the meaning of 'my voice'.

John 20: 27 & 28 Jesus removes Thomas' doubts about the Master's ability to resurrect his body.

"Then saith he (Jesus) *to Thomas, Reach hither thy finger, and behold my hands; and reach hither thy hand, and thrust it into my side: and be not faithless, but believing.*

"And Thomas answered and said unto him, My Lord and my God (Now I really understand that you, my Master, are an embodiment of Cosmic Consciousness).*"*

John 21: 15-17 Jesus empowers Peter to be the next Master: to look after his flock of disciples.

"So when they had dined, Jesus saith to Simon Peter, Simon, son of Jonas, lovest thou me more than these (the other disciples)*? He saith unto him, Yea, Lord; thou knowest that I love thee. He saith unto him, Feed my lambs.*

"He saith to him again the second time, Simon, son of Jonas, lovest thou me? He saith unto him, Yea, Lord; thou knowest that I love thee. He saith unto him, Feed my sheep.

He saith unto him the third time, Simon, son of Jonas, lovest thou me? Peter was grieved because he said unto him the third time, Lovest thou me? And he said unto him, Lord, thou knowest all things; thou knowest that I love thee. Jesus saith unto him, Feed my sheep." This touching scene belies the great power that was being transferred from the Master to the disciple in three stages, penetrating Peter's three bodies: physical, astral and causal.

Ephesians 5: 1 & 2 St. Paul records that Jesus took on the karmic burdens of his disciples to free them.

"Be ye therefore followers of God, as dear children;
"And walk in love, as Christ (Jesus the Christed one) *also hath loved us, and hath given himself for us an offering and a sacrifice to God for a sweet smelling savour* (and has allowed himself to be crucified so that we, his disciples, may become pure, free of karma)."

Colossians 1: 12-14 St. Paul gives thanks to God for the Master who brought the Light to the worthy.

"Giving thanks unto the Father, which hath made us meet (fit) *to be partakers of the inheritance of the saints in light* (to be able to follow the same path as the saints to enlightenment)*:*
"Who hath delivered us from the power of darkness, and hath translated us into the kingdom of his dear Son (Who has saved us from ignorance and transferred to us the same Christ Consciousness that is manifest in His son, Jesus, our Master)*:*
"In whom we have redemption through his blood, even the forgiveness of sins (Who has saved us by carrying our karmic debts and allowing himself to be crucified)*:"*

I Timothy 2: 5 It is a common and erroneous belief among devotees that their Master is the Only Way

"For there is one God, and one mediator between God and men, the man Christ Jesus." True understanding shows that each particular Master is 'the only mediator' for a particular group of disciples. Similar errors of understanding have arisen in most religions and, clearly, there must be some mistake. Those who claim that their Master, or Saviour, or Prophet, is the 'only one' cannot all be right.

I John 2: 1 & 2 Masters carry a portion of the sins or karmas of their disciples and of the world.

"My little children, these things write I unto you, that ye sin not. And if any man sin, we have an advocate with the Father, Jesus Christ the righteous:
"And he is the propitiation for our sins: and not for our's only, but also for the sins of the whole world." The Masters warn that this relationship exists between a Master and his immediate disciples only. It is not a contract between Jesus (or any Master) and mankind for all time. At least the possibility should dawn on those who claim

exclusive divinity for their own particular icon that the unlimited God leaves no child of His bereft of a Saviour suited to his/her special needs no matter what era that person is born into and irrespective of his/her culture or religion.

Part 5.

The Knowledge.

1

What is Knowledge?

Yea, if thou criest after knowledge, and liftest up thy voice for understanding; If thou seekest her as silver, and searchest for her as for hid treasures; Then shalt thou understand the fear of the Lord, and find the knowledge of God. For the Lord giveth wisdom: out of his mouth cometh knowledge and understanding.
(Proverbs 2: 3-6)

Today is such a happy day.
There is no room for sadness.
Today we drink the wine of trust
From the cup of knowledge.
We can't live on bread and water alone.
Let us eat a little from the hand of God.
(Rumi, 13th century Sufi)

The Knowledge the Masters give to their disciples is quite different from the intellectual process of collecting and retaining information about worldly matters, where the source of the information gained is separate from the person possessing the cognitive facility. In Enlightenment there is no 'two' only 'one'; the source of the experience, the experience itself, and the person experiencing it are one and the same.

Enlightenment is a state that the mind and intellect cannot understand or reach because 'it is above' them. The mind and intellect, having emanated from the soul, are coarser manifestations of soul-consciousness and hence are unable to grasp its essential subtlety. No amount of information, not even scriptural information, can produce enlightenment. Scriptures are important for they point the way but that is the limit of their usefulness, and this only if they have been interpreted correctly. When not properly understood they are as useless to the devotee as a broken walking stick to the lame.

Saint Pipa, thankful that the Lord sent Kabir when he did, was particularly scathing of man's reliance on the scriptures for enlightenment, pointing out that the combination of false scriptural understanding and the Dark Age of Ignorance (the Iron Age or Kali Yuga) guaranteed a living hell.

> *Had not Kabir come*
> *In this Iron Age,*
> *The scriptures and Kali Yuga*
> *In collusion would have driven*
> *Devotion to perdition.*
> (Pipa, 15th century Rajasthan saint)

It is also true that Secular Man thinks in terms of truths or information as being knowledge handed down in oral or written form from generation to generation. He believes, quite rightly in worldly cases, that identical ideas or material appearing in publications by different authors must have been copied at some stage by one of them. Similarly, and not surprisingly perhaps, it is quite common for unenlightened theologians to claim that the religious teachings of say the Hindus have been 'lifted' from Christianity and vice versa. Such potentially harmful opinions would not see the light of day if the claimants did but realise that Spiritual Truth wells up of its own accord out of the inner world of man, from the God-centre of his soul. And, because it is the Truth, it has to be the same by definition. Saints, sages and prophets of all ages do not have to learn spirituality from each other or from the scriptures. Once enlightened they **become** the Truth, having received it directly from the same Source, their Divine Father, as Jesus confirms:

> *Then answered Jesus and said unto them, Verily, verily,*
> *I say unto you, The Son can do nothing of himself, but*

what he seeth the Father do: for what things soever he doeth, these also doeth the Son likewise.
(John 5: 19)

In its spiritual context, the term 'Knowledge' is to know the Self, the soul, and to 'know' it so thoroughly as to become what one knows. The early Christians termed this 'gnosis'. As Kabir puts it:

> *If you know the One,*
> *Then know that you know all;*
> *If you know not the One,*
> *Then all your knowledge*
> *Is nothing but fraud.*
> (Kabir, 15th century Muslim saint)

Eventually all mankind is destined to be drawn back into the Creator but this can happen only through Knowledge, through direct experience of God, because that is His wish.

> *For this is good and acceptable in the sight of God our Saviour; Who will have all men to be saved, and come unto the knowledge of the truth.*
> (I Timothy 2: 3 & 4)

Nevertheless, because God has given mankind free will, He will not force the issue but is content to wait patiently for His errant children to turn to Him. As Kabir again says:

> *As long as mind is smeared with the filth of passions and cravings, one cannot become free from the bondage of the world. When mind becomes pure, the soul will merge into the Pure One.*
> (Kabir, 15th century Muslim saint)

The Truth or Knowledge the Masters bring to mankind consists of one or more of four manifestations of God: the Word, the Divine Light, the Breath (I AM HE), and the Nectar. In actuality all four are manifestations of the Holy Ghost, the creative power of the Almighty, and are not separate from God or from each other, although they appear to have different forms when viewed from the perspective of our sense perceptions.

Since this all-inclusiveness is known to the saints by direct realisation, they do not always adhere strictly to the same label for any particular phenomenon. Sometimes a saint may say 'Name', meaning the 'Word', and yet another saint may use 'Name' in the context of the essential nature of the Godhead as Pure Awareness or Being. It could be argued that clear distinctions cannot be drawn between God's attributes for all are One in essence anyway. In the following text, for the sake of clarity, 'Name' is used in the same context as the Word, the Holy Sound Vibration or Holy Ghost.

Enlightenment is not a matter therefore of gaining intellectual knowledge of spiritual matters. A man can read the scripture of his choice daily for lifetimes to no avail. Such information merely points the way to the Path. It is not the Path itself. Rather, Knowledge is to know God, to experience Him directly. Such Knowledge can be obtained only through the Grace of the Creator and the help of an Enlightened Master.

What the Bible Says About Divine Knowledge.

Knowledge is direct inner experience of God. No one can give Knowledge to the Truth-Seeker except his/her God-chosen Master. Though the techniques given by the Masters may vary in detail they lead to the same goal.

Numbers 24: 16 Balaam tells of how, because of the Knowledge, he had an ecstatic vision of God.
"He hath said, which heard the words of God, and knew the knowledge of the most High, which saw the vision of the Almighty, falling into a trance, but having his eyes open:" See the section on 'The Word' for the meaning of 'words'.

I Samuel 2: 3 Hannah says that pride and arrogance violate True Knowledge: direct experience of God.

"Talk no more so exceedingly proudly; let not arrogancy come out of your mouth: for the Lord is a God of knowledge, and by him actions are weighed (through Him karmic law is carried out)."

II Chronicles 1: 10 Solomon asks God for Wisdom and Knowledge so that he can be a wise and just king.

"Give me now wisdom and knowledge, that I may go out and come in (can be in the world but be spiritually minded) *before this people: for who can judge this thy people, that is so great."* Eastern Masters similarly advise their disciples (chelas) to be 'in the world but not of it'. A common analogy employed by them is that of the lotus plant which, though it is rooted in the mud at the bottom of the pond, its flower basks in the light of the sun.

Job 36: 1-4 Job's friend comforts him by saying that God, who is perfect in Knowledge, is within him.

"Elihu also proceeded (continued to advise Job)*, and said,*
"Suffer me a little, and I will shew thee that I have yet to speak on God's behalf (Wait a moment for I am about to tell you what God is imparting to me through my intuition).
"I will fetch my knowledge from afar (the experience of God's silent voice comes from deep inside my consciousness)*, and will ascribe righteousness to my Maker* (and will prove the credentials of my Maker).
"For truly my words shall not be false: he that is perfect in knowledge is with thee (He, God, that is the source of this Divine Knowledge is within you and will not let you down)."

Job 36: 12 Elihu advises Job that his enemies will not prosper spiritually or materially without Divine Knowledge.

"But if they (the wicked) *obey not, they shall perish by the sword* (their karmas will overtake them)*, and they shall die without knowledge* (they will die spiritually without having received Divine Knowledge from a Master, the only thing that could save them)." See also Job 37: 16 for a similar reference to Knowledge.

Psalm 94: 10 David observes that God both disciplines us and brings us back to Him through the Knowledge.

"He that chastiseth the heathen (God who punishes the ignorant

through the Law of Karma), *shall he not correct? he that teacheth man knowledge* (to bring man back to his Creator), *shall not he know?"*

Psalm 139: 5 & 6 Many people have felt the same way as David when they received the Knowledge.

"Thou hast beset me behind and before, and laid thine hand upon me.

"Such knowledge is too wonderful for me; it is high (it is at the highest level of spirituality), *I cannot attain unto it* (I fear it is too difficult for me to achieve)."

Proverbs 1: 7 The Law of Karma drives mankind to seek Knowledge.

"The fear of the Lord (respect for God's Law of Karma) *is the beginning of knowledge* (instigates the quest for Knowledge): *but fools* (ignorant worldly people) *despise wisdom and instruction."*

Proverbs 1: 29-31 Rejecters of Knowledge and spiritual instruction will be chastened by the Law of Karma.

"For that they hated knowledge, and did not choose the fear of the Lord (Because they hated Divine Knowledge and did not fear the Law of Karma):

"They would none of my council: they despised all my reproof (They would not take good advice).

"Therefore shall they eat of the fruit of their own way, and be filled with their own devices (Therefore they will continue to reap the fruits of their own folly)."

Proverbs 2: 3-6 Knowledge is given to worthy Truth–Seekers by God through His Enlightened Ones.

"Yea, if thou criest after knowledge, and liftest up thy voice for understanding;

"If thou seekest her as silver, and searchest for her as for hid treasures;

"Then shalt thou understand the fear of the Lord (karmic law), *and find the knowledge of God.*

"For the Lord giveth wisdom: out of his mouth cometh knowledge and understanding (The Word, which is Knowledge and bestows

wisdom, comes through the 'Mouth of God' into the human body)."
See also Matthew 4: 4 for a similar reference to 'out of his mouth' and refer to the section called 'The Word' for the explanation.

Proverbs 2: 10-12 Spiritual safety lies in the power of wisdom and discretion that come from Knowledge.

"When wisdom entereth into thine heart, and knowledge is pleasant unto thine soul (When wisdom and Knowledge seem sweet to you);
"Discretion shall preserve thee (protect thee), *understanding shall keep thee* (shall guide you correctly):
"To deliver thee from the way of the evil man, from the man that speaketh froward things (that indulge in unspiritual conversation);"

Proverbs 3: 19 & 20 The Lord has done all things through the power of His Knowledge and Wisdom.

"The Lord by wisdom hath founded the earth: by understanding hath he established the heavens (All material things come from the Holy Ghost Vibration guided by the intelligence inherent in the Christ Consciousness).
"By his knowledge (by the divinely manifested powers inherent in Him) *the depths are broken up, and the clouds drop down the dew."*

Proverbs 4: 7 Wisdom and understanding are attained through Knowledge: direct experience of God.

"Wisdom is the principal thing; therefore get wisdom: and with all thy getting get understanding."

Proverbs 8: 10 Initiation and the Knowledge imparted with it are more precious than material wealth.

"Receive my instruction (teachings), *and not silver; and knowledge* (and initiation into the Divine Knowledge) *rather than choice gold."*
See also the section called 'Initiation into the Path'.

Proverbs 9: 10 Respect for the Law of Karma makes us wise enough to seek Knowledge and understanding.

"The fear of the Lord is the beginning of wisdom: and the knowledge of the holy is understanding."

Proverbs 10: 14 The truly wise man practises the Knowledge.
"Wise men lay up knowledge (Wise men practise the Knowledge given by the Master): *but the mouth of the foolish is near destruction."*

Proverbs 11: 9 Those that seek the True Knowledge shall be freed from this world.
"An hypocrite with his mouth destroyeth his neighbour: but through knowledge shall the just be delivered."

Proverbs 12: 1 The love of spiritual teachings and the desire for True Knowledge go hand in hand.
"Whoso loveth instruction loveth knowledge (He who loves spiritual teachings will want to be given the Knowledge): *but he that hateth reproof is brutish* (but the one that avoids spiritual instruction fearing that it will reveal to him the error of his ways, is not living up to his full human potential)."

Proverbs 14: 6, 7 & 18 Solomon picks out some contrasts between spiritual and non-spiritual people.
"A scorner seeketh wisdom, and findeth it not: but knowledge is easy unto him that understandeth (practising Knowledge comes easily to those with understanding).
"Go from the presence of a foolish man, when thou perceivest not in him the lips of knowledge (avoid the foolish man when you detect that he has not been made wise by the Knowledge)."
"The simple inherit folly: but the prudent are crowned with knowledge (the wise earn initiation into the Knowledge)." See also Proverbs 15: 14 and the section on 'Initiation into the Path'.

Proverbs 15: 7 Masters give Knowledge but the ignorant cannot speak with wisdom.
"The lips of the wise (God's Enlightened Ones) *disperse knowledge* (impart Divine Knowledge to the worthy): *but the heart of the foolish doeth not so* (the foolish impart nothing of value)."

Proverbs 18: 15 Wise and thoughtful people seek and get True Knowledge.
"The heart of the prudent getteth knowledge; and the ears of the wise seeketh knowledge (the wise wish to listen to the sound of the Holy Ghost which the Master gives to them at the time of initiation)." See also Proverbs 20: 15; 21: 11; 22: 12 & 17; & 24: 4. Refer to the section called 'The Word' for the subtle meaning of 'the ears of the wise'.

Proverbs 24: 13 & 14 Solomon clearly has been given the Knowledge.

"*My son, eat thou honey* (Nectar), *because it is good* (it has great spiritual benefits); *and the honeycomb* (the Word which holds the Nectar), *which is sweet to thy taste:*

"*So shall the knowledge of wisdom be unto thy soul: when thou hast found it, then there shall be a reward, and thy expectation shall not be cut off* (and when you have found Knowledge you will not be disappointed)." See the sections on 'The Word' and 'The Nectar'.

Isaiah 5: 11-13 The Lord complains that the people are not fit to receive the Knowledge from His Masters.

"*Woe unto them that rise up early in the morning, that they may follow strong drink; that continue until night, till wine inflame them!*

"*And the harp, and the viol, the tabret, and pipe, and wine, are in their feasts* (God is even in music, food and enjoyment): *but they regard not the work of the Lord* (but they cannot see Him or praise Him for it), *neither consider the operation of his hands.*

"*Therefore my people are gone into captivity* (are imprisoned into the cycle of birth, death, and rebirth), *because they have no knowledge* (because they have not been given the Divine Knowledge which will enable them to escape from the Laws of Karma and Reincarnation): *and their honourable men are famished, and their multitude dried up with thirst* (and those who are yearning for liberation remain hungry and thirsty for the Knowledge)."

Daniel 2: 20 & 21 Daniel praises the Lord who brings Knowledge to those who can understand such a blessing.

"*Daniel answered and said, Blessed be the name of God for ever and ever: for wisdom and might are his:*

"*And he changeth the times and the seasons: he removeth kings, and setteth up kings: he giveth wisdom unto the wise, and knowledge to them that know understanding:*" See the section on 'The Word' for the meaning of 'the name of God'.

Hosea 6: 6 The desire for God's mercy and Knowledge is a hallmark of the Truth–Seeker.

"*For I desired mercy and not sacrifice; and the knowledge of God more than burnt offerings.*"

Christopher Mark Hanson

Apocrypha, The Wisdom of Solomon 8: 4 Through wisdom the Knowledge of God can be understood.
"For she (wisdom) *is privy to the mysteries of the knowledge of God, and a lover of his works."*

Mark 1: 14 & 15 The terms 'Kingdom of God' and the 'Gospel' refer to the Knowledge and the Teachings of the Masters.
"Now after that John (John the Baptist) *was put in prison, Jesus came into Galilee, preaching the gospel of the kingdom of God* (teaching people and initiating them into Divine Knowledge),
"And saying, The time is fulfilled, and the kingdom of God is at hand: repent ye, and believe the Gospel (Saying, shake off the chains of the world and come to me, Jesus, to receive the teachings and be initiated into the Divine Knowledge that will set you free).*"* To 'believe the Gospel' infers both the verbal discourse of the Master and the initiation that follows: See the section on 'Initiation into the Path'.

Romans 11: 33 St. Paul praises the great benefits of obtaining wisdom and Knowledge
"O the depth of the riches both of the wisdom and knowledge of God! how unsearchable are his judgements, and his ways past finding out!"

II Corinthians 2: 14 St. Paul praises God who brings both the Son and Knowledge into His Creation.
"Now thanks be unto God (Cosmic Consciousness), *which always causeth us to triumph in Christ* (who brings the glory of the Son or Christ Consciousness), *and maketh manifest the savour of his knowledge by us in every place* (and enables us to manifest and pass on to others the delights of the Knowledge).*"*

II Corinthians 6: 6 St. Paul identifies Knowledge as a means by which disciples become enlightened.
"By pureness, by knowledge, by longsuffering, by the Holy Ghost, by love unfeigned."

II Corinthians 10: 5 St. Paul points out that Truth-Seekers need sufficient humility to accept Knowledge.
"Casting down imaginations, and every high thing that exalteth itself against the knowledge of God (Casting out foolish imaginings and arrogance that get in the way of receiving Knowledge from

those qualified to give it), *and bringing into captivity every thought to the obedience of Christ* (and by bringing every thought under the control of the Christ Consciousness within us);"

Ephesians 3: 19 St. Paul points out that Enlightened Ones give Knowledge to mankind out of pure love.
"And to know the love of Christ (Jesus the Christ and all those who have been, are, and will be One with the Christ Consciousness), *which passeth knowledge* (who passed Divine Knowledge on to his disciples), *that ye might be filled with the fullness of God* (so that your 'cup' may be filled to overflowing when you receive your natural inheritance as children of the One God after being initiated by me)." See the section on 'Initiation' for the meaning of 'which passeth knowledge'.

Ephesians 4: 13 St. Paul confirms that Knowledge will transform us into the Christ Consciousness itself.
"Till we all come into the unity of the faith, and of the knowledge of the Son of God, unto a perfect man, unto the measure of the stature of the fullness of Christ (Till we all have sufficient faith in the Teachings to be initiated into Knowledge which will in due course lift our consciousnesses to the level of unity with the Son of God, the Christ Consciousness):"

Colossians 1: 10 God is pleased when we practise Knowledge and draw closer to Him.
"That ye might walk worthy of the Lord unto all pleasing, being fruitful in every good work, and increasing in the knowledge of God;"

Colossians 3: 9-11 St. Paul writes about the great benefits Knowledge will bring to the people.
"Lie not one to another, seeing that ye have put off the old man with his deeds (Don't lie to one another. Get rid of your old ways now that you have entered the spiritual path);
"And have put on the new man, which is renewed in knowledge after the image of him that created him (and have been transformed into new men by the Divine Knowledge who are perfect images of God who created mankind):
"Where there is neither Greek not Jew, circumcision nor

uncircumcision, Barbarian, Scythian, bond nor free: but Christ is all, and in all (The Christ Consciousness in each one of you is common to all and recognises no divisions of race, status, culture or anything else)."

I Timothy 2: 3 & 4 God wants everyone to experience the Knowledge of what they really are.
"For this is good and acceptable in the sight of God our Saviour;
"Who will have all men to be saved, and come unto the knowledge of the truth."

Hebrews 10: 26 Enlightened Ones will not help us if we reject the Knowledge and return to our old ways.
"For if we sin wilfully after that we have received the knowledge of the truth (If, after we have been initiated into the Knowledge, we continue to do things that separate us from God), *there remaineth no more sacrifice for sins* (our Enlightened Teacher will no longer carry our karmas but will leave us to the mercies of the world until such time as we have repented in earnest)." See the section on 'Initiation into the Path' for the meaning of 'received knowledge of the truth'.

II Peter 1: 2-6 St. Peter emphasises the importance of receiving and practicing the Knowledge.
"Grace and peace be multiplied unto you through the knowledge of God, and of Jesus our Lord (I pray that the Knowledge you have been given by God through His Enlightened One, Jesus, will bring you immeasurable grace and peace).
"According as his (God's) *divine power hath given unto us all things that pertain unto life and godliness, through the knowledge of him* (through Jesus who has passed on the Divine Knowledge to us) *that hath called us to glory and virtue:*
"Whereby are given to us exceedingly great and precious promises (Through receiving the Knowledge we have entered into the sacred and binding oaths of loyalty to God, the Path and His chosen emissary): *that by these ye may be partakers of the divine nature* (that by these you may unite with God), *having escaped the corruption that is in the world through lust* (having escaped the darkness of ignorance through lustful desires of the things of this world).

"And besides this, giving all diligence, add to you faith virtue; and to virtue knowledge;
"And to knowledge temperance; and to temperance patience; and to patience godliness;"

2

The Word.

> *Amazing grace! How sweet the sound*
> *That saved a wretch like me.*
> *I once was lost but now am found,*
> *Was blind but now I see.*
> (Christian Hymn)

> *Thy Name is the lamp, Thy name the wick,*
> *Thy Name is the oil which I pour therein.*
> *Of Thy Name I have kindled the Light,*
> *With its illumination my entire home is bright.*
> (Ravidas, 15th century Indian saint)

Saints of every religion proclaim the importance of the sound issuing from God into His Creation and have adopted many different names to describe this awesome power. Among the many biblical appellations given to this Divine Sound are: Word, Holy Ghost, Logos, Name, Comforter, Witness, Voice and Watchword. In addition, the Bible contains many other words that attempt to describe the noise it makes: rushing wind, beating of wings, many waters, thunder, trumpet blast etc; but perhaps the most intriguing and the most overlooked is 'Amen'.

> *And blessed be his* (God's) *glorious name for ever: and let the whole earth be filled with his glory: Amen, and Amen.*
> (Psalm 72: 19)

When Amen is intoned loudly and continuously (as at the end of a prayer) it gives a sound identical to the AUM and OM of the Hindus and the Buddhists. Amen, OM and AUM are simply word-sounds that attempt to mimic the real sound of the Word as heard by saints in meditation: that 'sweet sound' that saves us from the blindness of our true nature which we mention every time we sing Amazing Grace.

Kabir refers to the Word as the 'Shabd', a Sound that is the origin of all sounds, all shabds. Though the world's scriptures make much of it, Kabir points out that few know what it is and where it comes from.

> *The Vedas and scriptures*
> *Extol the merits of Shabd-*
> *The Shabd that sustains*
> *All shabds in the world.*
> *Men, sages and gods*
> *Sing its praises*
> *Yet its mystery they know not.*
> *Imprint that Shabd*
> *In your heart, O friend.*
> (Kabir, 15th century Muslim saint)

But Kabir and all the saints have always been aware that the Word is the noise made by the vibration of God's Consciousness creating and maintaining Creation and that it is no different from God. It is God.

> *In the beginning was the Word, and the Word was with God, and the Word was God. The same was in the beginning with God. All things were made by him; and without him was not any thing made that was made.*
> (John 1: 1-3)

The Word has a dual purpose. It is not just the supreme creative force. It is also the Voice of God calling His children to return to their Celestial Home,

> *I (God) have sworn by myself, the word is gone out of my mouth in righteousness, and shall not return, That unto me every knee shall bow, every tongue shall swear.*
> (Isaiah 45: 23)

which is why the saints and scriptures repeatedly encourage earnest devotees to listen to (call upon) this Sound, God's Name.

> *And in that day shall ye say, Praise the Lord, call upon his name, declare his doings among the people, make mention that his name is exalted.*
> (Isaiah 12: 4)

> *But the word of the Lord endureth forever. And this is the word which by the gospel is preached unto you.*
> (I Peter 1: 25)

Ever since mankind and Creation were formed, the Word has been in existence. It is in fact the very life-force that animates the human body. Man is not separate from it. His soul, life and body are an integral part of it. Man exists because of it.

> *That which was from the beginning, which we have heard, which we have seen with our eyes, which we have looked upon, and our hands have handled, of the Word of life;*
> (I John 1: 1)

It is also true that every living being is being replenished constantly by Cosmic Energy from this source. Our bodies are sustained not solely by the food (bread) we eat but by the energy of the Word issuing from the 'mouth of God' situated at the base of man's cranium opposite the site of the Single Eye.

> *But he (Jesus) answered (Satan) and said, It is written, Man shall not live by bread alone, but by every word that*

proceedeth out of the mouth of God.
(Matthew 4: 4)

All substances consist of the Word or Holy Ghost vibrating at different frequencies to produce the quality of the particular substance in manifestation whether it is solid, liquid or gas. But the Holy Vibration would not know what to do by itself. It needs direction and this is provided by the intelligence of the Christ Consciousness. And the Christ Consciousness, or Son, is also God in Creation.

This link between matter, the Holy Ghost, the Christ Consciousness and God-the-Father is not accidental. It is not some process that has randomly evolved over a long period of time. It has been designed to be so and to operate in two ways. Man entered matter by this route: God-the-Father to God-the-Son to God-the-Holy Ghost; and must ascend back to God by the reverse sequence.

> *Go ye therefore, and teach all nations, baptizing them in the name of the Father, and of the Son, and of the Holy Ghost: Teaching them to observe all things whatsoever I have commanded you: and, lo, I am with you always, even unto the end of the world. Amen.*
> (Matthew 28: 19 & 20)

Mankind, bogged down in matter, is obliged to attach his consciousness in meditation to the Sound, Word or Holy Ghost. The Holy Ghost then raises his consciousness to the Christ Centre from where the Christ Consciousness carries his attention up to God-the-Father or Cosmic Consciousness; all of which happens within the body, particularly in the higher spiritual centres in the head.

This process is symbolised in the tolling of the church bell, with the bell representing the sound of the Word reverberating at the site of the Single Eye in man's forehead (the steeple) drawing his consciousness inward (into his body: the 'church') to God.

Though this and much other spiritual Knowledge has been lost during the rise of Christian orthodoxy, an understanding of the creative and unifying power of the Word (the golden bell) seems to have survived in isolated pockets of the western world as the following work of Goethe attests:

All things into one are woven, each in each doth act and dwell
As cosmic forces, rising, falling, charging up this golden bell,
With heaven-scented undulations, fill they universal time!
Amidst life's tides in raging motion.
        (Goethe).

Nevertheless it is a great pity that the enormous importance of 'The Word' as the Path back to God has been forgotten by the Christian world in general and its significance trivialised to the chanting of Amen at the end of a prayer and the occasional tolling of the church bell.

What the Bible Says About the Word.

The soul has descended into a material body formed out of the vibrating consciousness of God and must re-ascend to God through merging into that same Word. Listening to the Word of God, the Amen, is the universal route back to God: the starting point of 'real religion'.

Exodus 19: 19 Moses hears the Word resounding like a trumpet which becomes audible as a voice.
"*And when the voice of the trumpet* (the Word) *sounded long, and waxed louder and louder, Moses spake* (talked to God), *and God answered him by a voice* (The vibratory power of the Word formed itself into audible words).*"*

I Samuel 12: 14 Samuel advises the people to obey the Word of God in order to be in harmony with God Himself.
"*If ye will fear the Lord, and serve him, and obey his voice* (If you will follow the guidance that comes to you from meditating on the Word), *and not rebel against the commandment of the Lord* (and

not rebel against the divine advice coming to you through your awakening intuition), *then shall both ye and also the king that reigneth over you continue following the Lord your God:"*

II Samuel 22: 14 David experienced the thunderous sound of the Word.
"The Lord thundered from heaven (from the subtle astral heavens), *and the most High uttered his voice."* The thundering sound made by the Word, Amen, or OM, is often referred to by the saints as the Voice of God.

II Samuel 22: 31 God brings perfect justice, comfort and trust to the devotee through the Word.
"As for God, his way is perfect; the word of the Lord is tried (The Amen or Holy Vibration is a tried and tested way of reaching God)*: he is a buckler* (support) *to all them that trust in him* (that trust in Him as the Word or Holy Ghost)."

Job 36: 29 & 30 Elihu talks to Job about the Light and Sound of God in creation.
"Also can any understand the spreading of the clouds, or the noise of his tabernacle (sound of the Word in Creation and in the human body)*?*
"Behold, he spreadeth his light upon it, and covereth the bottom of the sea." See the section on 'The Divine Light' for the meaning of 'his light'.

Job 37: 1-5 Elihu tells Job about the wonders of God's Voice, the Word or Holy Ghost Vibration.
"At this also my heart trembleth, and is moved out of his place.
"Hear attentively the noise of his voice (the Word)*, and the sound that goeth out of his mouth.*
"He directeth it under the whole heaven, and his lightning unto the ends of the earth.
"After it a voice roareth: he thundereth with the voice of his excellency; and he will not stay them when his voice is heard.
"God thundereth marvellously with his voice; great things doeth he, which we cannot comprehend." See the text for an explanation of the 'mouth of God'.

Job 40: 9 The Lord makes a point to Job about His omniscience and the power of the Word, OM, Amen, or Holy Ghost.

"Hast thou an arm like God? Or canst thou thunder with a voice like him?"

Psalm 8: 1 The Name of God is a heavenly Power that is the foundation of all matter.

"O Lord our Lord, how excellent is thy name (the Word) *in all the earth! who hast set thy glory above the heavens."*

Psalm 9: 10 Those who can hear the sound of the Word have proof of the existence of God.

"And they that know thy name (the Word) *will put their trust in thee: for thou, Lord, hast not forsaken them that seek thee."*

Psalm 29: 2 & 3 God as the Word or Holy Ghost is the energy that upholds the world and is worthy of worship.

"Give unto the Lord the glory due unto his name (the Word)*; worship the Lord in the beauty of holiness.*

"The voice of the Lord is upon the waters (The Word as the Holy Vibration stirs into life the subtle energies underlying and pervading all matter)*: the God of glory thundereth: the Lord is upon many waters."*

Psalm 52: 9 The Saints. the Enlightened Ones, love the Name and listen to it constantly.

"I will praise thee (God) *for ever, because thou hast done it* (brought mercy to the believer)*: and I will wait on thy name* (I will listen patiently to the Word)*; for it is good before thy saints."*

Psalm 54: 1 Listening to the sound of the Holy Name in meditation saves one from the pull of the world.

"Save me, O God, by thy name (the Word)*, and judge me by thy strength."*

Psalm 68: 33 David describes the Word as a great voice.

"To him (God) *that rideth upon the heavens of heavens* (who exists beyond the subtle realms from which solid earth materialises)*, which were of old* (created when the world began)*; lo, he doth send out his voice* (the Word out of which all Creation issues forth)*, and that a mighty voice* (is powerful and all–pervading)*."*

Psalm 72: 17 The Word is the source of Creation and is the force that draws us back to God.

"His name (the Word) *shall endure for ever: his name shall be continued as long as the sun: and men shall be blessed in him* (and men shall reach God by immersing their minds in this Holy Sound)*: all nations shall call him blessed."*

Psalm 72: 19 David praises the Word, the Name, which is also called the Amen or OM.

"And blessed be his (God's) *glorious name for ever: and let the whole earth be filled with his glory: Amen, and Amen."*

Psalm 89: 15 & 16 David praises the sound emitted by the Word that brings the Light of God.

"Blessed is the people that know the joyful sound (the Word, OM or Amen)*: they shall walk, O Lord, in the light of thy countenance* (they will be guided by the Divine Light visible to the Single Eye).

"In thy name (Bathed in the Word) *shall they rejoice all the day: and in thy righteousness shall they be exalted* (be lifted up spiritually to enlightenment)*."* See also the section on 'The Divine Light'.

Psalm 119: 160 The Word is related to the Law of Karma or righteous judgements.

"Thy word is true from the beginning: and every one of thy righteous judgements endureth forever."

Proverbs 13: 13 Those who despise the Word will remain prisoners in this world.

"Whoso despiseth the word shall be destroyed (Those who scoff at the Word will lose their spiritual life)*: but he that feareth the commandment* (but he who responds to the inward pull of the Word) *shall be rewarded* (will be rewarded with enlightenment and God's gifts)*."*

Proverbs 18: 10 The Truth Seeker takes refuge in the stronghold of the Word.

"The name (the Word) *of the Lord is a strong tower: the righteous runneth into it, and is safe."*

Song of Solomon 1: 3 The pure in heart love the Name of God, the Word.

"Because of the savour of thy good ointments Thy name (the soothing sound of the Word or Holy Ghost) *is as ointment poured*

forth, therefore do the virgins (virgin souls uncontaminated by evil) *love thee."*

Song of Solomon 2: 8 Solomon expresses the uplifting nature of the Word or Holy Ghost Vibration in poetic terms.
"The voice of my beloved (the Holy Sound of God)! *behold, he cometh leaping upon the mountains, skipping upon the hills* (the Holy Sound, the Word, descends from the Crown Chakra and the Christ Centre)."*

Isaiah 2: 3 The Law of Karma and the Word come out of the Cosmic Consciousness of God.
"...for out of Zion (Cosmic Consciousness) *shall go forth the law* (the Law of Karma), *and the word* (the Holy Ghost) *of the Lord from Jerusalem* (from God within creation, the Christ Consciousness)."*
Refer back to the section on 'The Captivity' for details of the Law of Karma and to the section on 'The Higher Spiritual Centres' for the meaning of the Cosmic and Christ Consciousnesses.

Isaiah 5: 24 Isaiah describes the fate of those who reject the Holy Word.
"Therefore as the fire devoureth the stubble, and the flame consumeth the chaff, so their root shall be as rottenness, and their blossom shall go up as dust: because they have cast away the law of the Lord of host, and despise the word of the Holy One of Israel (Those who disregard the Law of Karma and sneer at the teachings about the Word or Holy Ghost Vibration, will continue to burn with unquenchable desires)."*

Isaiah 12: 4 When the Master comes people are drawn to the Name or Word.
"And in that day shall ye say, Praise the Lord, call upon his name (listen to the sound of the Word resounding within you), *declare his doings among the people* (tell the people of the benefits of doing so), *make mention that his name is exalted* (tell them that His Holy Word is of extreme spiritual benefit)."*

Isaiah 30: 20 & 21 God's chosen ones bring the Word to lead us back to Him.
"And though the Lord give you the bread of adversity, and the water of affliction (And though God brings you adversity through the Law of Karma), *yet shall not thy teachers be removed into a corner any more* (yet His spiritual teachers will always be with you), *but thine*

eyes shall see thy teachers (and the particular Teacher or Enlightened One that God has chosen for you will appear before you in body form):
"And thine ears shall hear a word (You will hear the Holy Ghost Vibration) *behind thee* (inside yourself: in the opposite direction to the usual outward way), *saying* (guiding you), *This is the way, walk ye in it, when ye turn to the right hand, and when ye turn to the left* (It will be calling you back to the Holy Father from whom the Holy Vibration comes. Let it guide you in everything that you do)."

Isaiah 45: 23 The Word issues from the mouth of God to guide His children back to Him.
"I (God) *have sworn by myself* (have issued the Sound), *the word* (the Holy Vibration) *is gone out of my mouth* (out of the realm of Spirit beyond Creation and into the human body) *in righteousness, and shall not return, That unto me every knee shall bow, every tongue shall swear."* See the text for the meaning of 'out of my mouth'.

Isaiah 52: 6 Through knowing God's Name one can experience God as the 'I AM HE' or simply as the 'I'.
"Therefore my people shall know my name (the Word): *therefore they shall know in that day that I am he that doth speak: behold, it is I."* See also the section called 'I Am He'.

Isaiah 52: 8 Through Isaiah God tells us that by listening to His Voice or Word we will attain enlightenment.
"Thy watchmen (the Enlightened Ones of the world) *shall lift up the voice* (shall issue forth the Sound Vibration of the Word); *with the voice together shall they sing* (all Masters are in tune with the Holy Vibration and among themselves): *for they shall see eye to eye, when the Lord shall bring again Zion* (all men shall be in agreement with each other when they follow the Divine Voice or Word to the Holy State of enlightenment)."

Isaiah 55: 11 The Holy Vibration is the Voice of God, calling His errant children back to Him. He will not fail.
"So shall my word (the Holy Ghost Vibration) *be that goeth forth out of my mouth* (the back entrance to the Single Eye centre): *it shall not return unto me void* (shall not return to Me empty handed),

but it shall accomplish that which I please, and it shall prosper in the thing whereto I sent it (and it will never fail to carry out Divine Will)."

Isaiah 56: 5 & 7 The Lord promises to send His Holy Name to the righteous.
"*...I will give them an everlasting name, that shall not be cut off* (I, God, will send the Holy Word to them via My Enlightened Ones)."
"*Even them* (Those contacting My Holy Ghost Vibration) *will I bring to my Holy Mountain* (I will draw inwards into the higher spiritual centres in the crown of their heads) *and make them joyful in my house of prayer...*" Meditation on the Word is said by the Masters to be true prayer. See also the section on 'Meditation'.

Jeremiah 7: 2 Jeremiah advises us to listen to the Word at the Gate of the Single Eye.
"*Stand in the gate of the Lord's house* (Place your focus at the Single Eye, the gateway to God), *and proclaim there his word* (and concentrate until His Holy Sound comes to you in the silence of meditation), *and say* (bear witness), *Hear the word of the Lord, all ye of Judah, that enter in at these gates to worship the Lord.*"

Jeremiah 10: 13 The sound of the Word activates the subtle energies that create matter and all nature.
"*When he* (God) *uttereth his voice* (the vibrational voice of the Holy Word), *there is a multitude of waters* (energies) *in the heavens, and he* (God as the Word or Holy Ghost) *causeth vapours* (subtle forces) *to ascend from the ends of the earth* (to manifest in all the earthly realms); *he maketh lightnings with rain and bringeth forth the wind out of his treasures.*" This passage also has a deeper meaning related to the Holy Sound and the flashes of Light one sees at the higher levels of meditation.

Ezekiel 1: 24 & 25 The prophet attempts to describe the sound made by the Word.
"*And when they* (the four angles) *went, I heard the noise of their wings, like the noise of great waters, as the voice of the Almighty, the voice of speech, as the noise of an host: when they stood, they let down their wings.*
"*And there was a voice from the firmament that was over their heads* (The Holy Sound came from a higher and subtler realm), *when they stood, and had let down their wings.*" The reference to 'wings' appears to be a description of the changing shape of the astral energy field around the angels.

Ezekiel 3: 12 The prophet hears the Word as an audible voice speaking to him.
"Then the spirit took me up, and I heard behind me (inside myself) *a voice of a great rushing, saying, Blessed be the glory of the Lord from his place* (emitting from His Cosmic Consciousness, His place of abode)."

Malachi 1: 11 God says through Malachi that non–Jews shall become familiar with the Holy Vibration in time.
"For from the rising of the sun even unto the going down of the same my name (the Word) *shall be great among the Gentiles* (the non–Jews); *and in every place incense* (the sweet incense of devotion) *shall be offered unto my name, and a pure offering: for my name shall be great among the heathen* (those currently non–believers), *saith the Lord of hosts."*

Apocrypha, II Edras 6: 13, 14 & 17 The prophet describes his experience of the Holy Word.
"So he (God) *answered and said unto me, Stand up upon thy feet, and hear a mighty sounding voice* (the holy vibrations of the Word).
"And it shall be as it were a great motion (It shall seem to be shaking the foundations of the earth); *but the place where thou standest shall not be moved."*
"And it happened, that when I had heard it I stood up upon my feet, and hearkened, and, behold, there was a voice that spake, and the sound of it was like the sound of many waters."

Apocrypha, The Wisdom of Solomon 16: 26 Man cannot live without the Word. It is the life of men.
"That thy children, O Lord, whom thou lovest, might know, that it is not the growing of fruits that nourisheth man: but it is thy word, which preserveth them that put their trust in thee (it is Thy Word which sustains those who make the effort to contact Thee in meditation)."
See also a similar reference to the Word as 'food' in Matthew 4: 4 below.

Apocrypha, Ecclesiasticus 1: 5 The quality of Divine Wisdom lies in the bosom of the Holy Word.
"The word of God most high is the fountain of wisdom; and her ways are everlasting commandments (Wisdom lies in the bosom of the Word and should be followed to the letter)."

Matthew 3: 17 God's Holy Ghost Vibration or Word formed itself into an audible voice.
"And lo a voice from heaven, saying, This is my beloved Son (This is the Master with the Christ Consciousness), *in whom I am well pleased."* See also Mark 1: 11.

Matthew 4: 4 Jesus confirms that man lives by the Word coming out of the mouth of God.
"But he (Jesus) *answered* (Satan) *and said, It is written, Man shall not live by bread alone, but by every word that proceedeth out of the mouth of God* (but by the life-energy of the Holy Ghost that enters the human body through the back entrance of the Medullar Chakra, the mouth of God)."

Matthew 6: 9 Jesus teaches his disciples to pray on the Word.
"After this manner therefore pray ye: Our Father which are in heaven (who is in the realm of Cosmic Consciousness), *Hallowed be thy name* (Holy be Thy Word for it will carry me back to You)."

Matthew 8: 8 & 10 Faith in the power of God's Word comes from an unusual source.
"The centurion answered and said, Lord, I am not worthy that thou shouldest come under my roof: but speak the word only (send out your Divine Vibrations), *and my servant shall be healed."*
"When Jesus heard it, he marvelled, and said to them that followed, Verily I say unto you, I have not found so great faith, no, not in Israel."

Matthew 28: 19 & 20 Jesus refers to the Trinity and emphasises the importance of the Holy Ghost, the Amen.
"Go ye therefore, and teach all nations, baptizing them in the name of the Father, and of the Son, and of the Holy Ghost (initiating those that are ready, giving them, according to their ability to receive, an experience of the three aspects of God living within them: Cosmic Consciousness, Christ Consciousness and the Word or Holy Ghost):
"Teaching them to observe all things whatsoever I have commanded you: and, lo, I (the Christ Consciousness that is within me) *am with you always, even unto the ends of the world. Amen."* This is the only occasion on which Jesus is recorded as having spoken directly of the Trinity. See also the section on 'Initiation into the Path' for the meaning of 'baptizing'.

John 1: 1-3 St. John identifies the Word as the origin of all Creation and as being no different from God Himself.

"In the beginning was the Word, and the Word was with God, and the Word was God.

"The same (the Word) *was in the beginning with God.*

"All things were made by him (God as the power of the Word); *and without him was not any thing made that was made."*

John 5: 25 The Master brings the Holy Word to lead seekers back to God.

"Verily, verily, I say unto you, The hour is coming, and now is (I tell you that this is a very opportune moment for a Master is with you), *when the dead* (those who were previously spiritually dead) *shall hear the voice of the Son of God* (shall be able to hear the vibrational power of the Word which is with the Christ Consciousness in Creation): *and they that hear shall live* (those that are receptive to it shall become aware that they are immortal souls, perfect in every way)."

John 5: 37 & 38 Jesus point out that worldly people are ignorant of God's Voice or Word.

"And the Father himself, which hath sent me (the Master, Jesus), *hath borne witness of me* (through the teachings and miracles). *Ye have neither heard his voice at any time, nor seen his shape* (You have not heard the vibrational sounds of His Holy Word nor seen the Light–form of God).

"And ye have not his word abiding in you: for whom he hath sent, him ye believe not (If you had been in the habit of meditating on the Holy Word, you would have made enough spiritual progress to be able to recognise a Master intuitively)." See the section on 'The Divine Light' for the meaning of 'his shape' as the Light-form of God.

John 8: 31 & 32 Jesus says that it is necessary to continue to meditate on the Word.

"Then said Jesus to those Jews which believed on him, If ye continue in my word, then are ye my disciples indeed (Only those who continue to listen to the Word in meditation can count themselves among my disciples);

"And ye shall know the truth, and the truth shall make you free (Meditating on the Word will lead to the Supreme Truth, God–the–

Father, and that union will free you from the cycles of death and rebirth)."

John 12: 28 & 29 The Word formed itself into an audible voice to answer Jesus' prayer.
"Father, glorify thy name (Holy Father, bring to others the glory of Yourself through Your Holy Word). *Then came there a voice from heaven, saying, I have both glorified it, and will glorify it again.*
"The people therefore, that stood by, and heard it, said that it thundered: others said, An angel spake to him."

John 12: 48 The one who rejects the Word the Master has come to give him will regret it at death.
"He that rejecteth me (the Christ Consciousness in me), *and receiveth not my words* (the teachings or Knowledge), *hath one that judgeth him: the word* (the Holy Ghost Vibration) *that I have spoken* (that is behind every word that I utter), *the same shall judge him in the last day* (The Truth within the Word will reveal his errors to him when he reviews his life at the moment of death)." The Master's say that at the moment of death every person judges the quality of his life using the purity of the soul as the standard. This is the real Day of Judgement.

John 14: 16 Jesus calls the Word the Comforter as its presence gives immeasurable comfort to the devotee.
"And I will pray the Father, and he shall give you another Comforter (Though I will soon be crucified, God will comfort you by sending to you another comforter, the Holy Word), *that he may abide with you for ever* (That through this Holy Word you will know that God is always with you);"

John 14: 26 Jesus specifically identifies the Comforter as the Holy Ghost or Word.
"But the Comforter, which is the Holy Ghost, whom the Father will send in my name (whom God will send because I am united to the Holy Ghost or Word itself), *he* (the voice of God heard through your intuition) *shall teach you all things, and bring all things to your remembrance, whatsoever I have said unto you* (By meditating on the Holy Ghost or Word you will remember clearly every detail of everything I have told you)."

John 15: 3 Jesus has freed his disciples from karma through the agency of the Word.
"Now ye are clean through the word (the Holy Word or Holy Ghost) *which I have spoken unto you* (which is reverberating within my body)."

John 15: 26 & 27 Jesus tells his disciples what to expect when the Comforter, the Word, comes to them.
"But when the Comforter is come (When you begin to hear the Holy Sound in meditation), *whom I will send unto you from the Father* (which I will send to you when I am united to the Father in Cosmic Consciousness), *even the Spirit of truth, which proceedeth from the Father, he shall testify of me* (you will realise from its testimony that it comes from God and I am one with Him):
"And ye also shall bear witness, because ye have been with me from the beginning (You will know this truth with all the power of your souls because you have been with me from the beginning of my ministry)."

John 16: 8 The Comforter or Word brings judgement to the world.
"And when he (the Comforter) *is come, he will reprove the world of sin* (the Word or Amen will reveal the real nature of sin and those who become one with it will be cleansed), *and of righteousness* (and establish the rule of right conduct), *and of judgement* (through the Law of Karma):"

John 16: 23 & 24 Jesus assures his disciples that the Comforter will confer its power of omniscience upon them.
"And in that day ye shall ask me nothing. Verily, verily, I say unto you, Whatsoever ye shall ask the Father in my name, he will give it you (When the Comforter or Word has come all your queries will be answered for divine wisdom will be yours).
"Hitherto have ye asked nothing in my name: ask, and ye shall receive, that your joy may be full (Up to now you have been insufficiently advanced spiritually to be able to ask the Holy Ghost or Word for anything but from here on, through regularly 'asking' in meditation, you will be able to get anything you need and you will receive the divine joy of God–union)."

John 17: 17 & 20 Jesus prays for the spiritual success of all those who follow his advice to listen to the Word.

"Sanctify them through thy truth: for thy word is truth (Enlighten them, Father, through the Holy Ghost, Thy True Word).*"*

"Neither pray I for these alone, but for them also which shall believe on me through their word (I pray also for all those who believe in the Christ Consciousness through listening to the Word reverberating inside themselves);*"*

John 17: 26 Jesus tells the Lord he has initiated the disciples with the Holy Name so that they can become 'Love'.

"And I have declared unto them thy name (the Word), *and will declare it: that the love wherewith thou hast loved me may be in them, and I in them."* See the section on 'Initiation into the Path' for the meaning of 'I have declared unto them thy name'.

Acts 2: 2 & 3 By focusing the attention on the Single Eye the Light of the Eye is revealed along with the Word.

"And suddenly there came a sound from heaven as of a rushing mighty wind (the Holy Ghost or Word), *and it filled the house where they were sitting* (meditating).

"And there appeared unto them cloven tongues like as of fire (And they saw a vision of a burning yellow ring with the blue circle and the bright star in the middle), *and it sat upon each of them* (which each one of them saw within himself).*"* See the section on 'The Higher Spiritual Centres' for further details of the Single Eye.

Romans 10: 8 The Holy Word vibrates in all speech and in the heart of everyone.

"But what saith it? The word is nigh thee (The Holy Vibration is so close to you, not far away at all), *even in thy mouth* (being the basis of all sound, it is even in the words you speak), *and in thy heart* (in the feelings of your heart): *that is the word of faith, which we preach."* Like so many divine things, the Holy Word has to be experience before it can be understood.

Romans 14: 17 St. Paul spells out the meaning of the Kingdom of God.

"For the kingdom of God is not meat and drink (has nothing to do with the material pleasures of this world); *but righteousness, and peace, and joy in the Holy Ghost* (but is spiritual joy achieved through meditating on the Holy Ghost or Word).*"*

I Corinthians 4: 20 St. Paul talks of the power of the Word, the Holy Ghost Vibration.
"For the kingdom of God is not in word (not a spoken word), *but in power* (but a power)."

Hebrews 4: 12 St. Paul speaks of the qualities of the Word, imbued with the intelligence of the Christ Consciousness.
"For the word of God is quick, and powerful, and sharper than any twoedged sword, piercing even to the dividing asunder of soul and spirit, and of the joints and marrow, and is a discerner of the thoughts and intents of the heart."

James 1: 21 St. James, the disciple of Jesus, refers to the Word as being inseparable as if engrafted on to man.
"Wherefore lay apart all filthiness and superfluity of naughtiness, and receive with meekness the engrafted word, which is able to save your souls."

I Peter 1: 25 St. Peter says that the Word of the Lord endures forever and is the foundation of all spiritual teachings.
"But the word of the Lord endureth for ever. And this is the word which by the gospel is preached unto you (this Word is given to you along with the Teachings at the time of initiation.)." See the section called 'Initiation into the Path' for the meaning of 'Gospel'.

I John 1: 1 St. John describes the Word that can be heard and seen and touched: the basis of all Creation.
"That which was from the beginning, which we have heard, which we have seen with our eyes, which we have looked upon, and our hands have handled, of the Word of life;"

I John 2: 7 St. John confirms that the Word is not a new idea. It has been with us since the beginning of time.
"Brethren, I write no new commandment unto you, but an old commandment which ye had from the beginning. The old commandment is the word which ye have heard from the beginning."

Revelation 1: 10 St. John experienced the Word when he went into meditation.
"I was in the Spirit on the Lord's day (I was in communion with God

in meditation), *and heard behind me* (and heard in the interior of my body) *a great voice, as of a trumpet."*

Revelation 3: 14 Revelation refers to the Word as the Amen: the Faithful and True Witness of God.
"And unto the angel of the church of the Laodiceans write; These things say the Amen, the faithful and true witness, the beginning of the creation of God;" See also Revelation 1: 18.

Revelation 3: 20 God explains that He is forever waiting to reveal Himself as the Amen at the Christ Centre.
"Behold, I stand at the door (I am always waiting at the Christ Centre), *and knock* (I try to attract the meditator's attention)*: if any man hear my voice* (If during meditation any one hears My Holy Sound, the Word), *I will come in to him, and will sup with him, and he with me* (I, the Formless God, will appear to him and we will be united in Spirit)."* See the section on 'Meditation' for the meaning of 'knock'.

Revelation 14: 2 Some more of the sounds made by the Holy Ghost as it passes through the chakras.
"And I heard a voice from heaven, as the voice of many waters, and as the voice of a great thunder: and I heard the voice of harpers harping with their harps:" Refer back to the section on 'The Tree of Life' for the sounds made by the chakras.

Revelation 19: 6 Many Enlightened Ones have attempted to describe the sounds emitted by the Word.
"And I heard as it were the voice of a great multitude, and as the voice of many waters, and as the voice of mighty thunderings, saying Alleluia: for the Lord God Omnipotent reigneth (for God's omnipotence is expressed through the Word or Holy Ghost)."*

Revelation 22: 4 & 5 The angelic form reveals to St. John the location of the Light & Sound: in the forehead.
"And they (the devotees of God) *shall see his face* (shall see the Light-form of God)*; and his name shall be in their foreheads* (they will hear the holy vibrations of the Word when they focus their meditative attention on the Single Eye).

"And there shall be no night there (the darkness of ignorance and also

day and night do not exist in God's Realm of Cosmic Consciousness); and they need no candle, neither light of the sun; for the Lord God giveth them light: and they shall reign (and they do not need light of any kind because God's Light will be in them and they shall enjoy the state of absolute freedom in Cosmic Consciousness) *for ever and ever."* See the section on 'The Divine Light'.

3

The Divine Light.

Whereupon as I went to Damascus with authority and commission from the chief priests, At midday, O king, I saw in the way a light from heaven, above the brightness of the sun, shining round about me and them which journeyed with me.
(Acts 26: 12 & 13)

If a thousand suns appeared simultaneously in the sky, their light might dimly resemble the splendour of that Omnific Being!
(God Talks With Arjuna Ch XI: 12, page 818)

Wherever there is vibration, there is sound and light. Thus God's Holy Vibrating Consciousness produces the Word and the Divine Light together. Clearly then the Light is also God.

This then is the message which we have heard of him (from Jesus), *and declare unto you, that God is light, and in him is no darkness at all.*
(I John 1: 5)

It follows therefore that just as Creation sprang from the Word all things also sprang from God as Light.

And God said, Let there be light: and there was light.
(Genesis 1: 3)

Because our souls are sparks of God, then the same Divine Light is also in man

> *In him* (God as the Word) *was life; and the life was the light of men.*
> (John 1: 4)

and, just like the Word, the Light is able to lead mankind back to the Godhead.

> *Thy word is a lamp unto my feet, and a light unto my path.*
> (Psalm 119: 105)

As part of the Christ Consciousness, the intelligence of God in creation, the Divine Light is wisdom and enlightenment,

> *For she* (wisdom) *is the brightness of the everlasting light, the unspotted mirror* (pure reflection) *of the power of God, and the image of his goodness.*
> (Apocrypha, The Wisdom of Solomon 7: 26)

> *I have even heard of thee, that the spirit of the gods is in thee, and that light and understanding and excellent wisdom is found in thee.*
> (Daniel 5: 14)

and the non-recognition that the Divine Light is in the world as a creative force and the life of man constitutes ignorance or darkness.

> *And the light shineth in darkness; and the darkness comprehended it not.*
> (John 1: 5)

Thus the spiritual function of the Light is to dispel the darkness of ignorance and, in its place, ensconce the Light of Wisdom which brings enlightenment. This is eventually achieved when the devotee is able to fully focus his attention in the Single Eye and his consciousness is thereby uplifted by the sound of the Word and/or Light to the highest spiritual centre (holy hill) in his body (the 'tabernacle' of God).

> *O send out thy light and thy truth: let them lead me; let them bring me unto thy holy hill, and to thy tabernacles.*
> (Psalm 43: 3)

When man thus raises the centre of his consciousness to the spiritual realms, the darkness of ignorance is dispelled forever and he can live in this world (the land of the shadow of death) with equanimity

> *The people that walked in darkness have seen a great light: they that dwell in the land of the shadow of death, upon them hath the light shined.*
> (Isaiah 9: 2)

and all his fears and anxieties fall away.

> *The Lord is my light and my salvation; whom shall I fear? the Lord is the strength of my life; of whom shall I be afraid?*
> (Psalm 27: 1)

In the East, the Master has been traditionally called the Guru, which means the one who leads the disciple from darkness (gu) to light (ru). He is the 'Lit Candle' who passes his Light on to all his worthy disciples. But because the term is now commonly used to mean any teacher, the one capable of leading others from the darkness of ignorance to enlightenment is sometimes called the True Guru or the Perfect Master. Thus we find Jesus, as a Perfect Master, saying:

> *I am the light of the world: he that followeth me shall not walk in darkness, but shall have the light of life.*
> (John 8: 12)

Two thousand years after the advent of Jesus most Christians have come to regard the term 'light' as a figure of speech. Others don't think about it at all. Even the orthodox religion that has evolved over the course of time from the true teachings of the Perfect Master, Jesus, has transformed this vital inner spiritual experience and its real power into a mere symbol: the church candle.

The verses recorded by Dadu, a 16th century Indian saint, show that he was able to connect with the Light in a way that cannot be attained by mere ritual.

> *The ground is of Light,*
> *The House is of Light,*
> *Of Light alone is my beloved Groom.*
> *The union is of Light,*
> *The game is of Light,*
> *Only Light is, and I dwell in Light.*
> *I am in love with Light,*
> *I am drunk with Light,*
> *I thrive on Light-*
> *Thy Light, O Lord.*
> (Dadu 16th century Indian saint)

In future, instead of lighting an external candle and placing it on a physical altar in a church built of bricks and mortar, we Christians must light the inner candle on the altar of love in the temple of our bodies. That is the correct way to worship the Supreme Being who gives life and light to all.

What the Bible Says About the Divine Light.

The Divine Light is the life and consciousness of God in man. It manifests when the Word lifts his consciousness up to the Single Eye or Christ Centre between the two 'little hills' of the eyebrows. And that same Light has the power to raise the consciousness of the devotee even higher: to the Holy Hill of the Crown Chakra, the seat of God-consciousness.

Genesis 1: 3 All creation is made out of the Light emitted by the Word.
"And God said (And God sent out the primal energy of creation as the Word), *Let there be light: and there was light* (and the vibratory light of all energy and matter appeared)."

Exodus 3: 2 Astral or heavenly beings can appear for specific purposes on earth in their bodies of light energy.
"And the angel of the Lord appeared unto him (Moses) *in a flame of fire out of the midst of a bush: and he looked, and, behold, the bush burned with fire, and the bush was not consumed."*

II Samuel 22: 29 David affirms that the Divine Light leads the devotee back to God and dispels the darkness of ignorance.
"For thou art my lamp, O Lord: and the Lord will lighten my darkness."

Job 3: 23 Job wonders why the Divine Light is given even to the man who lives in the darkness of ignorance.
"Why is light given to a man whose way is hid (who is ignorant of the meaning of life), *and whom God hath hedged in* (and who is imprisoned by his karmas)?" The Masters teach that the Divine Light is in all men without exception where it manifests as life; but that it also manifests as wisdom and divinity in the Enlightened Man.

Psalm 18: 28 David acknowledges that the Lord is the Light of enlightenment that shines in pure souls.
"For thou wilt light my candle (for You will bring the means for me to see the Light within me): *the Lord my God will enlighten my darkness* (He will remove the darkness of spiritual ignorance from me)."

Psalm 27: 1 David acknowledges the Divine Light of God to be the source of life in him and the destroyer of fear.
"The Lord is my light and my salvation; whom shall I fear? the Lord is the strength of my life; of whom shall I be afraid?"

Psalm 36: 9 David acknowledges that God is life and that the Divine Light leads to enlightenment.

"For with thee is the fountain of life: in thy light shall we see light (shall we be enlightened)." See also John 1: 4 & 5 below for God as life and Light.

Psalm 43: 3 David prays for the Light that draws the devotee upward to the highest spiritual centres.

"O send out thy light and thy truth (Let me see the Divine Light emanating from Thy Cosmic Consciousness)*: let them lead me; let them bring me unto thy holy hill, and to thy tabernacles* (Let Truth and Light bring me to the holy places in the 'hill' of my head so that my consciousness can reside forever in the centres of Christ and Cosmic Consciousness within me)."*

Psalm 89: 15 & 16 David praises the sound emitted by the Holy Word that brings the Light of God.

"Blessed is the people that know the joyful sound (the Word or Holy Ghost)*: they shall walk, O Lord, in the light of thy countenance* (they will be guided by the Divine Light visible at the Single Eye).
"In thy name (Bathed in the Holy Word or Amen*) shall they rejoice all the day: and in thy righteousness shall they be exalted* (be lifted up spiritually to enlightenment)."*

Psalm 104: 2 God 'clothes' His universal body of matter by means of the Divine Light.

"Who coverest thyself with light as with a garment: who stretchest out the heavens like a curtain:"

Psalm 119: 105 The psalmist links the Divine Light and the Word together.

"Thy word is a lamp unto my feet, and a light unto my path." The Light and Sound are two inseparable facets of the Holy Word or Holy Ghost.

Proverbs 4: 18 & 19 Spiritual people follow the Divine Light to God–union but the ignorant live in the darkness of ignorance.

"But the path of the just is as the shining light, that shineth more and more unto the perfect day (to enlightenment).
"The way of the wicked is as darkness: they know not at what they stumble (they do not understand why they are beset by problems)."*

Isaiah 9: 2 Isaiah says that the Christ Consciousness comes with the Light to dispel ignorance.

"The people that walked in darkness (The people that lived in the darkness of satanic ignorance) *have seen a great light* (have been shown the Light of God within themselves): *they that dwell in the land of the shadow of death* (the dwellers of this earth, burdened by both spiritual and bodily death), *upon them hath the light shined* (have received the Divine Light from God's Emissary)." Isaiah himself was an Enlightened One who gave the Knowledge to the people of his time. It is commonly assumed by the church, quite wrongly, that the above and similar references made in the book of Isaiah refer only to the abilities of the future Messiah.

Isaiah 60: 1-3 Isaiah says that God's Light is available to all through Masters like himself.

"Arise, shine; for thy light is come, and the glory of the Lord is risen upon thee.

"For, behold, the darkness shall cover the earth (though the Cosmic Satan covers the world in the darkness of duality), *and gross darkness the people* (and gross individual ignorance affects the people)*: but the Lord shall rise upon thee, and his glory shall be seen upon thee.*

"And the Gentiles (the unbelievers) *shall come to thy light, and kings* (kingly souls) *to the brightness of thy rising."*

Isaiah 60: 19 & 20 Isaiah describes the state wherein the worthy man will be guided by the Divine Light.

"The sun shall be no more thy light by day; neither for brightness shall the moon give light unto thee: but the Lord shall be unto thee an everlasting light, and thy God thy glory (and you will achieve unity with God)*.*

"Thy sun (the direct Light of God) *shall no more go down; neither shall thy moon* (the mirrored Light of God as our souls) *withdraw itself: for the Lord shall be thine everlasting light, and the days of thy mourning shall be ended* (you will no longer need to yearn for God-union for it will be yours)*."*

Daniel 5: 14 The testimony of Belshazzar king of Babylon concerning the captive Daniel.

"I have even heard of thee, that the spirit of the gods is in thee,

and that light and understanding and excellent wisdom is found in thee."

Micah 7: 9 Micah does not mind paying his dues to the Law of Karma provided it allows the Light to come to him.
"I will bear the indignation of the Lord (I will gladly pay my karmic dues to the world), *because I have sinned against him, until he plead my cause, and execute judgement for me: he will bring me forth to the light, and I shall behold his righteousness* (I know that the time will come when I will be sufficiently pure for the vision of His Light to appear in my Single Eye)."

Apocrypha, The Wisdom of Solomon 7: 26 Solomon points out that Wisdom and Light are inseparable.
"For she (wisdom) *is the brightness of the everlasting light, the unspotted mirror* (pure reflection) *of the power of God, and the image of his goodness."*

Matthew 4: 16 The Master, Jesus, brought the Divine Light to those lost in the darkness of spiritual ignorance.
"The people which sat in darkness saw great light; and to them which sat in the region and shadow of death light is sprung up (To those fumbling in the darkness of spiritual ignorance and bodily death, Jesus brought the opportunity of enlightenment)." See also Luke 1: 79.

Matthew 5: 14 & 16 Jesus tells his disciples that the Divine Light shining in them will have wide influence.
"Ye are the light of the world. A city that is set on a hill cannot be hid."
"Let your light so shine before men, that they may see your good works, and glorify your Father which is in heaven."

Matthew 6: 22 Jesus tells his disciples about the Single Eye, the Light of which is found at the Christ Centre.
"The light of the body is the eye: if therefore thine eye be single, thy whole body shall be full of light." See also Luke 11: 34.

Matthew 17: 1-3 Divine Light has shone out of the face of many saints before and after Jesus; see the note below.

"And after six days Jesus taketh Peter, James, and John his brother, and bringeth them up into a high mountain apart (to the higher spiritual centres in the head).

"And was transfigured before them: and his face did shine as the sun, and his raiment was white as the light.

"And behold, there appeared unto them Moses and Elias (Elijah) *talking with him."* The appearance of these two should afford no surprise: Moses The Law Giver was the first major Enlightened One of Israel and Elijah was Jesus' Master during his previous lifetime and in this lifetime too when he appeared as John the Baptist – see Matthew 11: 12-14. When Moses came down from mount Sinai having received the Ten Commandments from God Exodus 34: 29 & 30 records that his face shone so brightly that the people were afraid to come near him.

Luke 2: 30-32 Luke records that Simeon foresaw that Jesus would be a Light to mankind.

"For mine eyes have seen thy salvation.

"Which thou hast prepared before the face of all people;

"A light to lighten the Gentiles, and the glory of thy people Israel."

John 1: 4 & 5 The Divine Light comes from the Word and manifests as the life force within the human body.

"In him (the Word) *was life; and the life was the light of men* (the Light is the life and consciousness in man).

"And the light shineth in darkness (The Light is hidden by the darkness of duality and individual ignorance); *and the darkness comprehended it not* (and ignorance neither acknowledges its presence nor seeks to understand it)."

John 3: 19 Divine Light shines on all creation to spiritualise it but men choose evil and turn away from it.

"And this is the condemnation, that light is come into the world, and men loved darkness rather than light, because their deeds were evil."

John 5: 35 Jesus pays homage to his beloved Master who also brought Divine Light into the world of men.

"He (John the Baptist) *was a burning and a shining light: and ye were willing for a season to rejoice in his light."*

John 8: 12 In the tradition of many Enlightened Teachers, Jesus speaks from the heights of Christ Consciousness.

"Then spake Jesus again unto them, saying, I am the light of the world (I AM the Light of Christ Consciousness): *he that followeth me shall not walk in darkness, but shall have the light of life* (He that unites himself to the Christ Consciousness, the Only Begotten Son of God that is reflected truly in me, shall never live in the darkness of ignorance)."* See also John 9: 5.

John 12: 36 All Enlightened Ones are the Light, bring the Light, and give the Light to the deserving.

"While ye have the light, believe in the light, that ye may be the children of light. These things spake Jesus, and departed, and did hide himself from them."

Acts 26: 12 & 13 The Divine Light transformed St. Paul from an enemy of the followers of Jesus into a believer.

"Whereupon as I went to Damascus with authority and commission from the chief priests (to persecute the followers of the crucified Jesus),

"At midday, O king, I saw in the way a light from heaven, above the brightness of the sun, shining round about me and them which journeyed with me."

Ephesians 5: 14 St. Paul issues the clarion call of all Enlightened Ones to sleeping humanity: Wake up! Wake up!

"Wherefore he (God) *saith, Awake thou that sleepest* (Awake, all of you who are asleep in ignorance), *and arise from the dead* (arise from spiritual death), *and Christ shall give thee light* (attain the Light of the Christ Centre or Single Eye)."

I John 1: 5-7 Jesus, the Master, showed his disciples the Divine Light of God which is within everyone.

"This then is the message which we have heard of him (from Jesus), *and declare unto you, that God is light, and in him is no darkness at all* (God manifests in the World as Divine Light, in whom the darkness of ignorance, the consciousness of duality, does not exist).
"If we say that we have fellowship with him (God), *and walk in darkness* (and yet do evil things), *we lie, and do not the truth.*

Christopher Mark Hanson

"But if we walk in the light, as he is in the light, we have fellowship one with another, and the blood of Jesus Christ his Son cleanseth us from all sin (But if we attune ourselves to the Light that is in us, we will be in unity one with the other, and the sacrifice to karmic law that Jesus made will cleanse us, his disciples, from all past wrongdoing)."

Revelation 22: 4 & 5 St. John is shown that God's Light & Name can be located in the forehead.

"And they (the devotees of God) *shall see his face; and his name shall be in their foreheads* (and they will hear the vibrational sound of the Holy Word resounding at the Single Eye).

"And there shall be no night there; and they need no candle, neither light of the sun; for the Lord God giveth them light: and they shall reign (and they shall be in the Light of Cosmic Consciousness) *for ever and ever."*

4

The 'I AM HE'.

Ye are my witnesses, saith the Lord, and my servants whom I have chosen: that ye may know and believe me, and understand that I AM HE: before me there was no God formed, neither shall there be after me.
(Isaiah 43: 10)

In every heart,
With every breath,
God! God! God!
(Sufi song)

Genesis records that when God made man, the archetypal Adam, He 'breathed' Himself into the human body to make individualised souls.

And the Lord God formed man of the dust of the ground, and breathed into his nostrils the breath of life; and man became a living soul.
(Genesis 2: 7)

The Perennial Philosophy however, provides much more detail. It points out that when man is fully relaxed and breathing naturally, his breath makes the sound So-hum which means 'I AM HE'. Thus approximately 20 times a minute throughout his life, man is affirming his real nature: 'I Am God'. Through this affirmation in the breath, we are God's witnesses to the fact that He exists as the all-powerful Creator and that He resides within us.

> *Ye are my witnesses, saith the Lord, and my servants whom I have chosen: that ye may know and believe me, and understand that **I am he**: before me there was no God formed, neither shall there be any after me. Yea, before the day was **I am he**; and there is none that can deliver out of my hand: I will work, and who shall let it?*
>
> (Isaiah 43: 10 & 13)

The current Indian Avatar, Sathya Sai Baba, says that the word Soham is not of any language but a sound of divine origin and meaning. He goes on further to describe that though the breath is constantly affirming Soham during the day, in deep sleep the sound becomes that of the Aum or Amen. This corresponds to the teachings of many other saints who have pointed out that in deep sleep man is in contact with his soul and therefore with God. Thus, in deep sleep, man is constantly affirming his essential nature as soul: the Amen, Aum or Holy Ghost, which, as was discussed earlier in the section on The Word, is no different from God Himself.

Because of this relationship between the breath and the Aum or Word, Masters often refer to the breath as the Name of God (Nam).

> *With arms raised Kabir calls:*
> *Repeat,*
> *Repeat the Lord's Name*
> *Each day, with each breath,*
> *For Nam alone will be your saviour*
> *At the perilous hour of death.*
>
> (Kabir, 15th century Muslim saint)

But, after the 'Fall' described in Genesis, when man began to follow the dictates of his ego and fear and anxiety began to leave its mark on his daylight hours, he lost the art of natural breathing, which became rapid and erratic. This, in turn, influenced the state of his mind.

> *For the changeableness and waywardness of the human mind is ineluctably bound up with man's breathing*

patterns. *The Glory of India's ancient sages is that they discovered the liberating truth: to control the breath is to control the mind.*
(God Talks With Arjuna, page 639)

'Control' in this context does not infer force of any sort. Enlightened Ones warn against anyone trying to calm their breathing forcefully as this is likely to cause both physical and mental harm. To control the breath in the spiritual sense means to follow meditation practices that return the breath to its natural relaxed rhythm.

Being of divine origin, the breath provides an additional means for man to reclaim his divine stature and return to his Celestial Home. In Sufi tradition, mankind's situation and salvation is illustrated by a wonderful analogy between a dry reed and the plight of mankind. The story tells of how a soul had become body-identified and had lost its connection with God (the reed had been torn from the reed-bed). Covered in the dust of karmas, empty and dry of any divine qualities, the body-bound soul lay for eons unrecognised for what it was until, one day, a passing Master recognised its worth and began to transform it into an instrument fit to experience the breath of God once more. When, as God's representative, the Master blew through it, the sounds of divine melodies, the vibrations emitted by the spiritualise chakras, filled the air and entranced everyone passing by. The reed lived again.

> *A reed was torn from its reed bed and lay in the dust. To everyone passing by it was just a dry, hollow stick. One day a Master craftsman stopped to rest by the water's edge and noticed the forgotten reed. Taking pity upon it he lovingly carved it into a flute and blew through it. To everyone's amazement the abandoned stick gave forth the most wonderful divine melodies.*
> (A Sufi story)

When the devotee becomes enlightened under the Master's stewardship, he can experience his real nature as the 'I AM HE'. This declaration, which originates from the Word or Holy Name, has the awesome power of God behind it as the officers of the High Priest intent on arresting Jesus found to their cost.

> *Jesus therefore, knowing all things that should come upon him, went forth, and said unto them* (the arresting officers), *Whom seek ye? They answered him, Jesus of Nazareth. Jesus saith unto them,* **I am he**. *And Judas also, which betrayed him, stood with them. As soon then as he had said unto them,* **I am he**, *they went backwards and fell to the ground.*
> (John 18: 4–6)

An alternative expression of this Ultimate Reality, which appears frequently in the Bible, is 'I am That' or 'I am'. This declaration, commonly appearing in all the world's scriptures, is expressed in the Indian Vedas as *Tat twam asi*: 'That Thou Art'.

> *And God said unto Moses, I AM THAT I AM: and he said, Thus shalt thou say unto the children of Israel, I AM hath sent me unto you.*
> (Exodus 3: 14)

These three expressions, 'I am That', 'I am' and, more powerfully, 'I am He' provide the definitive answer to the question of the jnana yogi: 'Who am I?' Once having experienced his real essence, the liberated devotee can truly attest:

> *I am Pure Awareness, beyond all forms and thoughts, and yet out of which all Creation and humanity came forth.*

What the Bible Says About 'I AM HE'.

With every breath man takes, he is reaffirming the Truth of who and what he really is: God in human form. When the meditator has merged his consciousness in God then he can say as Jesus did 'I am He'.

Genesis 2: 7 God 'breathed' Himself into our bodies as individualised souls, inseparable parts of His Oneness.
"And the Lord God formed man of the dust of the ground, and breathed into his nostrils the breath of life; and man became a living soul." See the main text for an explanation of the relationship between the breath and the 'I AM HE'.

Exodus 3: 14 God identifies Himself to Moses as the 'I AM'.
"And God said unto Moses, I AM THAT I AM: and he said, Thus shalt thou say unto the children of Israel, I AM hath sent me unto you."

Deuteronomy 32: 39 Moses reports God as saying that He is the 'I AM HE' that is the source of life and death.
"See now that I, even I, am he, and there is no god with me (there is no other spiritual power besides Me)*: I kill and I make alive* (I take away the body at death and bring it back at rebirth)*; I wound, and I heal* (I punish and reward through the Law of Karma)*: neither is there any that can deliver out of my hand* (No one can take a soul away from Me)*."*

Psalm 33: 6 David notes the connection between the Word and the Breath in all living creatures.
"By the word (the Holy Ghost) *of the Lord were the heavens made* (the Astral and Causal Worlds)*; and all the host of them by the breath of his mouth* (and all living entities were made from His Breath)*."*

Isaiah 41: 4 Through Isaiah the Lord identifies Himself as the all in all: the I AM HE.
"Who hath wrought and done it, calling the generations from the beginning? I the Lord, the first, and with the last; I am he."

Isaiah 43: 10 & 13 The Lord identifies Himself to Isaiah as 'I AM HE', the only One.
"Ye are my witnesses, saith the Lord, and my servant whom I have chosen: that ye may know and believe me, and understand that I am he: before me there was no God formed, neither shall there be any after me."
"Yea, before the day was I am he; and there is none that can deliver out of my hand: *I will work* (forming, maintaining and destroying Creation), *and who shall let it* (and who shall prevent it)?"

Isaiah 46: 4 The Lord tells Isaiah that as the 'I AM HE' He is the Creator, Preserver and Deliverer of mankind.
"And even to your old age I am he; and even to hoar hairs will I carry you: I have made, and I will bear; even I will carry, and will deliver you."

Isaiah 48: 12 The prophet, speaking with the voice of Cosmic Consciousness, identifies with the 'I AM HE'.
"*Hearken unto me, O Jacob and Israel, my called* (My people whom I have consistently called back to Me)*; I am he; I am the first, I also am the last.*"

Isaiah 51:12 Once again, through Isaiah, God refers to Himself in terms of 'I AM HE'.
"I, even I, am he that comforteth you: who art thou, that thou shouldest be afraid of a man that shall die, and of the son of man which shall be made as grass?"

Isaiah 52: 6 The expression of God as the real 'I' is the ultimate teaching of non-duality given by the Enlightened.
"*Therefore my people shall know my name* (shall unite with Me through the Word)*: therefore they shall know in that day that I am he that doth speak* (that issues forth the Holy Vibration of the Word)*: behold, it is I.*" See the section called 'Paths to God' for a description of non–dualistic teachings.

Matthew 18: 20 Jesus assures his disciples that the 'I AM' will be with them in group meditation.
"*For where two or three are gathered together in my name* (meditating on the Holy Word), *there am I* (there is the I AM, God) *in the midst of them.*" The vibrational power of the Word is intensified in group meditation.

John 4: 26 From his oneness with God Jesus tells the woman at the well that he is the 'I AM HE'.

"*Jesus saith unto her* (the woman of Samaria), *I that speak unto thee am he.*"

John 6: 47 & 48 Jesus, one with the 'I AM', speaks from the level of the Christ Consciousness.

"*Verily, verily, I say unto you, He that believeth on me hath everlasting life.*
"*I am that bread of life.*"

John 8: 24 Jesus tells his critics they will die spiritually if they do not believe that he is one with the 'I AM HE.'

"*I said therefore unto you, that ye shall die in your sins* (spiritual death)*: for if ye believe not that I am he, ye shall die in your sins.*" Jesus is informing his audience that they will continue to suffer in spiritual ignorance as a result of their accruing karmas if they do not take initiation from him, the current Master.

John 8: 28 Jesus reiterates that his consciousness is one with the 'I AM HE': united to God.

"*Then said Jesus unto them, When ye have lifted up the Son of man* (When you have spiritualised your consciousness), *then shall ye know that I am he* (then you will know that I am one with God, the I AM HE)*, and that I do nothing of myself; but as my Father hath taught me, I speak these things* (that I speak with the silent voice of unadulterated intuition arising from my complete unity with God)*.*"

John 8: 58 Jesus knew that his essential nature was soul, one with Cosmic Consciousness, the 'I AM'.

"*Jesus said unto them, Verily, verily, I say unto you, Before Abraham was, I am* (I was in existence as the soul, one with God, long before the person you know as Abraham came on earth)*.*"

John 9: 5 Again, from his oneness with Cosmic Consciousness, Jesus identifies himself with the 'I AM'.

"*As long as I am in the world, I am the light of the world.*" The primary meaning of this verse is that as long as the Cosmic Consciousness, the I AM, is in the world as Divine Light, the world will remain in existence. An underlying second meaning is that while the Master is in the world he is able to give the Divine Light to his disciples but he cannot perform that function when he has left the body.

John 13: 19 Yet again Jesus confirms his Oneness with the Cosmic Christ: the 'I AM HE'.
"Now I tell you before it come, that, when it come to pass, ye may believe that I am he."

John 14: 6 Jesus now confirms that the Christ Consciousness, one with the 'I AM', is the only way to God.
"Jesus saith unto him, I am the way, the truth, and the life: no man cometh unto the Father, but by me."

John 18: 4–6 The power of the 'I AM HE' threw the arresting officers to the ground.
"Jesus therefore, knowing all things that should come upon him, went forth, and said unto them (the arresting officers), *Whom seek ye?*
"They answered him, Jesus of Nazareth. Jesus saith unto them, I am he. And Judas also, which betrayed him, stood with them.
"As soon then as he had said unto them, I am he, they went backwards and fell to the ground (The power of the declaration 'I AM HE' threw them to the ground)."

John 20: 22 From the level of his Oneness with the Father, Jesus breathes the Holy Ghost into his disciples.
"And when he had said this, he breathed on them, and saith unto them, Receive ye the Holy Ghost."

Revelation 1: 17 & 18 While in ecstasy St. John experiences God 'I AM' with power over life and death.
"And when I saw him, (the ascended Jesus) *I fell at his feet as dead* (fell into an ecstatic trance). *And he laid his right hand upon me, saying unto me, Fear not; I am the first and the last* ('I am' one with God, the one who made everything that is).
"I am he that liveth, and was dead (My soul, the I AM HE', once suffered the death of ignorance but is now alive in Spirit); *and, behold, I am alive forevermore, Amen; and have the keys of hell and of death* (and now as the 'I am' I have power over ignorance and death. Amen)." See the section on 'The Word' for the meaning of 'Amen'.

Revelation 2: 23 God as the 'I AM HE' is Master over the Law of Karma too.
"And I will kill her children with death (I will kill the desire in you

and all the offspring of desire); *and all the churches shall know that I am he which searcheth the reigns and hearts* (and all the chakras in your subtle bodies of light shall be purified by your unity with the I AM HE): *and I will give unto every one of you according to your works."* Earlier verses refer to Jezebel, symbolising lust, whose offspring (all the evil tendencies arising from lust) are 'killed off' by God as the devotee advances in spirituality.

5

The Nectar.

My son, eat thou honey, because it is good; and the honeycomb, which is sweet to thy taste: So shall the knowledge of wisdom be unto thy soul: when thou hast found it, then there shall be a reward, and thy expectation shall not be cut off.
(Proverbs 24: 13 & 14)

*Kabir, the Lord's slave, has discovered
An ocean filled with the Nectar of love;
But I find no one disposed to taste it.
When men do not believe my words,
Words from my own experience,
What else can I say to convince them?*
(Kabir, 15th century Muslim saint)

The Nectar, called 'Amrit' in the East, is the least known of the four divine manifestations or 'forms' of God that man can experience while in the human body. On the relatively few occasions the term is referred to in spiritual literature, it is often difficult to distinguish whether 'Nectar' is being used in its literal sense or as a metaphor for something pleasant or sweet. But sometimes it is clear, as in the above poem by Saint Kabir and in the following one by Saint Ravidas, that the saints are referring to an actual substance and are not merely employing the term as a literary device.

*Obtained is the Divine Nectar.
The one in the taste of which*

I remain immersed.
And I ever keep it on my tongue.
Drinking this Nectar,
I am steeped in the Divine Ambrosia.
And I remain absorbed day and night.
(Guru Ravidas, 15th century Indian saint)

Not only can confusion arise from the possibility that the word 'nectar' is being used as a metaphor for something sweet but the reverse can occur also. The saints often substitute alternative terms such as honey, elixir, ambrosia, dew, sugar or sweetness when actually alluding to the Divine Nectar. In the quotation below, for example, the land 'flowing with milk and honey' that is obtained by going within ('go in and possess the land') is not a physical country but a spiritual state in which the honey-like Nectar flows down from the nourishing Word (milk) heard when in deep communion with God.

Therefore shall ye keep all the commandments which I command you this day, that ye may be strong, and go in and posses the land, whither ye go to posses it; And that ye may prolong your days in the land, which the Lord sware unto your fathers to give unto them and to their seed, a land that floweth with milk and honey.
(Deuteronomy 11: 8 & 9)

Nectar is pure condensed Cosmic Energy distilled from the Holy Word or Holy Ghost and this accounts for the two phenomena being commonly linked together in the scriptures as in the above verses from Deuteronomy (milk and honey). In the following verses, Solomon refers to the Nectar as 'honey' and to the Word as the honeycomb:

My son, eat thou honey, because it is good; and the honeycomb, which is sweet to thy taste: So shall the knowledge of wisdom be unto thy soul: when thou hast found it, then there shall be a reward, and thy expectation

shall not be cut off.
(Proverbs 24: 13 & 14)

whereas Isaiah, while also using the term 'honey' when alluding to the Divine Nectar, adopts 'butter' for the Word presumably because it has a soothing effect on man's nature by teaching him to avoid evil and choose good.

Butter and honey shall he eat that he may know to refuse the evil and choose the good.
(Isaiah 7: 15)

The following verses from Deuteronomy give more details on the nature of the inner 'land that floweth with milk and honey'. It is a land that is quite different from the material world where man sows the seeds and reaps the harvests of his actions (symbolically the captivity in Egypt). This land consists of the bumps and folds (hills and valleys) in the human brain; more specifically the higher spiritual centres from where the heavenly Nectar (water of the rain of heaven) descends. In addition it is a place particularly close to God because 'the eyes of the Lord thy God are always upon it':

For the land, whither thou goest in to posses it, is not as the land of Egypt, from whence ye came out, where thou sowest thy seed, and waterest it with thy foot, as a garden of herbs: But the land, whither ye go to posses it, is a land of hills and valleys, and drinketh water of the rain of heaven: A land which the Lord thy God careth for: the eyes of the Lord thy God are always upon it, from the beginning of the year even unto the end of the year.
(Deuteronomy 11: 10-12)

The following description by Paramahansa Yogananda succinctly adds additional details.

In samadhi meditation (the state of temporary divine

ecstasy)*, the conjunction of these currents produces a thrill of divine joy, and also a secretion of Nectar into the mouth. Nourished by this Nectar, the yogi can keep his body immobile indefinitely in the state of ecstasy.*
(From God Talks With Arjuna, page 792)

Even though the Nectar is rarely alluded to directly in the scriptures, its value should not be underestimated. The spiritual discipline for accessing this internally produced 'honey', helps the devotee to redirect his focus from the outside material world to the inner spiritual world. And the Nectar itself, being the purest form of 'food', offers far-reaching benefits to the Truth Seeker, revivifying him physically and mentally as well as bringing him closer to God.

The appearance of Nectar in the mouth of the meditating devotee is regarded as a reward from the Lord to those striving earnestly to unite with Him. This is the meaning at the end of the previous quotation from Proverbs 24: 13 & 14:

when thou hast found it, then there shall be a reward,

indeed God's devotees cannot possibly be disappointed when this divine gift manifests within them for the above quotation from Proverbs ends by affirming:

and thy expectation shall not be cut off.

What the Bible Says About the Nectar.

Nectar or Amrit is the condensed consciousness of God, sweet beyond imagining. It is the 'nectar of immortality', the real 'ambrosia of eternal youthfulness', which is savoured by those who reach even a temporary state of unity with the divinity resident within them.

Exodus 16: 11-15 The manna from heaven that the Israelites lived on for forty years in the desert was solidified Nectar.

"And the Lord spake unto Moses, saying,

"I have heard the murmurings of the children of Israel: speak unto them, saying, At even ye shall eat flesh, and in the morning ye shall be filled with bread; and ye shall know that I am the Lord your God.

"And it came to pass, that at even the quails came up, and covered the camp: and in the morning the dew lay round about the host (the food blessed by God).

"And when the dew that lay was gone up, behold, upon the face of the wilderness there lay a small round thing, as small as the hoar frost on the ground.

"And when the children of Israel saw it, they said one to another, It is manna: for they wist not what it was. And Moses said unto them, This is the bread which the Lord hath given you to eat." From the descriptions given, this manna seems to have been a crystallised form of Nectar as it was said to consist of small, hard, round objects formed from condensation of the 'dew', sweet to the taste, and to have melted in the sun. See Psalm 78: 23-25 below for a description by David of the angel's food – an expression highly fitting for the Nectar.

Deuteronomy 11: 8-12 The new land of milk & honey was not a physical land but a spiritual one.

"Therefore shall ye keep all the commandments which I command you this day, that ye may be strong, and go in and posses the land (and go inside yourselves, wrest power from the ego and allow your souls to take control of your bodily kingdoms once more), *whither ye go to posses it;*

"And that ye may prolong your days in the land, which the Lord sware unto your fathers to give unto them and to their seed (so that you can remain in the land of God–communion), *a land that floweth with milk and honey* (that flows with the nourishing milk of the Word and the sweetness of Divine Nectar).

"For the land, whither thou goest in to posses it, is not as the land of Egypt (This inner land is not a physical land nor is it the same as the captivity the soul experiences when trapped in this world through karmic actions), *from whence ye came out, where thou sowest thy seed, and waterest it with thy foot, as a garden of herbs* (where you sowed and reaped the seeds of earthly desires):

"But the land, whither ye go to posses it, is a land of hills and valleys (But the place I, your Lord, am directing you to is an inner domain lying in the higher spiritual centres in the top of the head), *and drinketh water of the rain of heaven* (and upon which falls the 'rain' of Cosmic Consciousness from God):
"A land which the Lord thy God careth for: the eyes of the Lord thy God are always upon it, from the beginning of the year even unto the end of the year (It is a land which God is always watching over because it is the seat of Cosmic Consciousness in every man)."

Psalm 78: 23-25 God sent Nectar, aptly called angel's food, for the people to eat in the 'wilderness'.
"Though he (God) *had commanded the clouds from above, and opened the doors of heaven* (God had used His divine power to enable a miracle to take place),
"And had rained down manna upon them to eat, and had given them the corn of heaven (And fed the children of Israel with Nectar and quails).
"Man did eat angels' food: he sent them meat to the full (This heavenly food filled them to satisfaction)."

Psalm 133: 3 The Nectar descends from the higher spiritual centres in the brain: the mountains of Zion
"As the dew of Hermon, and as the dew that descended upon the mountains of Zion (Just as moisture forms on the hill tops so does the dew of heaven, the Nectar, descend from the mountains of Cosmic Consciousness): *for there the Lord commanded the blessing, even life for evermore* (from Zion, the seat of Cosmic Consciousness in man's head, the blessed Nectar descends and from there also God grants eternal life)."

Proverbs 3: 20 Solomon appears to be referring to the Knowledge of the Masters and to the Nectar.
"By his knowledge the depths are broken up, and the clouds drop down the dew."

Proverbs 24: 13 & 14 Eating Nectar and listening to the Holy Word brings wisdom.
"My son, eat thou honey (Nectar), *because it is good* (it has great

spiritual benefits); *and the honeycomb* (the Word which holds the Nectar), *which is sweet to thy taste:*
"So shall the knowledge of wisdom be unto thy soul: when thou hast found it, then there shall be a reward, and thy expectation shall not be cut off (and you will not be disappointed).*"* God gives the Nectar as a reward to persevering devotees. The most propitious time to taste it is at the end of meditation.

Song of Solomon 4: 6 Solomon refers to the Crown Chakra from which the Nectar flows down.
"Until the day break, and the shadows flee away, I will get me to the mountain of myrrh (the Crown Chakra, source of the Nectar), *and to the hill of frankincense* (and to the fragrance of the Christ Centre).*"*

Song of Solomon 5: 1 & 5 Solomon sings of his experiences in meditation with the Nectar.
"I am come into my garden (I have entered into my meditation where I grow my spiritual flowers), *my sister, my spouse* (my soul)*: I have gathered my myrrh with my spice* (I have tasted the Nectar with its distinctive flavour)*; I have eaten my honeycomb with my honey* (I have absorbed the Word with the Nectar)*; I have drunk my wine with my milk* (I have imbibed the wine of bliss which brings ineffable peace)*: eat, O friends; drink, yea, drink abundantly, O beloved."*
"I rose up to open to my beloved (My concentration rose to the higher spiritual levels in my head)*: and my hands dropped with myrrh, and my fingers with sweet smelling myrrh, upon the handles of the lock* (I tasted the Nectar after unlocking the secret inner door where it is kept).*"*

Song of Solomon 5: 2 Solomon describes the state of ecstatic communion in which the Nectar descends.
"I sleep (in ecstatic communion), *but my heart waketh: it is the voice of my beloved* (the Holy Word or Voice of God) *that knocketh, saying, Open to me, my sister, my love, my dove* (the Single Eye), *my undefiled: for my head is filled with dew, and my locks with the drops of the night* (my 'cup' runneth over with Nectar).*"*

Isaiah 7: 15 The Divine Nectar, hidden within the honeycomb of the Holy Ghost or Word, destroys the evil in us.

"Butter (The delicious sound of the Holy Ghost or Word) *and honey* (Nectar) *shall he eat that he may know to refuse the evil and choose the good."*

Isaiah 12: 3 & 4 Meditation on the Holy Name causes the Divine Nectar to flow from our wells of salvation.

"Therefore with joy shall ye draw water out of the wells of salvation (The Divine secretion of Nectar, a gift of God, brings an experience of sublime joy or bliss).
"And in that day shall ye say, Praise the Lord, call upon his name (listen to the Holy Word reverberating within you), *declare his doings among the people, make mention that his name is exalted* (praise the Word that takes us to that receptive spiritual level)."

Ezekiel 3: 3 Through a vision Ezekiel was given an experience of the Nectar which appeared in his mouth.

"And he (the voice in the vision) *said unto me, Son of man, cause thy belly to eat, and fill thy bowels with this roll* (a metaphysical parchment or book of divine knowledge) *that I give thee. Then did I eat it; and it was in my mouth as honey for the sweetness."* See also Revelation 10: 8-11 below for a similar reference.

Joel 3: 17 & 18 The Lord tells Joel that he will find Nectar and many other wonders by going inside himself.

"So shall ye know that I am the Lord your God dwelling in Zion (sitting in the seat of Cosmic Consciousness in the crown of your head), *my holy mountain: then shall Jerusalem be holy, and there shall no strangers pass through her any more* (then shall the body be holy and shall not be sullied by error any more).
"And it shall come to pass in that day, that the mountains shall drop down new wine (Then the Nectar and other wonders will drop down from the Holy Mountains in your head), *and the hills shall flow with milk, and all the rivers of Judah shall flow with waters* (and all the subtle channels in the astral body shall flow with divine energy), *and a fountain shall come forth of the house of the Lord, and shall water the valley of Shittim* (and your subtle and physical bodies will be revived by a great outpouring of spiritual energy)."

Amos 9: 13-15 The Lord promises spiritual gifts to His people including 'sweet wine' from the Divine Mountains.

"Behold, the days come, saith the Lord, that the plowman shall overtake the reaper, and the treader of grapes him that soweth seed (it will be a time of spiritual plenty)*; and the mountains shall drop sweet wine, and all the hills shall melt* (and Nectar will flow down from the seat of Cosmic Consciousness in the mountains of the head and all the spiritual centres will experience the sweet bliss that accompanies it).

"And I will bring again the captivity of my people of Israel (I will release my people once more from captivity in the world)*, and they shall build the waste cities* (the cities of their bodies will be spiritualised)*, and inhabit them; and they shall plant vineyards, and drink the wine thereof; they shall also make gardens, and eat the fruit of them* (their 'Trees of Life' and 'gardens' of the spiritual centres will flourish and they will enjoy the fruits of divinely spiritual perceptions growing there).

"And I will plant them upon their land, and they shall no more be pulled up out of their land which I have given them, saith the Lord thy God (They will be firmly rooted in God-consciousness).*"*

John 4: 13 & 14 Jesus compares the value of ordinary water to the spiritual benefits of Divine Nectar.

"Jesus answered and said unto her (the woman of Samaria)*, Whosoever drinketh of this water shall thirst again* (If you drink ordinary water from this well dug into the earth you will be thirsty again after a time)*:*

"But whosoever drinketh of the water that I shall give him shall never thirst; but the water that I shall give him shall be in him a well of water springing up into everlasting life (But I will show you how to draw Divine Water from a well that is inside your own body and when you drink from it all your desires, spiritual and material, will be satisfied).*"*

Revelation 10: 8-11 The Voice from Heaven opened St. John's 7th chakra and gave him Nectar.

"And the voice which I heard from heaven spake unto me again, and said, Go and take the little book (a metaphysical book of spiritual

knowledge) *which is open in the hand of the angel which standeth upon the sea and upon the earth* (the Cosmic Force which stands between the astral and physical worlds).

"And I went unto the angel, and said unto him, Give me the little book. And he said unto me, Take it, and eat it up; and it shall make thy belly bitter, but it shall be in thy mouth sweet as honey.

"And I took the little book out of the angel's hand, and ate it up; and it was in my mouth sweet as honey: and as soon as I had eaten it, my belly was bitter.

"And he said unto me, Thou must prophesy again before many peoples, and nations, and tongues, and kings." **The knowledge of all his past sins that is revealed to the advanced meditator can be bitter but this is more than compensated by the sweetness of the Divine Nectar that is part of God's reward.**

Part 6.

How to Escape the World.

1

Initiation into the Path.

And as they were going down to the end of the city, Samuel said to Saul, Bid the servant pass on before us, [and he passed on,] but stand thou still a while, that I may show thee the word of God.
(I Samuel 9: 27)

Blessed indeed is the day, the hour,
The precious moment, when
The man of God, my Master,
Came and graced my home.
(Kabir, 15th century Muslim saint)

Enlightened Ones point out that the karmas keeping mankind earthbound have been accumulated over thousands of lifetimes and now form such a tangled web of desires, deceits, attachments and emotions that man cannot possibly escape, without help, from the shackles that bind him.

Lures and passions
Are a burning lamp.
Men the heedless moths –
They come circling
And plunge into the flame;
Those rare ones escape, O Kabir,
Who receive from the Master
The precious boon of Nam.
(Kabir, 15th century Muslim saint)

Furthermore, these karmas, the Masters are at pains to point out, have been incurred while the person has been incarnate on earth (born of water) and can only be paid back in the same realm. Therefore, the quickest and most reliable way of paying our dues to the world is to be initiated by a Master (to be born of Spirit).

> *Jesus answered, Verily, verily, I say unto thee, Except a man be born of water and of the Spirit, he cannot enter into the kingdom of God.*
> (John 3: 5)

Contrary to the most cherished tenets of the orthodox religions, the Masters teach that death does not automatically qualify anyone to enter into the kingdom of God. Neither can any ordinary person 'see' God after death. These rights have to be fully earned. As God, through the ascended Jesus, pointed out to St. John in the book of Revelation, only those who successfully overcome the temptations of the world will be released (shall go no more out).

> *Him that overcometh will I make a pillar in the temple of my God, and he shall go more out: and I will write upon him the name of my God, and the name of the city of my God.*
> (Revelation 3: 12)

Those still engrossed in worldly desires and their offshoots (uncleanliness and violence) will not find the highway even though it is ever-present. Only those who have been 'redeemed' by a Master can walk this High Way.

> *And an highway shall be there, and a way, and it shall be called The way of holiness; the unclean shall not pass over it; but it shall be for those: the wayfaring men, though fools, shall not err therein. No lion shall be there, nor any ravenous beast shall go up thereon, it shall not be found there: but the redeemed shall walk there:*
> (Isaiah 35: 8 & 9)

Kabir quite clearly agrees:

> *Many study, ponder and labour to the point of death; many undertake varied practices, such as yoga, yagna and penances – all in vain. O Kabir, without a perfect Master they cannot obtain the Lord, though a million ways they adopt.*
> (Kabir, 15th century Muslim saint)

The meeting between the Master and the disciple is without doubt the greatest of all events in the long, tumultuous, journey of our many lives for it marks the real beginning of the path Home.

So significant is it that the disciple often becomes profoundly changed in an instant. In the case of one of Islam's greatest saints, Mawlana Rumi, it is said that after he met his Master, Shams-i-Tabriz, he became intoxicated with love, though he drank only the wine of Divine Light.

> *Lovers drink wine all day and night and tear the veils of the mind. When drunk with love's wine body, heart and soul become one.*
> (Rumi 13th century Sufi)

The necessity of being guided to God by someone who knows the way cannot be over-emphasised. One who has travelled the High Way himself and has come face to face with his Creator knows both the Truth and The Way.

> *My Master has revealed to me The mirror within my own body; Now I'll sing and dance in ecstasy. My true Lord I have come to behold, None knows of this wealth within the body.*
> (Mira, 16th century Indian saint)

Many people wonder how they can recognise their Master should they meet him, but such events are not in our hands. Though some pointers have been given earlier on in the section called 'The Nature of Enlightened Ones', the common human faculties of sight and mind are not infallible guides. In fact they can be the greatest hindrance. In actuality, the bond between Master and disciple is purely intuitive, a recognition between two souls. Which is precisely why Jesus' disciples instantly dropped everything and followed after him.

> *And Jesus, walking by the sea of Galilee, saw two brethren, Simon called Peter, and Andrew his brother, casting a net into the sea: for they were fishers. And he saith unto them, Follow me, and I will make you fishers of men. And they straightway left their nets, and followed him. And going on from thence, he saw other two brethren, James the son of Zebedee, and John his brother, in a ship with Zebedee their father, mending their nets; and he called them. And they immediately left the ship and their father, and followed him.*
> (Matthew 4: 18-22)

Though immersion in pure water is beneficial because of the divine energies in water, which is a most vital constituent of life, true baptism is by 'fire': the divine Light of the Holy Ghost.

> He (Jesus) *shall baptize you with the Holy Ghost and with fire:*
> (Matthew 3: 11)

Today in the West, baptism with the Holy Ghost is commonly known as 'initiation' and in the East as 'diksha'. During initiation, those fortune enough to be accepted as disciples by a Perfect Master are empowered to practise the meditation techniques given to him/her by the Master. Of this process Yogananda says:

> *This real baptism cleanses the consciousness of the initiate with the Holy Light of the spiritual eye and the sacred sound of Aum. Whosoever can see the life current*

of the spiritual eye changing and spiritualising the brain cells and the very composition of the mind of the initiate is one who baptizes with the Holy Ghost. He sees the light of the spiritual eye and throws that Light of Spirit onto the consciousness of the devotee. When that vibratory power passes through the initiate, it cauterises present bad habits and past karmic seeds lodged in the brain. By the consciousness of God which is within him, a great spiritual soul can transfer to others who are receptive an experience of some of his own God-consciousness.
(The Second Coming of Christ, page 114)

The term 'disciple' infers that the earnest Truth-Seeker is more than willing, out of love, to accept the spiritual practices given to him by his Master and take on the task of disciplining himself. Among the world's greatest disciples are Hanuman, Arjuna, St. John and Mira, beloved followers of Ram, Krishna, Jesus and Ravidas respectively.

For the very true beginning of her (wisdom) *is the desire of discipline* (to discipline oneself); *and the care of discipline is love* (love is the motivation of the devotee);
(Apocrypha, The Wisdom of Solomon 6: 17)

In turn, the Master assures the devotee that he will lead him back to God for, as Jesus told his disciples, it is God's 'good pleasure' that he should do so.

Fear not, little flock; for it your Father's good pleasure to give you the kingdom……
(Luke 12: 32)

Initiation should not be taken lightly. The bond forged is eternal and serious spiritual promises are made. On his part, the disciple promises to practise with devotion the methods of contacting the manifestations of God shown to him by the Master and undertakes not to reveal these methods to non-initiates. This is because non-initiates might well become confused and frustrated, especially as the techniques will not be effective without the transfer of spiritual energy from the Master to the disciple. While on his part, the Master solemnly undertakes to lead the disciple back to God no matter how long that may take.

What the Bible Says About Initiation.

Initiation is given by God through a Master to those He deems worthy to return to Him. Man is born of water in his mother's womb and returns to God by being baptised in the 'fire' of the Divine Light through the instrumentality of the Holy Ghost. This is the second birth.

Leviticus 9: 23 Moses initiates the people after they had been purified of sin.
"And Moses and Aaron went into the tabernacle of the congregation, and came out, and blessed the people (Moses performed a group initiation)*: and the glory of the Lord appeared unto all the people* (and the people had divine experiences).*"*

Deuteronomy 21: 5 The sons of Levi are empowered to bless or initiate others into the Lord's Name.
"And the priests the sons of Levi shall come near; for them the Lord thy God hath chosen to minister unto him, and to bless in the name of the Lord; and by their word shall every controversy and every stroke be tried:" See the earlier section on 'The Word' for the meaning of the 'name of the Lord' and 'word'.

Deuteronomy 32: 3 Moses declares that God has authorised him to initiate in His Name.
"Because I will publish the name of the Lord: ascribe ye greatness unto our God (Because God has given me the power to initiate others and give them the Word, do not praise me but God).*"*

I Samuel 9: 27 Samuel the Prophet initiates Saul into Knowledge of the Word.
"And as they were going down to the end of the city, Samuel said to Saul, Bid the servant pass on before us, [and he passed on,] but stand thou still a while, that I may show thee the word of God."

I Kings 19: 16 & 19 The Lord instructs Elijah to initiate Elisha to be his successor as a prophet.
"...and Elisha the son of Shaphat of Abel–meholah shalt thou anoint (you shall initiate Elisha) *to be prophet in thy room* (to replace you).*"*
"So he departed thence, and found Elisha the son of Shaphat, who was ploughing with twelve yoke of oxen before him, and he with the twelfth: and Elijah passed by him, and cast his mantle upon him (Elijah passed some of his spiritual power to Elisha).*"*

Psalm 68: 11 David notes that the Word issues forth from God and is shown to others by the Enlightened Ones.
"The Lord gave the word: great was the company of those that published it."

Isaiah 28: 9 Isaiah bemoans the fact that the people are so steeped in evil that few are fit for initiation.
"Whom shall he teach knowledge (To whom shall God teach Divine Knowledge through His Masters)*? and whom shall he make to understand doctrine? them that are weaned from the milk, and drawn from the breasts* (only the childlike, very innocent and pure, are fit to receive Knowledge).*"*

Isaiah 35: 8 & 9 God tells Isaiah of the time when men will be initiated into the Holy Highway.
"And an highway shall be there (the Holy Highway within the body)*, and a way, and it shall be called The way of holiness; the unclean* (the sinful) *shall not pass over it; but it shall be for those: the wayfaring men, though fools, shall not err therein* (but it shall be for the imperfect seekers who want to redeem themselves).
"No lion shall be there, nor any ravenous beast shall go up thereon (No violent or angry person will be able to travel up the Holy Highway)*, it shall not be found there* (these people will not find the Way)*: but the redeemed shall walk there* (but earnest Truth–Seekers

will find it through their Masters and will travel along the Holy Path);"

Apocrypha, The Wisdom of Solomon 6: 17 Solomon stresses the importance of being a disciple.
"For the very true beginning of her (wisdom) *is the desire of discipline* (to discipline oneself); *and the care of discipline is love* (love is the motivation of the devotee);"

Matthew 3: 11 Enlightened Ones initiate their devotees into the Holy Ghost and the Divine Light.
"I (John the Baptist) *indeed baptize you with water unto repentance: but he* (Jesus) *that cometh after me is mightier than I, whose shoes I am not worthy to bear: he shall baptize* (initiate) *you with the Holy Ghost* (the Word) *and with fire* (the Divine Light):" See also Mark 1: 9. It is customary for the disciples of the outgoing Master to be adopted by the incoming Master. It is also routine practice for the outgoing Master to heap praises on to his successor to give the transferring disciples faith to continue on the Path under the care of the new Master. In actuality no Master is greater or less than any other.

Matthew 3: 16 The moment Jesus was initiated by John the Baptist his 'Single Eye' opened.
"And Jesus, when he was baptized (initiated by his Master, John the Baptist), *went up straightway out of the water: and, lo, the heavens were opened unto him, and he saw the spirit of God descending like a dove, and lighting upon him* (His concentration was immediately drawn to his Christ Centre and he saw the 'door' to three spiritual worlds opening like a dove descending on him out of the heavenly realms)." See also Mark 1: 10 and the earlier section called 'The Higher Spiritual Centres'.

Matthew 4: 18-22 Jesus' disciples intuitively recognised their Master and did not hesitate to join him.
"And Jesus, walking by the sea of Galilee, saw two brethren, Simon called Peter, and Andrew his brother, casting a net into the sea: for they were fishers.
"And he saith unto them, Follow me, and I will make you fishers of men.
"And they straightway left their nets, and followed him.
"And going on from thence, he saw other two brethren, James the

son of Zebedee, and John his brother, in a ship with Zebedee their father, mending their nets; and he called them.
"And they immediately left the ship and their father, and followed him."

Matthew 11: 27 Jesus emphasises the importance of receiving the Knowledge from the Master.
"All things are delivered unto me of my Father (God gives me power over all things)*: and no man knoweth the Son, but the Father* (No ordinary person has experienced Christ Consciousness except God); *neither knoweth any man the Father, save the Son, and he to whomsoever the Son will reveal him* (and no ordinary person knows God except a Master who is united to the Christ Consciousness and those fortunate ones who have been initiated by a Master)*."*

Matthew 16: 19 The Master initiates the worthy disciple into the Knowledge.
"And I (Jesus your Master) *will give unto thee* (Peter my disciple) *the keys of the kingdom of heaven* (the methods of contacting God)*..."*
To this day the meditation techniques given by the Master at initiation are referred to as 'keys' because their function is to unlock the door of the Single Eye.

Matthew 28: 19 & 20 Jesus gave his disciples power to baptise or initiate people into the spiritual path.
"Go ye therefore, and teach all nations, baptising them in the name of the Father, and of the Son, and of the Holy Ghost (Initiate those that are ready, giving them, according to their ability to receive, an experience of the three aspects of God living within them: Cosmic Consciousness, Christ Consciousness and the Holy Ghost or Word)*:*
"Teaching them to observe all things whatsoever I have commanded you: and, lo, I (the Christ Consciousness that is within me) *am with you always, even unto the end of the world. Amen."* This is the only occasion on which Jesus is reported to have spoken directly of the Trinity.

Mark 4: 3-25 The Parable of the Sower describes how humankind responds in different ways to the 'Word' sown by the Masters in those fit karmically to be initiated. The Enlightened Ones know that some are ready in this lifetime to fully receive the Word and meditate upon it but others are not. Nevertheless the seed of the Word which has been 'sown' in them during initiation will bear fruit in another lifetime. See also Luke 8: 5-15.

Mark 8: 35 & 36 Jesus teaches that initiation is all-important to the spiritual life in man.

"For whosoever will save his life (Those who become entirely engrossed in material life) *shall lose it* (will lose their spiritual identity), *but whosoever shall lose his life* (but those willing to be initiated and to cast off material ignorance) *for my sake and the gospel's* (for the sake of the teachings and the spiritual path), *the same shall save it* (they shall overcome both the world and death and realise themselves to be immortal souls).

"For what shall it profit a man, if he shall gain the whole world, and lose his own soul (What will a person really gain if he loses his spirituality in pursuit of fame, notoriety and riches)?"

Mark 15: 43 One of Jesus' initiates, Joseph of Arimathaea, begs Pilate for the body of Jesus.

"Joseph of Arimathaea, an honourable councillor, which also waited for the kingdom of God (who had been initiated and was meditating to achieve God-consciousness), *came, and went in boldly unto Pilate, and craved the body of Jesus."*

Luke 12: 31 & 32 The Master assures his disciples that God has chosen them for initiation into the kingdom.

"But rather seek ye the kingdom of God; and all these things shall be added unto you.

"Fear not, little flock; for it your Father's good pleasure to give you the kingdom (God wants you to be initiated so that you can return to Him)."

John 1: 33 John the Baptist initiates Jesus into the Knowledge and into the Master/disciple relationship.

"And I knew him not (I, John the Baptist, could not with mortal eyes see the Christ Consciousness in Jesus)*: but he* (God) *that sent me to baptize with water, the same said unto me* (spoke to me through my intuition), *Upon whom thou shalt see the Spirit descending* (By divine sight, the one who becomes permanently established in the Christ Consciousness when you initiate him), *and remaining on him, the same is he which baptizeth with the Holy Ghost* (is the World Teacher who will initiate many people into the Word)." Part of the

reason why John the Baptist played down his role as a Master was because his task was to initiate a select band of disciples whereas Jesus was a World Teacher.

John 1: 51 Jesus, the Master, promises to open the Single Eye of the disciple.

"And he (Jesus) *saith unto him* (Nathanael), *Verily, verily, I say unto you, Hereafter ye shall see the heaven open* (You will have divine sight when your Single Eye is opened during initiation), *and the angels of God ascending and descending upon the Son of man* (and you shall see emanating from God the subtle energies responsible for creating and enlivening your own body)."

John 3: 3 & 5 Jesus explains the need for initiation to Nicodemus. This is the true 'second birth'.

"Jesus answered and said unto him, Verily, verily, I say unto thee, Except a man be born again (be initiated by his God-chosen Master), *he cannot see the kingdom of God* (he cannot experience the divine manifestations that will carry his consciousness back to God)."

"Jesus answered, Verily, verily, I say unto thee, Except a man be born of water (has a human birth) *and of the spirit* (and then receives spiritual empowerment through his Master), *he cannot enter into the kingdom of God."* See also John 8: 12 where Jesus spells out that he has the Divine Light and is qualified to give it to the worthy by virtue of being at One with God's Light of Creation: 'I am the light of the world...'

John 4: 14 Jesus talks about initiation to the woman of Samaria.

"But whosoever drinketh of the water (divine current) *I shall give him shall never thirst* (will find all his burning earthly desires satisfied); *but the water that I shall give him shall be in him a well of water springing up into everlasting life* (If you take this initiation I am offering to you, you will realise that you are the immortal spirit and not the human body; and you will taste the divine Nectar that comes from contact with God)."

John 6: 65 A Truth–Seeker needs to have made some spiritual progress to earn initiation.

"And he (Jesus) *said, Therefore said I unto you, that no man can come unto me* (no one can come can come to the Master and be initiated), *except it were given unto him of my Father* (except the one who has earned the Grace of God)."

Acts 14: 21 & 22 Barnabas and Paul give the teachings and initiate new disciples.

"And when they had preached the gospel (given the teachings and initiated the worthy) *to that city, and had taught many, they returned back to Lystra, and to Iconium and Antioch,*

"Confirming the souls of the disciples (bolstering up the courage of new disciples they had previously initiated), *and exhorting them to continue in the faith, and that we must through much tribulation enter into the kingdom of God* (and that we must persevere on the Path in spite of any difficulties we may meet)."

Acts 26: 16-18 The ascended Jesus tells St. Paul that he, Paul, is destined to preach and initiate people.

"But (the disembodied Jesus said to St. Paul out of the Holy Light) *rise, and stand upon thy feet: for I have appeared unto thee for this purpose, to make thee a minister and a witness both of these things which thou hast seen* (the vision of me you have just experienced), *and of those things in the which I will appear unto thee* (and of all those things you will learn about in due course);

"Delivering thee from the people and from the Gentiles, unto whom now I send thee (Fear not for I will protect you from the Jews and Gentiles who will try to harm you),

"To open their eyes (I send you to open their Spiritual or Single Eyes), *and to turn them from darkness to light* (to save them from the darkness of ignorance and turn them towards the Divine Light shining within them), *and from the power of Satan unto God* (and from the illusion of duality, the Cosmic Satan, to the Unity of the Godhead), *that they may receive forgiveness of sins* (that they may be freed from their karmas), *and inheritance among them which are sanctified by faith that is in me* (and give them their inheritance as worthy Sons of God)."

Ephesians 1: 15-18 St. Paul prays that God will arrange for the Ephesians to be initiated.

"Wherefore I also, after I heard of your faith in the Lord Jesus, and love unto all the saints (and love for all the Saints who come to help suffering humanity),

"Cease not to give thanks for you, making mention of you in my prayers;

"That the God of our Lord Jesus Christ, the Father of glory, may give unto you the spirit of wisdom and revelation in the knowledge of him (That God may arrange for you to receive wisdom, initiation and the gifts of divine experience handed down to us, Jesus' direct initiates, by divine Grace):

"The eyes of your understanding being enlightened (Your Single Eyes of Wisdom being opened by initiation); *that ye may know what is the hope of his calling, and what the riches of the glory of his inheritance in the saints* (that you may appreciate the wonders of the great spiritual inheritance that you are receiving and which all the Enlightened Ones who came before you also enjoyed),"

Ephesians 3: 19 St. Paul clearly points out that Enlightened Ones give Knowledge to mankind out of pure love.

"And to know the love of Christ (And to know the love of Jesus the Christ and all those who have been, are, and will be One with the Christ Consciousness), *which passeth knowledge* (who initiate mankind into the Divine Knowledge), *that ye might be filled with the fullness of God* (so that your 'cup' may be filled to overflowing when you receive your natural inheritance as children of the One God)."

I Peter 1: 25 St. Peter encourages Truth–Seekers to be initiated by him into the Word.

"But the word of the Lord endureth for ever. And this is the word which by the gospel is preached unto you (this is the Word that is given to you during initiation)."

I John 1: 1-3 St. John praises his Master who, by initiating his disciples, made them into Masters too.

"That which was from the beginning (God's Cosmic Light), *which we have heard* (as the Word), *which we have seen with our eyes* (which we have seen through our opened Single Eyes), *which we have looked upon, and our hands have handled, of the Word of life* (the Word in form as the Master);

"For the life (the Light as the life of men) *was manifested, and we have seen it, and bear witness, and shew unto you that eternal life* (and now show to you your immortality in Spirit by initiating you into the Path), *which was with the Father* (which Light originates

from God beyond Creation), *and was manifest unto us* (shown to us by the Master at initiation);

"That which we have seen and heard declare we unto you, (The Light and Word the Master showed to us we are now able to give to you) *that ye may also have fellowship with us* (so that you too can be disciples of God just like us): *and truly our fellowship is with the Father, and with his Son Jesus Christ* (Truly our fellowship is with God and the Christ Consciousness that was in Jesus our Master, the fully fledged Son of God)."

I John 2: 27 St. John writes helpful advice to recently anointed initiates.
"But the anointing which ye hath received of him abideth in you (The initiation you have received from me by the grace of the crucified Jesus is a lasting thing), *and ye not that any man teach you* (and no one has to teach you anything else for the Knowledge you have received is complete in itself): *but as the same anointing teacheth you of all things, and is truth, and is no lie, and even as it hath taught you, ye shall abide in him* (and the same initiation or anointing will bring all things to you in due course provided you keep faith with the Master's teachings)." Disciples always initiate in the name of either their Master or of God. Jesus' disciples always initiated in the name of their Master even after they had become free of karma themselves and had collected around them their own disciples.

Revelation 3: 12 The ascended Jesus describes to St. John the end result of initiation into the Path: enlightenment.
"Him that overcometh (the temptations of the world) *will I make a pillar in the temple of my God, and he shall go more out* (he need not leave the heavenly realms again and reincarnate on earth): *and I will write upon him the name of my God* (the Holy Word), *and the name of the city of my God* (Cosmic Consciousness) ...."

2

Meditation.

> *And they shall see his face; and his name shall be in their foreheads. And there shall be no night there; and they need no candle, neither light of the sun; for the Lord God giveth them light: and they shall reign for ever and ever.*
> (Revelation 22: 4 & 5)

> **The gratifying form of my Master is on my forehead; Now wherever I look, I see him always with me, His lotus feet are my life, my support.**
> (Guru Arjan Dev, Sikh saint, 1563-1606)

The mind is the most important tool a human being possesses and the most neglected. But while our educationalists focus on the limited function of filling the minds of their students with mere information, Enlightened Ones such as Isaiah, Jesus, Krishna, Buddha, Guru Nanak, Kabir and modern Masters dedicate their lives to the task of leading their disciples into the inner world where all true potential lies and where man can fulfil his ultimate destiny: enlightenment. Just as information is the primary medium of the educationalist, meditation is the indispensable tool of Enlightened Ones.

The object of meditation is therefore to explore and cultivate the mind's almost limitless qualities and ultimately lead the Truth-Seeker into the presence of God who resides within the human body. As God promises through one of His enlightened Masters, Isaiah, those who are karmically ready but currently ignorant of Reality (the spiritually blind) will be led into an unfamiliar inner world where darkness is turned to light and all thoughts, words and deeds come into harmony with Divine Will.

> *And I shall bring the blind by a way they knew not; I will lead them in paths they have not know: I will make darkness light before them, and crooked things straight. These things will I do unto them, and not forsake them.*
> (Isaiah 42: 16)

This 'inner Way' was more succinctly expressed by Jesus as:

> *Neither shall they say, Lo here! or, lo there! for, behold, the kingdom of God is within you.*
> (Luke 17: 21)

The primary goal of meditation is to quieten the mind for it is the noisy chatter of the mind that obscures the 'Silence' wherein the qualities that make us truly *human* are to be found.

> *Be still, and know that I am God: I will be exalted among the heathen, I will be exalted in the earth.*
> (Psalm 46: 10)

The word *human* is, in itself, very revealing for *Hu* is an ancient name for God and the word *man* originates from the Sanskrit 'manas' meaning mind. Thus 'man' is in actuality 'God with the mind'. This being the case, it is fair to say that almost all humanity is operating well below its full potential.

As discussed in earlier sections the first step on the Truth-Seeker's Path or Way is the meeting with the Master and the initiation that follows. During this initiation the Master instructs the disciple in the art of meditation. The process of meditation, of 'finding the kingdom of God within you', is described in both Old and New Testaments in the form of the analogy of entering a room or closet and 'closing off' the senses from the outside world. Isaiah, for example, stresses that the meditator should set up a regular practice of entering the 'chamber' of the body and shutting the 'doors' to the five senses (seeing, hearing, tasting, smelling and touch) until the 'indignation' (the unseemly demands of the mind and senses) is overcome:

> *Come, my people, enter thou into thy chambers, and shut thy doors about thee: hide thyself as it were for a little moment, until the indignation be overpast.*
> (Isaiah 26: 20)

Jesus likens this same process to entering into a closet, shutting the doors and experiencing the heavenly perceptions that lie within us.

> *But thou, when thou prayest, enter into thy closet, and when thou hast shut thy door, pray to thy Father which is in secret; and thy Father which seeth in secret shall reward thee openly.*
> (Matthew 6: 6)

Masters advise their disciples to set up a regular routine of meditation, morning and evening, always picking the same spot away from worldly distractions; the best time of all being during the early hours of the morning before the bustle of the world has begun.

> *Stand in awe, and sin not: commune with your own heart upon your bed, and be still.*
> (Psalm 4: 4)

> *Until the day break, and the shadows flee away, I will get me to the mountain of myrrh, and to the hill of frankincense.*
> (Song of Solomon 4: 6)

Enlightened Teachers also point out that, though age is no bar to the Path, the earlier one starts in life the better. Later in life bodily aches and pains can be distracting.

I love them that love me; and those that seek me early shall find me.
(Proverbs 8: 17)

They also stress the need for the meditator to be on his guard against the tricks of the mind. It is all too easy to put off meditation. Of this tendency Kabir says:

> *Today you say, 'I'll meditate tomorrow';*
> *When tomorrow comes you say,*
> *'Not now, next day'.*
> *Saying 'tomorrow, tomorrow',*
> *This golden chance will pass away.*
> (Kabir, 15th century Muslim saint)

The secret to bringing the mind to heel, the Masters say, is to give it a taste of something far sweeter than anything the world has to offer. That 'something' is an experience of the divinity or Knowledge within us, which is attained by faithfully practising the meditation techniques provided by the Master. With perseverance, these techniques not only calm the mind but also develop the power of concentration so that the consciousness can rise to the site of the Single Eye located between the 'hills' of the eyebrows, the gateway to God-realisation.

> *I will lift up mine eyes unto the hills, from whence cometh my help. My help cometh from the Lord, which made heaven and earth.*
> (Psalm 121: 1 & 2)

When instructing his disciples in meditation Jesus called the Single Eye 'the strait gate' and 'the narrow way' for the mind has to be taken in hand and focussed at a particular point. He contrasted this to the normal condition of the worldly man, whose attention spreads outwards into the world ('the broad way') and becomes enslaved by the very many earthly temptations on offer.

> *Enter ye in at the strait gate: for wide is the gate, and broad is the way, that leadeth to destruction, and many there be which go in thereat: Because straight is the gate, and narrow is the way, which leadeth unto life, and*

few there be that find it.
(Matthew 7: 13 & 14)

When the attention has become settled at the Single Eye, the Divine Light and Sound manifest and are 'seen' and 'heard' via intuitive perception.

The light of the body is the eye: if therefore thine eye be single, thy whole body shall be full of light.
(Matthew 6: 22)

And they shall see his face; and his name (the Word) *shall be in their foreheads. And there shall be no night there; and they need no candle, neither light of the sun; for the Lord God giveth them light: and they shall reign for ever and ever.*
(Revelation 22: 4 & 5)

This experience brings with it a feeling of pure bliss, a drop of which, say the Masters, is so sweet that it transcends anything the world has to offer. In the following passage Isaiah says that if we lift up our eyes to the heavenly realms found by entering the Single Eye, even the pleasures of the astral heavens will fade into insignificance by comparison with the divine delights of God-communion.

Lift up your eyes to the heavens, and look upon the earth beneath: for the heavens shall vanish away like smoke, and the earth shall wax old like a garment, and they that dwell therein shall die in like manner: but my salvation shall be for ever, and my righteousness shall not be abolished.
(Isaiah 51: 6)

This 'redemption' is free of charge, even though we have sold our souls to the world and become prisoners therein. Indeed, no one can pay for it because it is priceless.

> *Shake thyself from the dust; arise, and sit down, O Jerusalem: loose thyself from the bands of thy neck, O captive daughter of Zion. For thus saith the Lord, Ye have sold yourselves for nought; and ye shall be redeemed without money.*
> (Isaiah 52: 2 & 3)

Moreover, this Divine Path is available to everyone no matter what their age, gender, race, religion or culture. No one who yearns for this Knowledge and is fit to receive it is ever turned away.

> *For I know their works and their thoughts: it shall come, that I will gather all nations and tongues; and they shall come, and see my glory.*
> (Isaiah 66: 18)

Masters usually insist that their disciples and prospective disciples attend weekly group meetings called Satsangs. Group meditation is very powerful as the Christ Consciousness increases with the number and abilities of those present.

> *For where two or three are gathered together in my name, there am I in the midst of them.*
> (Matthew 18: 20)

Over the years, as his meditation deepens, the aspirant will be blessed with many experiences, among the first being the manifestation of one or more of the four 'forms' of God mentioned in the earlier section on 'The Knowledge': the Divine Light, the Word, the 'I AM HE' and the Nectar.

> *Hearken unto this, O Job: stand still, and consider the wondrous works of God. Dost thou know when God disposed them, and caused the light of his cloud to shine?*
> (Job 37: 14 & 15)

Eventually these divine manifestations will lead him to the ultimate gaol.

What the Bible Says About Meditation.

Meditation is the means by which man gains control over his mind, enters the inner silence, penetrates his consciousness into the Single Eye, meets the Universal Christ, and merges his soul with God.

Deuteronomy 11: 8-12 Moses speaks to the people in the language of the Masters of those days telling them to meditate.

"Therefore shall ye keep all the commandments which I command you this day, that ye may be strong, and go in and posses the land, whither ye go to posses it (Keep the laws that God gave you as doing so will make you strong enough spiritually to go within yourselves and posses the spiritual 'land' lying there)*;*

"And that ye may prolong your days in the land, which the Lord sware unto your fathers to give unto them and to their seed, a land that floweth with milk and honey (If you keep divine law you will be able to stay in God–communion longer and experience the peace and bliss that is always waiting there for you).

"For the land, whither thou goest in to posses it, is not as the land of Egypt, from whence ye came out, where thou sowest thy seed, and waterest it with thy foot, as a garden of herbs (This land is not the worldly land of ignorance and mortality that you hitherto had sown for yourselves)*:*

"But the land, whither ye go to posses it, is a land of hills and valleys, and drinketh water of the rain of heaven (But is a heavenly land watered by the sweet energies emanating from the higher spiritual regions located in your brain)*:*

"A land which the Lord thy God careth for: the eyes of the Lord thy God are always upon it, from the beginning of the year even unto the end of the year (This inner land is a realm cared for by the

God, a garden which the Lord tends and which He is always looking after even though your ego feels that it is the one performing the actions)."

Joshua 5: 13-15 Joshua has a divine vision after lifting his eyes up to the Christ Centre in meditation.

"And it came to pass, when Joshua was by Jericho, that he lifted up his eyes and looked (Joshua focussed his eyes on his Christ Centre), *and behold, there stood a man over against him with his sword drawn in his hand: and Joshua went unto him, and said unto him, Art thou for us, or for our adversaries?*

"And he said, Nay; but as captain of the host of the Lord am I now come. And Joshua fell on his face to the earth, and did worship, and said unto him, What saith my Lord unto his servant?

"And the captain of the Lord's host said unto Joshua, Loose thy shoes from off thy foot; for the place whereon thou standest is holy. And Joshua did so." It was common in those days – and still is in the east - to take off one's shoes when meditating or entering into a temple to worship.

I Samuel 17: 32-49 The story of David and Goliath is an excellent example of how ancient scriptural writers would weave spiritual messages into historic fact. This is true of the entirety of the ancient Indian epic the Mahabharata and the Indian scripture called the Bhagavad Gita: the Song of God. In the story of David and Goliath, David represents the ideal devotee of God and the huge physical Goliath represents the desires of the world. In his youth David had already gained control of over his God-given senses (his Divine Father's sheep) by successfully controlling his anger (the bear) and any inner violence (the lion). Having done so he was ready for the last battle against worldly desires (Goliath) which he subsequently defeated. This he did by using the sling of meditation to cast his concentration (the pebble) up to his Christ Centre (Single Eye) in the middle of his forehead. This, the Enlightened Ones assure us, is the way to kill the giant of desires.

I Chronicles 21: 16 David and the elders have a vision after David had lifted his eyes up to the Christ Centre.

"And David lifted up his eyes, and saw the angel of the Lord stand between the earth and the heaven, having a drawn sword in his hand stretched out over Jerusalem. Then David and the elders of Israel, who were clothed in sackcloth, fell upon their faces."

Job 37: 14 & 15 Elihu advises Job to meditate and experience the wonders of God in the inner world.

"Hearken unto this, O Job: stand still (still your body and mind in meditation), *and consider the wondrous works of God* (experience

the wonders of the inner worlds).
"Dost thou know when God disposed them, and caused the light of his cloud to shine (Do you know when God first gave you these things or when He first caused the Divine Light to shine within you)*?"*

Psalm 1: 2 David praises the righteous man who delights in meditating on the Law or Holy Ghost of God.
"But his delight is in the law of the Lord; and in his law doth he meditate day and night."

Psalm 2: 11 & 12 The way to overcome karma is by connecting with the Christ Consciousness in meditation.
"Serve the Lord with fear (fear of His Law of Karma), *and rejoice with trembling* (rejoice in the vibration of the Holy Ghost).
"Kiss the Son (Unite with the Christ Consciousness in meditation), *lest he be angry* (in case you slip from the Path and alienate Him), *and ye perish from the way* (and you slip back into the darkness of ignorance)..."*

Psalm 4: 4 Enlightened Teachers advise that the best time to meditate is in the early hours of the morning.
"Stand in awe, and sin not: commune with your own heart upon your bed, and be still." In the language of the saints, the 'heart' refers to the soul, the centre of Being.

Psalm 5: 1 Since it appears throughout Psalms, there is no reason for Christians to fear the word 'meditation'.
"Give ear to my words, O Lord, consider my meditation." See also Psalm 19: 14; 49: 3; 63: 6; 77: 12; 104: 34; 119: 15, 23, 48, 78, 97, 99 & 148; and 143: 5.

Psalm 23: 1-6 David describes the state the meditator attempts to achieve.
"The Lord is my shepherd; I shall not want (The Lord is my inner teacher who will not leave me without guidance or anything else I really need in life).
"He maketh me to lie down in green pastures: he leadeth me beside the still waters (God leads me into the pleasant stillness within my Self).
"He restoreth my soul (God puts me back in contact with my soul)*:*

he leadeth me in the paths of righteousness for his name's sake (He leads me back on to the Path by means of His Holy Word).
"Yea, though I walk through the valley of the shadow of death (Though I travel through this world with its danger of spiritual death), *I will fear no evil: for thou art with me; thy rod* (the punishing rod of karma) *and thy staff* (the spine that keeps the body of the meditator upright) *they comfort me* (they lead me ever into Your comforting presence, my Lord).
"Thou preparest a table before me in the presence of mine enemies (You prepare the Way so that I do not fall prey to the army of evil temptations): *thou anointest my head with oil; my cup runneth over* (You bring the sublime oil of peace, joy and bliss to my consciousness until I am full to the brim with it).
"Surely goodness and mercy shall follow me all the days of my life: and I will dwell in the house of the Lord for ever (Surely, therefore, I shall reach enlightenment)."

Psalm 46: 10 The meditator has first to still his mind so that it can become filled with God.
"Be still, and know that I am God (Be still in body, senses and mind, and experience the Divine Being within you): *I will be exalted among the heathen* (meditation will lead the unenlightened to Me), *I will be exalted in the earth* (I will be praised within Creation)."

Psalm 48: 9 David says that he experiences God's loving kindness inside the temple of his body.
"We have thought of thy lovingkindness, O God, in the midst of thy temple (the bodily temple)." See also I Corinthians 3: 16 "Know ye not that ye are the temple of God..." and II Corinthians 6: 16.

Psalm 104: 33 & 34 Enlightened Ones remember God all twenty four hours of the day all life long.
"I will sing unto the Lord as long as I live: I will sing praise to my God while I have my being.
"My meditation of him shall be sweet: I will be glad in the Lord."

Psalm 121: 1 & 2 David promises to continually struggle to keep his consciousness at the Christ Centre.
"I will lift up mine eyes unto the hills (I will keep my attention on

the Christ Centre which resides between the two little hills of my eyebrows), *from whence cometh my help* (from where comes the spiritual experiences which help me through life).
"My help cometh from the Lord (These experiences are manifestations of God and naught else), *which made heaven and earth."*

Proverbs 8: 17 The God of Love promises that we shall unite with Him in this life if we seek Him from youth.
"I love them that love me; and those that seek me early shall find me."

Ecclesiastes 12: 1 The Preacher advises us to start early on the spiritual path before the world ensnares us.
"Remember now thy Creator in the days of thy youth, while the evil days come not, nor the years draw nigh, when thou shalt say, I have no pleasure in them;"

Song of Solomon 4: 6 Solomon vows to meditate all night until he experiences God within himself.
"Until the day break, and the shadows flee away, I will get me to the mountain of myrrh, and to the hill of frankincense (I will meditate all night until I reach the Christ Centre and then the Centre of Comic Consciousness in the crown of my head)*."*

Song of Solomon 5: 1 & 5 Solomon sings of his experiences in meditation with the Nectar.
"I am come into my garden (I have entered my meditation in which I grow my spiritual flowers), *my sister, my spouse* (my soul, my spirit): *I have gathered my myrrh with my spice* (I have harvested the Nectar with its distinctive flavour); *I have eaten my honeycomb with my honey* (I have absorbed the Word with the Nectar); *I have drunk my wine with my milk* (I have partaken of the wine of bliss which brings ineffable peace): *eat, O friends; drink, yea, drink abundantly, O beloved."*
"I rose up to open to my beloved (My concentration rose to the higher levels); *and my hands dropped with myrrh, and my fingers with sweet smelling myrrh, upon the handles of the lock* (I tasted the Nectar after unlocking the door to where it is kept)*."* The Masters teach

a technique for harvesting the Nectar which those that have been initiated will recognise in the above description. See also the section on 'The Nectar'.

Isaiah 1: 18 When united to God through meditation even evil people can reach enlightenment.

"Come now, and let us reason together (Come! Let us commune with each other in meditation)*, saith the Lord: though your sins be as scarlet, they shall be as white as snow; though they be red like crimson, they shall be as wool* (No matter how evil you have been God–contact can make you pure: as white as wool).*"*

Isaiah 2: 2 & 3 Isaiah foretells of the time when most people will meditate to reach Cosmic Consciousness.

"And it shall come to pass in the last days (the 'last days' of the domination of evil in the world)*, that the mountain of the Lord's house* (that Cosmic Consciousness) *shall be established in the top of the mountains* (in the topmost spiritual centre in the head, or mountain, of man)*, and shall be exalted above the hills* (which lies above the two hills where the eyebrows are located, the Christ Centre or Single Eye)*; and all nations shall flow unto it* (all people shall be attracted to seek Cosmic Consciousness).

"And many people shall go and say, Come ye, and let us go up to the mountain of the Lord, to the house of the God of Jacob (let us lift our consciousnesses in meditation up to the higher spiritual centres attained by Jacob)*, and he* (God) *will teach us of his ways, and we will walk in his paths: for out of Zion* (Cosmic Consciousness) *shall go forth the law* (the Law of Karma)*, and the word of the Lord from Jerusalem* (and the Holy Word will be heard in meditation issuing forth from within the human body).*"* See also Micah 4: 1 & 2.

Isaiah 26: 20 The prophet exhorts the people to go within their bodies in order to dispel ignorance.

"Come, my people, enter thou into thy chambers (in meditation enter into your own bodies, the temple of God)*, and shut thy doors about thee* (and shut the doors of your senses)*: hide thyself as it were for a little moment* (retreat from worldly concerns)*, until the indignation be overpast* (until the unseemly state of ignorance be dispelled).*"*

Isaiah 40: 26 The Lord tells the people through Isaiah to enter the Christ Centre and experience His wonders.

"Lift up your eyes on high (Lift your focus up to the Christ Centre), *and behold who hath created these things* (and find your God who has formed the wonders of Creation out of His One Consciousness), *that bringeth out their host by number: he calleth them all by names by the greatness of his might, for that he is strong in power; not one faileth* (meditation is infallible; no persevering seeker fails)."

Isaiah 41: 1 & 2 God reminds us that we need to go into the silence, through the 'east' gate and upwards.

"Keep silence before me (Go into the inner Silence), *O islands* (My children floating in the sea of My cosmic consciousness)*; and let the people renew their strength: let them come near; let them speak: let us come near together to judgement* (let them commune with Me, their Creator, who will lead them to the perfect judgement).

"Who raised up the righteous man from the east (Who raised the Truth-Seeker up to the high spiritual levels when he contacted the Single Eye, the Star of the East)...." See the section on 'The Higher Spiritual Centres' for the meaning of 'east'.

Isaiah 42: 16 It is the Lord that guides us to Him through the unfamiliar inner paths.

"And I shall bring the blind (the spiritually blind) *by a way that they knew not* (by a method they have never heard of before)*; I will lead them in paths that they have not know* (the inner paths they have ignored previously in their flirtations with the outside world)*: I will make darkness light before them, and crooked things straight* (I will give them the Divine Light to lead them and the Truth to make straight their Path). *These things will I do unto them, and not forsake them."*

Isaiah 51: 6 Lift up your eyes to the Christ Centre and experience the bliss of Spirit.

"Lift up your eyes to the heavens, and look upon the earth beneath (Raise your consciousness up to the Christ Centre and compare the divine joys there to earthly attractions)*: for the heavens shall vanish away like smoke, and the earth shall wax old like a garment* (for both the astral heavens and the physical world are temporary manifestations and their attractions are also temporary and cannot compare to the permanent divine delights of God–communion), *and*

they that dwell therein shall die in like manner (earthly people will die a mundane earthly death)*: but my salvation shall be for ever, and my righteousness shall not be abolished* (but I will give you eternal life in Spirit)."

Isaiah 51: 9 Through Isaiah the Lord exhorts the people to wake up from the illusions of the world.
"Awake, awake, put on strength (Wake up out of your delusion! Grow spiritually!), *O arm of the Lord* (O offspring of God)*; awake as in the ancient days, in the generations of old* (regain the spirituality that you possessed at the beginning of time)."

Isaiah 52: 2 & 3 The Lord goes further and exhorts us to meditate. It costs nothing and we will lose nothing
"Shake thyself from the dust (Escape from the evil of the world)*; arise, and sit down, O Jerusalem* (lift your consciousnesses in meditation)*: loose thyself from the bands of thy neck* (free yourself from karmic ties that keep you returning to the world like slaves), *O captive daughter of Zion* (O people imprisoned by your own ignorance and not claiming your spiritual estate).

"For thus saith the Lord, Ye have sold yourselves for nought (You have sold your souls for a pittance and will gain nothing worthwhile from your worldly adventures)*; and ye shall be redeemed without money* (but the Path of redemption costs nothing and you will realise that you have, in reality, had to give up nothing to attain enlightenment)."

Isaiah 56: 5 & 7 The righteous are not far from enlightenment and even erstwhile sinners will be saved.
"...I will give them an everlasting name, that shall not be cut off (I, God, will continue to send the Holy Wordy to the righteous via a Master as I always have done since the world began)."
Even them (Even the lost ones who now turn to Me) *will I bring to my holy mountain* (will I lead to the higher spiritual centres in their heads) *and make them joyful in my house of prayer:"* Enlightened Ones point out that meditation is true prayer because the supplicant is asking God for nothing except for God Himself.

Isaiah 62: 10 Isaiah exhorts future Saviours to prepare themselves for their tasks.
"Go through, go through the gates (Go through the gates of your Single Eyes); *prepare ye the way of the people* (prepare yourselves to lead the people along that same Path); *cast up, cast up the highway* (raise your consciousnesses up the Way to the higher spiritual centres); *gather out the stones* (remove the obstacles to your spiritual progress); *lift up a standard for the people* (set up a high spiritual vibration that will draw your future disciples to you)."*

Isaiah 66: 18 The Lord confirms that meditation on the Knowledge is for all the people of the world.
"For I know their works and their thoughts: it shall come, that I will gather all nations and tongues; and they shall come, and see my glory (all mankind are destined to enter the spiritual realms inside themselves and experience Me)."*

Jeremiah 7: 2 God advises us to bear witness to the Holy Word at the Gate of the Single Eye.
"Stand in the gate of the Lord's house (Place your focus at the Single Eye, the gateway to God), *and proclaim there this word* (and concentrate there until the Holy Sound comes to you in the silence of meditation), *and say* (bear witness), *Hear the word of the Lord, all ye of Judah, that enter in at these gates* (the 'gates' of the Single Eye) *to worship the Lord."*

Jeremiah 13: 20 & 21 Jeremiah tells the people to look up to their Christ Centres and consider their losses.
"Lift up your eyes, and behold them that come from the north (Enter the Christ Centre and witness the splendid, obedient, sheep–like, powers given to you by God): *where is the flock that was given thee, thy beautiful flock* (what has happened to your divine inheritance since it was first given to you in perfect condition when you were created)?
"What will thou say when he (God through the Law of Karma) *shall punish thee: for thou hast taught them to be captains, and as chiefs over thee* (Instead of taking command of these powers of the senses you have let them rule you): *shall not sorrows take thee, as a woman in travail* (as a result you have suffered greatly in due season when

your bad karmas have born fruit)?" See also Lamentations 3: 48–51 for reference to the 'eye' that 'mourns' for the destruction of the daughter (virgin purity) of the people.

Ezekiel 8: 5 Ezekiel lifts his consciousness to the Crown Chakra in meditation and sees the seat of jealousy.

"Then said he (the angel) *unto me, Son of man, lift up thine eyes now the way towards the north* (lift up your eyes to the highest centre located in the north of the body, the head). *So I lifted up mine eyes the way towards the north, and behold northward at the gate of the altar this image of jealousy in the entry* (then I saw at the entrance to the Single Eye, the gateway to God, the astral location of the Cosmic Satan: the origin of the human emotion of jealousy)."

Ezekiel 43: 1 & 2 The prophet experienced the Holy Ghost Vibration at his Single Eye.

"Afterwards he (God) *brought me to the gate, even the gate that looketh towards the east* (The pull of God drew my concentration to focus on the Christ Centre which is on the eastern side of my body i.e. between the eyebrows, towards the east):

"And, behold, the glory of the God of Israel came from the way of the east: and his voice was like a noise of many waters: and the earth shined with his glory (The rumbling sound of the Word manifested at my Christ Centre and I saw the Divine Light that is the basis of all matter)." See also Ezekiel 11: 1; 44: 1; 46: 1; and 47: 1.

Daniel 4: 34 Every day Nebuchadnezzar focussed his attention on the Christ Centre and gained understanding.

"And at the end of the days I Nebuchadnezzar lifted up mine eyes unto heaven, and mine understanding returned unto me, and I blessed the most High, and I praised and honoured him that liveth for ever, whose dominion is an everlasting dominion, and his kingdom is from generation to generation:" See also Daniel 8: 3 and 10: 5.

Zechariah 1: 18 & 19 Zechariah's vision when he lifted his eyes up to the Christ Centre.

"Then lifted I up mine eyes, and saw, and behold four horns (four creative powers).

"And I said unto the angel that talked with me, What be these? And he answered me, These are the horns which have scattered Judah,

Israel and Jerusalem (these are the forces responsible for creating Cosmic Satan and Individual Delusion)." See also Zechariah 2: 1; 5: 1, 5 & 9; & 6: 1 and refer back to the section on 'Forming Creation' for details of the satanic forces.

Zechariah 2: 13 The Lord tells Zechariah to be silent and find God in His holy place inside himself.
"Be silent, O all flesh, before the Lord (Go into the Holy Silence within your body)*: for he is raised up out of his holy habitation* (for I, God, am found in the highest holy place within you: the Crown Chakra)."

Apocrypha, The Wisdom of Solomon 7: 7 & 11 Wisdom is won by sincere prayer: by meditation.
"Wherefore I prayed, and understanding was given me: I called upon God, and the spirit of wisdom came to me."
"All good things together came to me with her (along with wisdom)*, and innumerable riches in her hands."* The common experience of all who meditate deeply is that contact with the Source of wisdom in Creation, the Christ Consciousness, brings many blessings in its wake.

Apocrypha, The Wisdom of Solomon 16: 26 Man cannot live without the Word. It is the life of men.
"That thy children, O Lord, whom thou lovest, might know, that it is not the growing of fruits that nourisheth man: but it is thy word, which preserveth them that put their trust in thee (it is not food that spiritually nourishes man but it is the Holy Word that sustains those who make the effort to contact it in meditation)."

Matthew 2: 1-10 These verses tell the story of how the three wise men followed the Star of the Christ Centre or Spiritual Eye to Bethlehem, where the baby Jesus had been born. Clearly the wise men could not have been following a physical star shining in the east of the sky as they would have been travelling westward to get to Israel and, further, it is improbable that any star would, or could without a major miracle, hover in the sky above the place where the babe lay. The 'star in the east' is a euphemism for the Christ Centre and is a well-known term in the Hindu religion, in which married women are reminded of their spiritual nature by the red mark located over the Third or Single Eye. The wise men were following guidance given in meditation.

Matthew 6: 6 Go within and meditate in the secret silence after shutting out the distractions of the world.
"But thou, when thou prayest, enter into thy closet (When you meditate enter the privacy of your own body)*, and when thou hast*

shut thy door (and when you have closed off all your senses from contact with the outside world), *pray to thy Father which is in secret* (meditate in the secret silence within); *and thy Father which seeth in secret shall reward thee openly* (and God who sees all things, even secret internal ones, will reward you with His very evident spiritual qualities)."

Matthew 6: 22 & 23 Jesus clearly identifies the place where we must focus our attention to see the Divine Light.
"The light of the body is the eye: if therefore thine eye be single, thy whole body shall be full of light (God, manifesting in Creation and in the human body as the Divine Light, can be seen within the Single Eye at the Christ Centre).
"But if thine eye be evil, thy whole body shall be full of darkness. If therefore the light that is in thee be darkness, how great is that darkness (But if your bad actions cover up the Divine Light in you, as seen in your Single Eye, then your actions are bound to be evil and will draw you deeper into karmic debt)." See also Luke 11: 34.

Matthew 7: 13 & 14 Jesus elaborates on the 'narrow way' to God–union.
"Enter ye in at the strait gate (Obtain God through the difficult way of good behaviour and meditation): *for wide is the gate, and broad is the way, that leadeth to destruction* (for the world offers a wide array of temptations to drawn the seeker away from the spiritual path), *and many there be which go in thereat:*
"Because straight is the gate, and narrow is the way, which leadeth unto life, and few there be that find it (Follow the inner route to God through concentrating the attention inside yourselves as opposed to your normal situation where your concentration is being attracted outwards towards all the distractions the world has to offer)."

Matthew 18: 20 Jesus talks about the power of group meditation.
"For where two or three are gathered together in my name, there am I (there is the 'I AM' as the Christ Consciousness) *in the midst of them."* The vibrational power of the Word is intensified in group meditation.

Mark 1: 14 & 15 The real meaning of 'repentance' is to change the direction of your attention by the inner Path of meditation.

"Now after that John (John the Baptist) *was put into prison, Jesus came into Galilee, preaching the gospel of the Kingdom of God* (teaching the Knowledge),

"And saying, The time is fulfilled, and the kingdom of God is at hand: repent ye (turn your attention away from the world to the inner realms of the silence within you)*, and believe the* gospel (have faith in the teachings and initiation I have given to you).*"*

Mark 4: 30-32 Meditate and the little glimpses of the glorious divinity within will grow into a mighty force.

"And he (Jesus) *said, Whereunto shall we liken the kingdom of God? or with what comparison shall we compare it?*

"It is like a grain of mustard seed, which, when it is sown in the earth, is less than all the seeds that be in the earth (At first the devotee gets only little glimpses of God within)*:*

"But when it is sown, it groweth up, and becometh greater than all the herbs, and shooteth out great branches; so that the fowls of the air may ledge under the shadow of it (Eventually, with persistent meditation, the little glimpses grow into the mighty force of God-Realisation).*"* See also Matthew 13: 31 & 32

Mark 7: 21-23 Jesus associates an Evil Single Eye with a tendency for wickedness.

"For from within, out of the heart of men, proceedeth evil thoughts, adulteries, fornications, murders.

"Thefts, covertness, wickedness, deceit, lasciviousness, an evil eye (a Single Eye that has not the Light of God in it)*, blasphemy, pride, foolishness:*

"All these evil things come from within, and defile the man." See Matthew 6: 22 & 23 above.

Luke 17: 21 Jesus gives the clearest explanation of where God can be experienced: inside our bodies.

"Neither shall they say, Lo here! or, lo there! for, behold, the kingdom of God is within you."

Luke 21: 26-28 Jesus says that tribulations will drive mankind to look up to the Christ Centre.

"Men's hearts failing them for fear, and for looking after those things which are coming on the earth: for the powers of heaven shall be shaken (Great troubles will cause man to fear and lose his faith in material things).

"And then shall they see the Son of man coming in a cloud with power and great glory (And when that comes to pass, the ordinary person, the Son of man, will make the effort to go into the darkness behind closed eyes and find the glory of his soul).

"And when these things begin to come to pass, then look up, and lift up your heads; for the redemption draweth nigh (then raise your consciousness in meditation to the high spiritual centres wherein your salvation lies)."

John 1: 18 Jesus comments that one cannot unite with God except through the Christ Consciousness.

"No man hath seen God at any time; the only begotten Son (the first born of God when He made Creation by dividing His Cosmic Consciousness into God–the–Father and God–the–Son: the Christ Consciousness), *which is in the bosom of the Father* (which is part of God's infinite consciousness), *he hath declared him* (The Christ Consciousness 'declares' or heralds the presence of God–the–Father)."

John 3: 14 Jesus identifies an important spiritual process necessary to raise our spiritual level.

"And as Moses lifted up the serpent (raised the coiled spiritual power in the base of the spine from perception of earthly things to spiritual perception) *in the wilderness* (in the silence within where ego and the multitude of physical forms disappear), *even so must the Son of man be lifted up* (similarly, all people must do this in meditation in order to become enlightened):"

John 8: 31 & 32 Jesus says that it is necessary to continue to meditate on the Word.

"Then said Jesus to those Jews which believed on him, If ye continue in my word, then are ye my disciples indeed (Only those who continue to listen to the Word in meditation can count themselves among my

disciples);
"And ye shall know the truth, and the truth shall make you free (Meditating on the Word will lead to the Supreme Truth, God the Father, and union with Him will set you free of having to come back time and time again to this world)."

John 10: 4 Disciples intuitively recognise the voice of their Master and he also recognises them.
"And when he putteth forth his own sheep, he goeth before them, and the sheep follow him: for they know his voice."

John 17: 1 & 2 The Single Eye in the centre of the forehead is the gateway or door to the Christ Consciousness.
"These words spake Jesus, and lifted up his eyes to heaven (and lifted up his consciousness in meditation to the Christ Centre, the Single Eye), *and said, Father, the hour is come* (my time on earth is running out); *glorify thy Son* (glorify the Christ Consciousness in me), *that thy Son may also glorify thee* (that I and the Christ Consciousness in me may glorify You, God the Father, by my resurrection):
"As thou hast given him power over all flesh (As You have given the Christ Consciousness power over death), *that he should give eternal life* (so that it can give freedom from the dream of death) *to as many as thou hast given him* (to all those who have received the Christ Consciousness, as my disciples have through me)." See also John 11: 41 for another mention of Jesus looking to his Christ Centre when raising Lazarus from the dead.

Acts 7: 54 & 55 St. Stephen looks up to the Christ Centre and sees the astral form of his Master: Jesus.
"When they (the members of the synagogue) *heard these thing* (Stephen's severe criticism of them and their kind), *they were cut to the heart, and they gnashed on him with their teeth.*
"But he, being full of the Holy Ghost (hearing the holy sound of the Word drawing his attention inward), *looked up steadfastly into heaven* (raised his focus to the Christ Centre), *and saw the glory of God, and Jesus standing on the right hand of God."*

II Corinthians 9: 6 The Law of Karma dictates that what we put into meditation we also get out: no more, no less.
"But this I say, He which soweth sparingly shall reap also sparingly; and he which soweth bountifully shall reap also bountifully."

I Thessalonians 5: 4-6 St. Paul talks of meditation into the night hours.
"But ye, brethren, are not in darkness (you do not suffer from spiritual ignorance), *that that day should overtake you as a thief* (and because of that the day of evil will not come to you).
"Ye are all the children of the light, and the children of the day (You follow the Divine Light that gleams from behind the darkness of closed eyes)*: we are not of the night, nor of darkness.*
"Therefore let us not sleep, as do the others (the worldly people)*; but let us watch and be sober* (let us be awake in spirit through meditation)*."* It is possible that these verses have other meanings too: 'let us be continually watchful day and night in case we fall into sin', and 'let us meditate during the night when others are asleep'.

I Timothy 4: 14 & 15 St. Paul urges Timothy not to forget to meditate on the Christ Centre.
"Neglect not the gift that is in thee (Do not neglect to meditate on the Single Eye)*, which was given thee by prophecy* (which was given to you as a result of your good karma)*, with the laying on of the hands of the presbytery* (which was given to you by my touch during initiation).
"Meditate upon these things; give thyself wholly to them; that thy profiting may appear to all." The presbytery is the sanctuary at the eastern part of the chancel beyond the choir stalls. Since there were no churches in those days, it is apparent that St. Paul was referring to the sanctuary of the Single Eye, or Christ Centre, located in the east of the temple of the body.

Revelation 1: 10 St. John experienced the Word when he went into meditation.
"I was in the Spirit on the Lord's day (I was meditating on a certain day when I had a spiritual experience)*, and heard behind me* (in the darkness behind my closed eyelids) *a great voice, as of a trumpet* (the vibratory roar of the Holy Word)*."* The entire book of Revelation is an account of the event of St. John going within in meditation and, with his ascended Master's help, successfully spiritualising the seven major astral centres and 144, 000 sub-centres responsible for energising his body and raising his consciousness to God–union.

Revelation 3: 20 God, via the angel, explains that He is forever waiting to reveal Himself to the meditator.

"Behold, I stand at the door (I am always waiting at the door of the Single eye), *and knock* (and I try to attract the meditator's attention): *if any man hear my voice* (if during meditation any one hears My Holy Word), *I will come in to him, and will sup with him, and he with me* (I, God as the Christ and then Cosmic Consciousness, will appear to him and we will be united in Spirit)."

Revelation 22: 4 & 5 St. John reveals the location of the Divine Light & Sound: in the forehead.

"And they (the devotees of God) *shall see his face; and his name shall be in their foreheads* (and they will hear the sound of the Holy Word when they focus their meditative attention on the Single Eye).

"And there shall be no night there (the darkness of ignorance will disappear); *and they need no candle, neither light of the sun; for the Lord God giveth them light* (the Divine Light will light the way): *and they shall reign* (shall be in Cosmic Consciousness) *for ever and ever."*

3

Qualities for Success.

Is not this the fast that I have chosen? to loose the bands of wickedness, to undo the heavy burdens, and to let the oppressed go free, and that ye break every yoke? Is it not to deal thy bread to the hungry, and that thou should bring the poor that are cast out to thy house? when thou seest the naked, that thou cover him; and that thou hide not thyself from thine own flesh? Then shall thy light break forth as the morning, and thine health shall spring forth speedily: and thy righteousness shall go before thee; the glory of the Lord will be thy reward.
(Isaiah 58: 6–8)

> *Are you searching for your soul?*
> *Then come out of your prison.*
> *Leave the stream and join the river*
> *that flows into the ocean.*
> *Absorbed in this world*
> *you've made it your burden.*
> *Rise above this world.*
> *There is another vision.*
> (Rumi, 13th century Sufi)

To the disciple, loyalty to the Master is a vital quality. Time and time again throughout numerous lifetimes we have fallen prey to the wiles of the world. Having previously made a little progress along the Path we should be able to understand at a really deep level that we cannot of ourselves break free from the clutches of Individual Ignorance and Cosmic Satan without the help of a God-chosen Guide. Even though Jesus' disciples were very advanced spiritually, their Master was at pains to warn them that they could not go it alone.

> *Abide in me, and I in you. As the branch cannot bear fruit in itself, except it abide in the vine; no more can ye, except ye abide in me. I am the vine, ye are the branches: He that abideth in me, and I in him, the same bringeth forth much fruit: for without me ye can do nothing.*
> (John 15: 4 & 5)

Loyalty to the Master is, in itself, a God-given test. For if we cannot be loyal to God's chosen vessel, there is little chance that we will remain faithful to God in the long run. Loyalty to the Master does not infer blind obedience. It mainly means following the spiritual disciplines the Master has given us for this is the only way we will discover our True Selves.

> *Then said Jesus to those Jews which believed on him, If ye continue in my word, then are ye my disciples indeed; And ye shall know the truth, and the truth shall set you free.*
> (John 8: 31 & 32)

The great importance of deeply absorbing the Master's teachings and regularly practising them was graphically illustrated by Jesus in the ceremony during the Last Supper. In that touching scene, Jesus exhorted his disciples to ingest his teachings (bread) and drink of the spiritual life (wine) he had shown them while he was with them.

> *And as they were eating, Jesus took bread, and blessed it, and brake it, and gave it to the disciples, and said, Take, eat; this is my body. And he took the cup, and gave thanks, and gave it to them, saying, Drink ye all of it; For this is my blood of the new testament, which is shed*

> *for many for the remission of sins.*
> (Matthew 26: 26–28)

One of the results of following the Path with diligence is that faith in its ability to transform and uplift the devotee grows at a commensurate rate. Though one's faith may initially be a sapling, vulnerable to being damaged by the goats of this world, in time it will grow into a great tree capable of removing all doubts and of giving shelter to others.

> *Then said he (Jesus), Unto what is the kingdom of God like? And where-unto shall I resemble it? It is like a grain of mustard seed, which a man took, and cast into his garden; and it grew, and waxed a great tree; and the fowls of the air lodged in the branches of it.*
> (Luke 13: 18 & 19)

It is an unfortunate fact that we live in a 'quick-fix' world where everything must happen immediately. In the spiritual world nothing happens quickly. Patience is an essential quality.

> *To every thing there is a season, and a time to every purpose under the heaven:*
> (Ecclesiastes 3: 1)

Along with patience comes perseverance. Enlightened Ones teach that the attainment of Truth is bound to come to those who persist in their spiritual practice. It is not a matter of 'if' but 'when'.

> *Ask, and it shall be given you; seek, and ye shall find; knock, and it shall be opened up unto you.*
> (Matthew 7: 7)

Provided we make the necessary effort God cannot help but respond in like measure. He wants us back Home just as much, if not more, than we desire to return to Him. One should not give up even at the point of death. There is no time that can be considered to be too late.

Strive for the truth unto death, and the Lord shall fight for thee.
(Apocrypha, Ecclesiasticus 4: 28)

Man is bound to this world by his desires. He keeps on appearing in this multi-faceted theatre until all his desires have been worked out. The ability of the ego-mind to create desires is endless.

And he (Jesus) *said unto them* (his disciples), *Take heed, and beware of covetousness: for a man's life consisteth not in the abundance of the things which he possesseth.*
(Luke 12: 15)

More often than not, man has to repeatedly chase a desire before he reaches the understanding that no temporary material thing can possibly bring permanent happiness. Some progress has to have been made in this direction even to meet a Master as described in the section 'Qualities of the Truth-Seeker'. But for the individualised soul to regain its perfect Eden-like state the renunciation of desires has to be very deep indeed.

Jesus explains the extent of the renunciation of desires required in his characteristically colourful way by advising that it is better to remove (cut off) ourselves from the temptations of this world than to let our organs and limbs lead us towards spiritual death. In the more advanced stages of meditation this is achieved by disconnecting the inner life force from the senses of sight, touch, sound, taste and smell.

And if thy right eye offend thee, pluck it out, and cast it from thee: for it is profitable for thee that one of thy members should perish, and not that thy whole body should be cast into hell. And if thy right hand offend thee, cut it off, and cast it from thee: for it is profitable for thee that one of thy members should perish, and not

> *that thy whole body be cast into hell.*
> (Matthew 5: 29 & 30)

As soon as any desired object has been attained, the ego claims possession of it: 'this house, wife, money, child etc is **mine**'. Thus desire and the feeling of ownership are related. It does not seem to have dawned on us that no matter how powerful or rich we are, we cannot take anything material with us when we die. Eventually all of it has to be left behind at death. It is better by far to reject the temporary pleasures of the material world in favour of the permanent treasures that lie in the kingdom of heaven.

> *Lay not up for yourselves treasures upon earth, where moth and rust doth corrupt, and where thieves break through and steal: But lay up for yourselves treasures in heaven, where neither moth nor rust doth corrupt, and where thieves do not break through nor steal: For where your treasure is, there will your heart be also."*
> (Matthew 6: 19-21)

More often than not we cannot achieve this degree of detachment in one lifetime. It is more common for people to leave this earth feeling regret for the possessions and loved ones they have had to leave behind. This feeling of loss creates a strong desire to repossess the things we have had to let go of in our last life, an urge that inevitably draws us back into the world once more. These cycles of loss and desire to re-posses can be almost endless.

When, however, through meditation and leading a harmonious life, our consciousness expands so that the limited ego-feeling of 'mine' disappears, all things become ours. Then we begin to regard all mothers, fathers and children as our own. Similarly we begin to treat the property of others with the same degree of care and respect that we would have if they had belonged to us.

> *Then Peter said, Lo, we have left all, and followed thee. And he* (Jesus) *said unto them, Verily I say unto you, There is no man that hath left house, or parents, or brethren,*

or wife, or children, for the kingdom of God's sake, Who shall not receive manifold more in this present time, and in the world to come life everlasting.
(Luke 18: 28-30)

A natural outpouring of this all-inclusiveness of consciousness is compassion. The compassionate person is surely close to God. There is no greater proof of spiritual advancement than a love that is capable of embracing the concerns of even one's enemies.

If thine enemy be hungry, give him bread to eat; and if he be thirsty, give him water to drink:
(Proverbs 25: 21)

As working people with families and many obligations, we cannot simply opt out of worldly life. As Jesus puts it, we have to pay our dues to the world (Caesar) and also follow the spiritual path to God.

And Jesus answering said unto them, Render to Caesar the things that are Caesar's, and to God the things that are God's. And they marvelled at him.
(Mark 12: 17)

The balance between worldly actions and spiritual ones is often a fine one. It is particularly difficult when wrongdoing has become the norm. In today's world everything is pervaded by imperfection to some degree or another. We have to make choices but the choice is often between the 'bad' and the 'no-so-bad'. In such circumstances the advice given by Krishna in the Bhagavad Gita is invaluable: do everything for God and do not try to lay claim to the results whether they appear to be 'good' or 'bad' in our sight. In the Bible this same advice appears as:

Commit thy works unto the Lord, and thy thoughts shall be established.
(Proverbs 16: 3)

It is the intention with which we act that is the important factor rather than the deeds themselves. In the initial stages of the Path, the voice of the ego remains overwhelmingly loud and the right way is often 'too hard' for us to see. But with progress on the Path, the volume of the voice of ego diminishes and the silent voice of God begins to make its 'commands' known and our ability to live in harmony with Divine Law improves.

> *Seek not out the things that are too hard for thee, neither search the things that are above thy strength. But what is commanded thee, think thereupon with reverence; for it is not needful for thee to see with thine eyes the things that are in secret.*
> (Apocrypha, Ecclesiasticus 3: 21 & 22)

Very often a Master may advise a disciple to undertake some public service in order to further his/her spiritual progress. This may take many forms including feeding and clothing the poor. In the following moving passage Jesus exhorts his disciples to serve the God in man.

> *For I was an hungred, and ye gave me meat: I was thirsty, and ye gave me drink: I was a stranger and ye took ye in: Naked, and ye clothed me: I was sick and ye visited me: I was in prison, and ye came unto me.*
> (Matthew 25: 35 & 36)

Then again, Enlightened Ones advise all those who have been initiated, without exception, to continue coming to their meetings (Satsangs) not only to help themselves but particularly to encourage others who are new to the path.

> *He that walketh with wise men shall be wise: but a companion of fools shall be destroyed.*
> (Proverbs 13: 20)

Odd though it may seem at first sight, the highest service any disciple can perform for mankind is to enlighten himself; for, in doing so, he makes an invaluable contribution to uplifting not only those he comes into contact with on a daily basis but the whole world. This, in God's eyes, is the ultimate service.

Meditation may bring about no immediate noticeable change; changes there are indeed but they tend to be evolutionary not revolutionary. No matter how little progress the meditator feels he/she is making one should never give up. There are no failures in God's world. The techniques given by the Masters enable the mind gradually to steady and become focussed on the object of meditation. When this happens body, mind, and senses settle down into the Silence from which Divinity springs forth.

What the Bible Says About the Qualities for Success.

The main qualities required of the Truth-Seeker are: loyalty and faith in the Path and in one's God-chosen Guide; perseverance beyond normal requirements; the rejection of worldly desires in favour of spiritual perceptions; and complete surrender of the ego in favour of the guiding voice of divinity from within. God is 'jealous' and demands one's full attention.

Exodus 20: 5 Union with God requires whole-hearted devotion.
"Thou shalt not bow down thyself to them, nor serve them: for I the Lord thy God am a jealous God (a God who demands complete devotion).*"*

Deuteronomy 11: 1 Moses sets out the basic laws underlying right action.
"Therefore thou shalt love the Lord thy God, and keep his charge, and his statutes, and his judgements, and his commandments, alway".

Psalm 55: 22 Have faith in the divine processes and in the inherent Justice built into Creation.

"Cast thy burden upon the Lord (have faith and surrender all your worries to Him), *and he shall sustain thee* (He will give you strength): *he shall never suffer the righteous to be moved* (He will not allow the devout spiritual aspirant to be overcome by fear)."

Psalm 104: 33 & 34 Enlightened Ones remember God all twenty-four hours of the day.

"I will sing unto the Lord as long as I live: I will sing praise to my God while I have my being.
"My meditation of him shall be sweet: I will be glad in the Lord."

Proverbs 1: 14 & 15 Be careful of the company you keep for like creates like: attend the Master's meetings.

"Cast in thy lot among us (Stay in the company of good people); *let us all have one purse* (let us stick closely together)*:*
"My son, walk thou not in the way with them (evil people); *refrain thy foot from their path* (do not keep company with them)*:"*

Proverbs 4: 24-26 Wisdom advises us not to let our senses and limbs lead us away from the path to God.

"Put away from thee a froward mouth (Avoid coarse and unpleasant speech), *and perverse lips put far from thee* (avoid people who speak evilly).
"Let thine eyes look right on, and let thine eyelids look straight before thee (Don't allow your eyes to lust after things you should not have).
"Ponder the path of thy feet (Be careful where you decide to go), *and let thy ways be established* (and keep to the divine path)."

Proverbs 6: 2 Unwise words lead us into captivity.

"Thou art snared with the words of thy mouth, thou art taken with the words of thy mouth (Beware that your words do not cause you to be ensnared by the Law of Karma so that you become trapped into the cycle of birth, death and rebirth)." All words have the power of the Word, Aum or Amen behind them and can do good or ill accordingly.

Proverbs 8: 13 Good behaviour comes from a healthy respect for the Law of Causation or Karma.

"The fear of the Lord is to hate evil (Hate evil out of fear of the Law of Karma)*: pride, and arrogancy, and the evil way, and the froward mouth* (avoid coarse and unseemly speech)*, do I hate."*

Proverbs 13: 20 You become like the company you keep, so walk with good people not evil ones.

"He that walketh with wise men shall be wise: but a companion of fools shall be destroyed (in both character and spiritually)*."*

Proverbs 14: 17 Anger clouds wisdom and evil behaviour creates disharmony.

"He that is soon angry dealeth foolishly: and a man of wicked devices is hated."

Proverbs 16: 3 Do everything for God and the mind will become established in righteousness.

"Commit thy works unto the Lord, and thy thoughts shall be established."

Proverbs 16: 6 Evil tendencies can be removed from the mind by being merciful to others and truthful.

"By mercy and truth iniquity is purged: and by the fear of the Lord men depart from evil."

Proverbs 16: 8 It is better to obtain a little by right methods than riches by evil means.

"Better is a little with righteousness than great revenues without right."

Proverbs 16: 23 & 24 Wisdom leads to wise and pleasant words that help us, and others, along the Path.

"The heart of the wise teacheth his mouth, and addeth learning to his lips.

"Pleasant words are as an honeycomb, sweet to the soul, and health to the bones."

Proverbs 16: 32 To control anger and win soul perception is more important than gaining material power.

"He that is slow to anger is better than the mighty; and he that

ruleth his spirit than he that taketh a city."

Proverbs 17: 27 The one who has been given Knowledge seeks the silence of lonely places to meditate.
"He that hath knowledge (He who has been given the teachings and meditation techniques from an Enlightened One) *spareth his words* (likes his own company and quiet places)*: and a man of* (spiritual) *understanding is of an excellent spirit* (is happy and close to God)."

Proverbs 23: 2 Control your food intake or suffer the consequences.
"And put a knife to thy throat, if thou be a man given to (uncontrolled) *appetite."*

Proverbs 23: 9 Do not speak spiritual truths to an unbelieving person.
"Speak not in the ears of a fool: for he will despise the wisdom of thy words." See also Jesus' advice in Matthew 7: 6 'Give not that which is holy unto the dogs, neither cast ye your pearls before swine'.

Proverbs 23: 10 & 11 Do not throw away the old tried and trusted values; protect the orphans.
"Remove not the old landmark (of protecting the weak)*; and enter not into the fields of the fatherless* (do not steal from orphans for God is their protector through the Law of Karma).
"For their redeemer is mighty; he shall plead their cause with thee (He will see that justice is done and that the evil eventually become compassionate)."

Proverbs 25: 21 Show compassion even to your enemies..
"If thine enemy be hungry, give him bread to eat; and if he be thirsty, give him water to drink:"

Proverbs 29: 20 Rashness is more difficult to overcome than foolishness.
"Seest thou a man that is hasty in his words? There is more hope of a fool than of him."

Proverbs 29: 22 & 23 By the Law of Karma, aggression and pride lead to the cycle of death and rebirth.
"An angry man stirreth up strife, and a furious man aboundeth in

transgression (Anger causes angry reactions and leads to greater errors).
"A man's pride shall bring him low: but honour shall uphold the humble in spirit (An ego-less, humble, person shall be honoured by men as well as by God)."

Ecclesiastes 3: 1 Follow the voice of God within you, the silent voice of intuition.
"To every thing there is a season, and a time to every purpose under the heaven:" The voice of intuition knows what to do, when to do it and the way it should be done. It is the silent voice of God.

Isaiah 5: 20 & 21 Avoid lies, ignorance & hypocrisy.
"Woe unto them that call evil good, and good evil; that put darkness for light, and light for darkness; that put bitter for sweet and sweet for bitter!
"Woe unto them that are wise in their own eyes (who think they are clever when they are actually misleading themselves and other people), *and prudent in their own sight!"*

Isaiah 58: 6-8 Isaiah describes the type of behaviour that pleases the Lord.
"Is not this the fast that I (God) *have chosen* (for you, My children)? *to loose the bands of wickedness* (to free yourself from ignorance), *to undo the heavy burdens* (to lighten your karmic loads), *and to let the oppressed go free* (to free yourselves from the clutches of this world), *and that ye break every yoke* (that you manage to break everything holding you back from enlightenment)?
"Is it not to deal thy bread to the hungry (to feed the hungry), *and that thou bring the poor that are cast out to thy house* (to house the homeless)? *when thou seest the naked, that thou cover him* (to clothe the naked), *and that thou hide not thyself from thine own flesh* (and that you love and serve your family and your neighbour!)?
"Then shall thy light break forth as the morning (The Divine Light will manifest within you), *and thine health shall spring forth speedily* (and this pure Light will dispel all illness): *and thy righteousness shall go before thee* (God's Light in you shall be apparent to all people); *the glory of the Lord shall be thy reward* (and you will gain your rightful heritage as a child of God)."

Jeremiah 13: 15-17 Be humble enough to find the soul within you. Doing so will save you endless troubles.

"Hear ye, and give ear; be not proud: for the Lord hath spoken.

"Give glory to the Lord your God, before he cause darkness, and before your feet stumble upon the dark mountains, and, while ye look for light, he turn it into the shadow of death, and make it gross darkness (Find the Light inside yourself before the darkness of ignorance overtakes you).

"But if ye will not hear it, my soul shall weep in secret places for your pride (If you will not listen to the Voice of God as the Word then your soul will remain imprisoned in the body like a bird trapped in a cage), *and mine eyes shall weep sore, and run down with tears, because the Lord's flock is carried away captive* (because God's children are cast into bondage through the Laws of Karma and Reincarnation)."

Ezekiel 8: 5 Ezekiel 'sees' the seat of jealousy that prevents one from entering Cosmic Consciousness.

"Then said he (the angel) *unto me, Son of man, lift up thine eyes now the way towards the north* (lift up your eyes to the highest centre located in the north of the body, the head). *So I lifted up mine eyes the way towards the north, and behold northward at the gate of the altar this image of jealousy in the entry* (then I saw at the gateway of the Single Eye the astral location of Cosmic Satan, the origin of the human emotion of jealousy)." Jealously arises from thwarted desires.

Apocrypha, The Wisdom of Solomon 9: 6 Without wisdom mere cleverness is of no benefit.

"For though a man be never so perfect among the children of men, yet if thy wisdom (God's wisdom) *be not with him, he shall be nothing regarded."*

Apocrypha, Ecclesiasticus 1: 22–30; 2: 1–6 & 4: 1–10 The prophet advises us to cultivate patience, faith, compassion, generosity, cheerfulness and endurance; keep the commandments; fear the Law of Karma; and avoid anger, hypocrisy, pride, temptation and many others. In actuality these qualities arise naturally through persistent meditation on God but the process is speeded up if one's worldly actions support what you are trying to achieve in meditation.

Apocrypha, Ecclesiasticus 3: 21 & 22 Listen to and follow the intuition even when in doubt.

"Seek not out the things that are too hard for thee, neither search the things that are above thy strength (Do not try to exceed the limitations of the mind),

"But what is commanded thee, think thereupon with reverence: for it is not needful for thee to see with thine eyes the things that are in secret (but follow the guidance of intuitive wisdom which 'speaks' to you from the Silence deep within you)."

Apocrypha, Ecclesiasticus 4: 28 Make spiritual effort throughout life and earn Grace thereby.

"Strive for the truth (spiritual Truth) *unto death, and the Lord shall fight for thee."*

Apocrypha, Ecclesiasticus 6: 5 Sweetness of speech attracts true friends and uplifts all you contact.

"Sweet language will multiply friends: and a fairspeaking tongue will increase kind greetings."

Matthew 5: 14 & 16 The best way to serve God is through setting a good example.

"Ye (my disciples) *are the light of the world. A city that is set on a hill cannot be hid."*

"Let your light so shine before men, that they may see your good works, and glorify your Father which is in heaven."

Matthew 5: 29 & 30 Jesus, in the language of the saints, graphically warns us to learn to control the senses.

"And if thy right eye offend thee, pluck it out, and cast it from thee: for it is profitable for thee that one of thy members should perish, and not that thy whole body should be cast into hell (If your eyes are in danger tempting you to sin, remove your sight from the object of your desire and fix your gaze on something more beneficial to you).

"And if thy right hand offend thee, cut it off, and cast it from thee: for it is profitable for thee that one of thy members should perish, and not that thy whole body be cast into hell (If your limbs are in danger of tempting you to sin, restrain them and give them something to do that is more beneficial to you and to others)."

Matthew 5: 39 Jesus' teaching on non–violence in thought, word and deed.
"But I say unto you, That ye resist not evil (with evil)*: but whosoever shall smite thee on thy right cheek, turn to him the other also* (Do not return a bad deed with an equally bad one, but return good for evil, because eventually your persistent goodness will overcome the evil in others).*"*

Matthew 5: 44 & 45 Treat everyone with love for they too are the children of God.
"But I say unto you, Love your enemies, bless them that curse you, do good to them that hate you, and pray for them which despitefully use you, and persecute you;
"That ye may be the children of your Father which is in heaven (For these are God–like qualities necessary for you to imitate if you are to unite with the Godhead)*: for he maketh his sun to rise on the evil and on the good, and sendeth rain on the just and on the unjust* (for God sends His love to everyone equally though some experience it and can emulate it better than others).*"*

Matthew 5: 48 Jesus tells his disciples to be perfect as God is perfect: for perfection is their true estate as souls.
"Be ye therefore perfect, even as your Father which is heaven is perfect."

Matthew 6: 14 & 15 If we are not able to forgive others we hurt ourselves and shut God out of our lives.
"For if ye forgive men their trespasses, your heavenly Father will also forgive you:
"But if ye forgive not men their trespasses, neither will your Father forgive your trespasses (God forgives endlessly. He never harbours ill–will. If you want to be one with God you have to be endlessly forgiving just like He is).*"*

Matthew 6: 19-21 Put not your trust in the temporary things of the world but in the One who created it.
"Lay not up for yourselves treasures upon earth, where moth and rust doth corrupt, and where thieves break through and steal:
"But lay up for yourselves treasures in heaven, where neither moth nor rust doth corrupt, and where thieves do not break through nor

steal:
"For where your treasure is, there will your heart be also."

Matthew 6: 24 We have a choice: either worship the material world or turn towards God. No one can do both.
"No man can serve two masters: for either he will hate the one, and love the other; or else he will hold to the one, and despise the other. Ye cannot serve (both) *God and mammon* (the material world)*."*

Matthew 6: 26 Have faith in the laws and processes God has worked out in His plan for you and for the world.
"Behold the fowls of the air: for they sow not, neither do they reap, nor gather (the harvest) *into barns; yet your heavenly Father feedeth them. Are ye not much better than they* (Even though the world appears to be going awry, everything, even a little bird's fate, is ultimately in the care of the Father's hand)*?"* This does not mean that man should leave everything to God. Man must think and work but he should do it in harmony with God's Will and with faith in God's perfect justice.

Matthew 6: 33 Put God first and all else will fall into place.
"But seek ye first the kingdom of God, and his righteousness; and all these things (material necessities, as opposed to uncontrolled desires) *shall be added unto you."*

Matthew 7: 7 Be persistent in your search for God, particularly in meditation.
"Ask, and it shall be given you; seek, and ye shall find; knock, and it (the door to the kingdom of heaven at the site of the Single Eye) *shall be opened up unto you:"*

Matthew 7: 24 The Master warns that it is not sufficient to listen to the teachings. We must put them into practice.
"Therefore whosoever heareth these sayings of mine, and doeth them, I will liken him unto a wise man, which built his house upon a rock:" Being faithful to one's Master means to faithfully practice the meditation techniques he has given you.

Matthew 8: 8 & 10 Supreme faith & humility are necessary to reach the Godhead.
"The centurion answered and said, Lord, I am not worthy that thou shouldest come under my roof: but speak the word only (send out

your Holy Ghost vibrations), *and my servant shall be healed."*
"When Jesus heard it, he marvelled, and said to them that followed, Verily I say unto you, I have not found so great faith, no, not in Israel."

Matthew 10: 37 The Master teaches the principle of non-attachment to his disciples.
"He that loveth father or mother more than me (the Christ Consciousness) *is not worthy of me: and he that loveth son or daughter more than me is not worthy of me* (Be not attached to your family of the flesh; such attachment will bring you back into the world to join them again and again)." Jesus did not mean that we should not love our relatives but that we should not be selfishly and jealously attached to them from the ego perspective of 'I' and 'mine'.

Matthew 10: 38 It is necessary to take up the disciplined life the Master lays out for the disciple.
"And he that taketh not his cross (is not willing to discipline himself according to my teachings), *and followeth after me* (and reach enlightenment as I have done), *is not worthy of me* (is not worthy of the teachings and the Christ Consciousness I am offering him)."

Matthew 15: 18 Jesus emphasises the importance of good speech.
"But those things which proceed out of the mouth (your speech) *come forth from the heart* (have the vibrational power of the Word behind them); *and they defileth a man* (Bad words will act against your spiritual interest)."

Matthew 18: 1-4 Jesus emphasises the need to be open, innocent and without ego.
"At the same time came the disciples unto Jesus, saying, Who is the greatest in the kingdom of heaven (what kind of person is the most spiritually advanced)?
"And Jesus called a little child unto him, and set him in the midst of them,
"And said, Verily I say unto you, Except ye be converted (be changed through the spiritual path), *and become as little children* (become open and pure), *ye shall not enter into the kingdom of heaven* (you will not become enlightened).
"Whosoever therefore shall humble himself as this little child, the

same is greatest in the kingdom of heaven." Masters constantly remind their disciples to be open and absorbent like a child. Fixed concepts and dogmas obstruct the Truth.

Matthew 18: 21 & 22 Jesus teaches the importance of constant forgiveness.
"Then came Peter to him, and said, Lord, how oft shall my brother (my fellow man) *sin against me, and I forgive him? till seven times?*
"Jesus saith unto him, I say not unto thee, Until seven times: but, Until seventy times seven (You must forgive without end)*."*

Matthew 19: 23 & 24 Non–attachment to one's wealth is essential but difficult for the rich to achieve.
"Then said Jesus unto his disciples, Verily I say unto you, That a rich man shall hardly enter into the kingdom of heaven (It is difficult for the rich to be unattached to their wealth)*.*
"And again I say unto you, It is easier for a camel to go through the eye of a needle, than for a rich man (one who is attached to his wealth) *to enter into the kingdom of God."* The Masters do not say that wealth is evil but that it is attachment to wealth and comforts that brings us back into the world. King Solomon of Israel and King Janaka of India were extremely wealthy but this did not hinder their spiritual advancement.

Matthew 25: 1-13 Jesus' lengthy parable of the Ten Virgins warns devotees to be always thinking about God as the time of His arrival in our consciousness is unpredictable. The virgins, the pure in heart, who always keep the lamps of their bodies full of the oil of devotion and the wicks of their Single Eyes aflame with divine light are the wise ones. The others who allow their devotion to lapse are foolish. God, the bridegroom, will take only the wise ones into His bedchamber: into His Cosmic Consciousness.

Matthew 25: 34-40 In his moving parable of the King Jesus explains that having sufficient compassion to help the poor and needy is an essential quality for finding God. In the story, the king (God) explains that helping the poor is the same as helping Him for He is the soul inside each one of us.

Matthew 26: 26-28 Jesus explains that God can be found by absorbing the teachings and practising them.
"And as they were eating, Jesus took bread, and blessed it, and brake it, and gave it to the disciples, and said, Take, eat; this is my body (this bread is symbolic of my teachings)*.*
"And he took the cup, and gave thanks, and gave it to them, saying, Drink ye all of it;
"For this is my blood of the new testament (Drink deeply for this

wine is symbolic of the spiritual life I want you to continue living as you have done while I have been with you on earth), *which is shed for many for the remission of sins* (Also my body will be broken and my blood will be shed as a sacrifice to the Law of Karma so that the many I have helped in this lifetime will be free of their past sins)."

Mark 10: 19 Jesus reminds the young man of the need to obey the laws given in the commandments.
"Thou knowest the commandments, Do not commit adultery, Do not kill, Do not steal, Do not bear false witness, Defraud not, Honour thy father and thy mother."

Mark 10: 21 Jesus advises the Truth-Seeker to take up the challenge of self-discipline and reach enlightenment.
"……and come, take up the cross, and follow me."

Mark 10: 24 The rich man with much spiritual credit, cannot bring himself to give his wealth to the poor.
"And the disciples were astonished at his words (They were amazed that Jesus said that riches were a major obstacle on the spiritual path). *But Jesus answereth again, and saith unto them, Children, How hard it is for them that trust in riches to enter into the kingdom of God* (People who put their faith in their wealth have little faith left over for God)*!"* This teaching does not infer that everyone must give up their wealth. The young man in question wanted to become a close disciple of Jesus, a monk, one who had given up all material goods in order to devote his life to God. Such a person, in contradistinction to the householder, is required to give away all material possessions.

Mark 10: 28-30 Jesus explains to his disciples that those who have given up their attachment to parents, relatives and material possessions, will inherit a great deal more (an hundred fold) by reaching the pinnacle of enlightenment wherein all the gifts of God are attained; but he cautions that enlightenment cannot be achieved without effort and by overcoming obstacles (persecutions).

Mark 10: 43 & 44 Jesus teaches the importance of being humble, without ego.
"…but whosoever will be great among you, shall be your minister (The most spiritual one of you is he who is sufficiently without ego to serve the others)*:*
"And whosoever of you will be the chiefest, shall be the servant of all (The one who wants to be the top of the roost will find himself the lowest on the spiritual ladder)."

Mark 12: 17 Jesus cleverly uses the giving of taxes to teach people how to live in the world.

"And Jesus answering said unto them, Render to Caesar the things that are Caesar's (Do your duty in and to the world), *and to God the things that are God's* (but carry out your spiritual duties also). *And they marvelled at him."*

Luke 12: 15 Avoid the trap of desiring material possessions.

"And he (Jesus) *said unto them* (his disciples), *Take heed, and beware of covetousness: for a man's life consisteth not in the abundance of the things which he possesseth* (It is our desires that keep us bound to the world and away from the spiritual path. The quantity of material goods we posses should not be taken as a measure of the quality of our lives)."

Luke 13: 18 & 19 Plant the seed of spirituality and it will grow into a great force and shelter others.

"Then said he (Jesus), *Unto what is the kingdom of God like? And where unto shall I resemble it?*
"It is like a grain of mustard seed (It starts off with a tiny leap of faith), *which a man took, and cast into his garden* (which the devotee plants in his mind); *and it grew, and waxed a great tree* (in time and with experience faith becomes enlightenment); *and the fowls of the air lodged in the branches of it* (and the power of it gives shelter to the rest of struggling humanity)."

Luke 18: 28-30 Jesus explains the benefits of having an expanded consciousness.

"Then Peter said, Lo, we have left all, and followed thee.
"And he (Jesus) *said unto them, Verily I say unto you, There is no man that hath left house, or parents, or brethren, or wife, or children, for the kingdom of God's sake,*
"Who shall not receive manifold more in this present time, and in the world to come life everlasting (In the light of an expanded consciousness all the world becomes yours and you will reach enlightenment too)."

John 3: 18 & 19 Jesus advises us to escape the clutches of the world by believing in God and loving the Light.

"He that believeth on him (He who believes on God and the Master who is one with Him) *is not condemned: but he that believeth not is condemned already* (has no chance of making spiritual progress), *because he hath not believed in the name* (because he has rejected the Holy Word that the Master has brought) *of the only begotten Son of God* (that emanates from the Christ Consciousness of God).

"And this is the condemnation, that light is come into the world (both as Cosmic Light and the Light of the Masters), *and men loved darkness rather than light, because their deeds were evil* (evil people prefer to do evil things and make every excuse to avoid contacting the Divine Light)."

John 3: 21 People who are sincerely interested in spiritual advancement are naturally drawn to the Light.

"But he that doeth truth cometh to the light (The spiritual seeker is drawn to the Light of God), *that his deeds may be made manifest* (so that his spirituality is apparent by the quality of his actions), *that they are wrought in God* (that they come from his desire to please God and not from his ego)."

John 6: 27 Jesus advises us not to live on food alone but to seek the immortality of our souls from our Master.

"Labour not for the meat which perisheth (Do not concern yourself solely with working to buy food and material goods), *but for that meat which endureth unto everlasting life* (but put the necessary effort into gaining the native immortality of your soul), *which the Son of man shall give unto you* (which, being in body form, I can give you): *for him hath God the Father sealed* (because I, as an Enlightened One, have been given the power and authority to do so by the Holy Father)."

John 8: 31 & 32 Jesus exhorts his followers to be persistent in meditating on the Word.

"Then said Jesus to those Jews which believed on him, If ye continue in my word, then are ye my disciples indeed (If you continue to listen to the Holy Word in meditation then you can count yourselves among my disciples);

"And ye shall know the truth, and the truth shall make you free

(Meditating on the Word will lead to the supreme Truth, God-the-Father, and that union will set you free from having to come back time and time again to this world)."

John 8: 51 The Master assures his disciples that by following his teachings they will become free of the world.
"Verily, verily, I say unto you, If a man keep my saying (if anyone follows my teachings), *he shall never see death* (he shall not slide back into the death of spiritual ignorance and will eventually realise his immortality in God)."

John 12: 44-46 We need enough insight, faith and loyalty to recognise and follow our chosen Master.
"Jesus cried and said, He that believeth on me, believeth not on me, but on him that sent me.
"And he that seeth me seeth him that sent me.
"I am come a light into the world, that whoseover believeth on me should not abide in darkness."

John 14: 21 Jesus teaches the principle of union with God through love of the Master.
"He that hath my commandments (has been given my teachings) *and keepeth them* (and practises them), *he it is that loveth me* (will automatically come to love the Master and the Christ Consciousness in him): *and he that loveth me shall be loved of my Father* (and he who loves the Christ Consciousness will be loved by God, the Cosmic Consciousness), *and I will love him* (the earnest devotee), *and will manifest myself to him* (will bring him into oneness with the Christ Consciousness and Cosmic Consciousness that are in me)."
See John 15: 19-11 for a similar statement.

John 15: 4 & 5 Jesus warns his disciples to adhere to their Master and the spiritual path.
"Abide in me, and I in you (We must be at one with the Christ Consciousness). *As the branch cannot bear fruit of itself, except it abide in the vine* (As the disciple cannot reach enlightenment without the Master); *no more can ye, except ye abide in me.*
"I am the vine, ye are the branches: He that abideth in me, and I in him, the same bringeth forth much fruit (spiritual progress): *for without me* (for without the one with the Christ Consciousness

chosen by God to lead you back to Him) *ye can do nothing* (you cannot succeed)."

II Corinthians 4: 1 & 2 St. Paul points out the responsibilities of those who wish to return to God.
"Therefore seeing we have this ministry, as we have received mercy, we faint not (we do not avoid our responsibilities as apostles and become faint hearted);
"But have renounced the hidden things of dishonesty, not walking in craftiness, nor handling the word of God deceitfully; but by manifestation of the truth commending ourselves to every man's conscience in the sight of God (in order to fulfil our responsibility as Sons of God, heirs to the Word, we are called upon to manifest the spiritual qualities given to us by God through meditation)."

II Corinthians 12: 7-9 St. Paul wryly notes that weaknesses exist to make us stronger spiritually.
"And lest I should be exalted above measure through the abundance of the revelations, there was given to me a thorn in the flesh, the messenger of Satan to buffet me, lest I should be exalted above measure (I have a weakness that serves to keep my ego in check in case I get too full of pride at my spiritual achievements).
"For this thing I besought the Lord thrice, that it might depart from me (Nevertheless I prayed to God to remove it).
"And he said unto me, My grace is sufficient for thee (God told me that the Divine Power within me is sufficient to overcome any adversity): *for my strength is made perfect in weakness* (and it is only by flexing my spiritual muscles that I will become strong in God). *Most gladly therefore will I rather glory in my infirmities, that the power of Christ may rest upon me* (Therefore I, Paul, will rejoice that my weaknesses give me the opportunity to draw on the power of the Christ Consciousness which is stronger than the satanic forces of Cosmic Satan and Individual Delusion)."

I John 2: 15 St. John advises initiates not to love the world more than they love God.
"Love not the world, neither the things that are in the world. If any man love the world, the love of the Father is not in him." This is akin to Jesus' teaching that a man cannot serve two masters at the same time – see Matthew 6: 24

4

Enlightenment.

*I protest by your rejoicing which
I have in Christ Jesus our Lord, I
die daily.*
   (I Corinthians 15: 31)

*If one dies while living,
For him death is sweet;
Death is sweet for him
Who has experienced it
Through the Master's grace.*
(Kabir, 15th century Muslim saint)

Masters, such as Kabir, advise Truth-Seekers to 'die while living', which means to rise above the limitations of the bodily ego-consciousness by focusing the attention on the Christ Centre or the Single Eye. They point out that it is through Love that the ego dies, for the separate self can no longer exist in the person who has merged into his Beloved. In that sublime state the two have become One.

There is only God; but uniting with Him does not infer extinction or annihilation. Far from it! As the ego-self drops away, the infinite divine Self is freed from captivity to express itself fully. God created each one of us as individualised parts of His Supreme Essence: unique, perfect and ever-existent. That divine individuality is never lost for it is ever held in the mind of the One who never forgets.

As the demands of the ego give way to the voice of intuitive wisdom, the devotee's entire attention becomes fixed on achieving enlightenment. Filled with a burning desire to merge with his Creator, and having had at least a taste of divine bliss, worldly desires no longer hold him in this material prison we know as the world. He wants to be free, free forever: to overcome the cycle of birth, death and rebirth.

Often this portion of the Path is the most difficult. For a time it can appear to the disconsolate devotee that he is in limbo, neither fully enjoying material life nor the bliss of Spirit. It is at this juncture that many truth seekers give up when, had they but known it, they were on the very brink of achieving their hard-worked-for goal. It is the final test. God is forever asking the seeker "Do you really want Me or are you still entranced by My worldly trinkets?"

When the deeply meditating devotee is able to withdraw his consciousness from the world and its cares and focus his attention fully on the Christ Centre, the 'gateway' to God, the great hum of the Word (God-the-Holy Ghost) manifests in his astral ear drawing his consciousness into the Silence within him.

> *I was in the Spirit on the Lord's day, and heard behind me a great voice, as of a trumpet.*
> (Revelation 1: 10)

Then the 'dove' or 'apple' of the Single Eye appears as a golden yellow ring (the Astral World of light energy), surrounding an azure blue 'pearl' of the Causal World (the Christ Consciousness or God-the-Son) at the centre of which shines the five-pointed star of Cosmic Consciousness (God-the-Father).

When the meditator has developed sufficient concentration, his attention is able to penetrate into the yellow ring and gain access to the Astral Realm, wherein he is able to see his own astral body of light as well as that of his Master. This was precisely St. John's experience:

> *And I turned to see the voice that spake to me. And being turned, I saw seven golden candlesticks; And in the midst of the seven candlesticks, one like unto the Son of man, clothed with a garment down to the foot, and girt about the paps with a golden girdle.*
> (Revelation 1: 12 & 13)

In the midst of the 'tissues' of light comprising the astral body, the meditator sees the seven chakras as whirls of concentrated energy ('churches') shaped like candlesticks, each with a 'star' of cosmic energy at its centre.

> *Write the things which thou hast seen, and the things which are, and the things which shall be hereafter; The mystery of the seven stars which thou sawest in my right hand, and the seven golden candlesticks. The seven stars are the angels of the seven churches: and the seven candlesticks which thou saw are the seven churches.*
> (Revelation 1: 19 & 20)

It is in the Astral World that the devotee, with the help of his ever-present Master, undertakes the task of purifying his chakras and the 144,000 minor energy centres comprising his Tree of Life

> *He that hath an ear, let him hear what the Spirit sayeth unto the churches; To him that overcometh will I give to eat of the tree of life, which is in the midst of the paradise of God.*
> (Revelation 2: 7)

> *And I heard the number of them which were sealed: and there were sealed an hundred and forty and four thousand of all the tribes of the children of Israel.*
> (Revelation 7: 4)

On entering the blue pearl, the Causal World of the Christ Consciousness, the devotee experiences oneness with God-the-Son and realises, by intuitive perception, that his incarnate soul is none other than the Spirit of God within Creation. This principle of God-the-Son being the gateway to God-the-Father was expressed by Jesus from his elevated level of Oneness with the Christ Consciousness.

> *Jesus saith unto him* (Thomas), *I am the way, the truth,*

> *and the life: no man cometh unto the Father, but by me.*
> (John 14: 6)

On penetrating the brilliant star in the centre of the blue pearl, the Truth-Seeker then realises (also by intuitive perception) that his soul is a drop of the Divine Ocean of Cosmic Consciousness, God-the-Father. This is the state which Jesus expressed as:

> *I and my Father are one.*
> (John 10: 30)

Initially, the Truth-Seeker is likely to find that though he is able to reach God-perception while in the meditative state, his consciousness becomes enwrapped in worldly affairs once again as soon as he resumes his normal activities. But this is only a temporary condition and with further meditative effort he becomes able to retain God-consciousness on 'returning to earth'. Having reached this state of permanent God-realisation the Truth-Seeker finds that he can operate in the world with unbroken God-contact. He has in fact regained his estate in Eden where original man, as Adam, walked and talked with God. Having reached that point, his consciousness is always thereafter absorbed in the Christ Centre in his forehead.

St. John describes the inner state of the enlightened man at the end of the book of Revelation; a state he enjoyed after raising his completely purified consciousness up the inner Holy Highway to the seat of Cosmic Consciousness in the crown of his head:

> *And he* (the angel) *shewed me a pure river of water of life* (spiritual energy flowing out of God to maintain the human body and soul), *clear as crystal, proceeding out of the throne of God and of the Lamb* (flowing out of Cosmic Consciousness into Christ Consciousness). *In the midst of the street of it* (in the middle of the stream of it), *and on either side of the river, was there the tree of life, which bare twelve manner of fruits, and yielded her fruit every month* (within the stream of God-consciousness lay the purified Tree of Life which yielded the fruits of

Divine Realisation in the appropriate way and at the right time): *and the leaves of the tree were for the healing of the nations* (and the perceptions 'hanging' from the Tree of Life were put there for the purpose of spiritualising all people). *And there shall be no more curse: but the throne of God and of the Lamb shall be in it; and his servants shall serve him* (When each person's Tree of Life has been spiritualised and enlightenment reach, the Satanic Powers of Cosmic Duality and Individual Ignorance will have no more authority): *And they* (the devotees of God who have pure Trees of Life) *shall see his face* (shall see God's form of Light); *and his name shall be in their foreheads* (and they will hear the sound of the Holy Word when they focus their meditative attention on the Single Eye). *And there shall be no night there; and they need no candle, neither light of the sun; for the Lord God giveth them light* (and they shall live in and by the Divine Light): *and they shall reign* (and they shall be in Cosmic Consciousness) *for ever and ever.*
(Revelation 22: 1-5)

This is the final state of God-Consciousness in which all the reincarnation-making desires and attachments have been overcome with the assistance of the Christ Consciousness in the Master

> *For whatsoever is born of God overcometh the world: and this is the victory that overcometh the world, even our faith.*
> (I John 5: 4)

and the last enemy, mortality, has been defeated.

> *The last enemy that shall be destroyed is death.*
> (I Corinthians 15: 26)

The Masters say that the state of enlightenment cannot be expressed adequately in words. Oneness can be understood fully only by direct experience.

> *Such is the inner experience*
> *That it cannot be expressed.*
> *When the union with the Lord is attained,*
> *Then who can separate?*
> *God is in all, and all is in God,*
> *This is realised only by men of the Lord.*
> (Guru Ravidas, 15th century Indian saint)

Nevertheless, every one of us is capable of understanding that all the worlds and their populations have emerged from Love, are made of Love, are ever surrounded by Love and are destined to return to Love. Ironically, Love is the power that initially compels us to search recklessly in all the wrong places for the ultimate union; and yet it is also the force that draws us inexorably back to God. The final and highest realisation is: 'God is Love and I am Love.' That is why Jesus endorsed Love as the quality that encompasses all other laws and completely satisfies the teachings of the prophets.

> *Jesus said unto him, Thou shalt love the Lord thy God with all thy heart, and with all thy soul, and with all thy mind. This is the first and great commandment. And the second is like unto it, Thou shalt love thy neighbour as thyself. On these two commandments hang all the law and the prophets.*
> (Matthew 22: 37–40)

When a great saint was once asked to address a group of children, he got to his feet and simply repeated three times "Little children, love one another!" When the organiser of the event criticised him for saying so little, the great saint replied: "If they can but remember this small contribution, it will save them from mountains of sins."

What the Bible Says About Enlightenment.

A cave may remain in darkness for thousands of years but the gloom inside it can be dispelled in an instant as soon as a light is switched on. Enlightenment dispels the darkness of ignorance in an instant when man harnesses his mind to the Word and meets the Light of Christ Consciousness. Unity with the Universal Christ earns the Truth-Seeker the title of 'Son of God' and unity with God frees the soul from bondage to the otherwise unending cycles of death and rebirth.

Psalm 2: 7 The Lord calls David His 'son' as are all who reach oneness with the Christ Consciousness.
"I will declare the decree: the Lord hath said unto me, Thou art my Son; this day have I begotten thee (this day you have attained Christ Consciousness, the divine status of a 'Son of God')." See Ephesians 4: 13 for Jesus as a Son of God, one with the Christ Consciousness, who bestowed the fullness of the Christ Consciousness on his disciples.

Isaiah 2: 2 Enlightenment comes when God is seated in the crown of the head above the hills of the eyebrows.
"And it shall come to pass in the last days (in a person's last days of ignorance)*, that the mountain of the Lord's house* (the height of God-consciousness) *shall be established in the top of the mountains* (shall be established in the crown of the head)*, and shall be exalted above the hills* (which is located above the little hills of the Christ Centre)*; and all nations shall flow unto it* (and it is God's plan that everyone will eventually reach there)." For an almost exact repeat see Micah 4: 1 & 2.

Isaiah 2: 3 When people turn from the world to God in the highest spiritual centre, He will guide them.
"And many people shall go and say, Come ye, and let us go up to the mountain of the Lord (let us lift our consciousnesses up to the Crown Chakra)*, to the house of the God of Jacob* (to the spiritual level enjoyed by Jacob)*; and he* (God) *will teach us of his ways, and we will walk in his paths: for out of Zion* (Cosmic Consciousness)

shall go forth the law (the Law of Karma), *and the word* (the Holy Vibration) *of the Lord from Jerusalem* (from God within creation, the Christ Consciousness).*"* Refer back to the section on 'The Captivity' for details of the Law of Karma; to the section on 'The Higher Spiritual Centres' for the meaning of the Cosmic and Christ Consciousnesses; and to the section on 'The Word' for the meaning of 'word'.

Isaiah 45: 22 There is no permanence in the world. It is a sick illusion. True happiness lies in unity with God.
"Look unto me, and be ye save, all the ends of the earth: for I am God, and there is none else."

Isaiah 56: 1 Those who act rightly are not far from enlightenment.
"Thus saith the Lord, Keep ye judgement, and do justice: for my salvation is near to come, and my righteousness to be revealed."

Isaiah 60: 19 & 20 The Lord describes the experiences to be had when treading the inner path to God.
"The sun shall be no more thy light by day; neither for brightness shall the moon give light unto thee: but the Lord shall be unto thee an everlasting light (but the Divine Light will be your guide), *and thy God thy glory* (and you will achieve unity with the Godhead).
"Thy sun shall no more go down; neither shall thy moon withdraw itself: for the Lord shall be thine everlasting light, and the days of thy mourning shall be ended (you will yearn no more for God-realisation for you will be One with Him)."* This same theme is the subject of the entire sixtieth chapter of Isaiah.

Daniel 2: 22 Daniel praises the Lord for the hidden secrets He tells His prophets from the depths of their souls.
"He revealeth the deep and secret things: he knoweth what is in the darkness, and the light dwelleth with him."

Malachi 4: 2 The Lord proclaims that those who listen to His Holy Word will see the Divine Light.
"But unto you who fear my name (to you who listen to the Holy Word with attention and respect) *shall the Sun of righteousness arise with healing in his wings* (the Divine Light which heals all ills and destroys all karmas will arise in your consciousness, making you whole again); *and ye shall go forth, and grow up as calves of the stall."* Stall-fed calves are well looked after by their keepers.

Matthew 22: 37-40 Two of the main Paths to God are identified: love God and love man as His image.

"Jesus said unto him (a lawyer), *Thou shalt love the Lord thy God with all thy heart* (with complete devotion), *and with all thy soul* (with all the power of the soul in oneness with God), *and with all thy mind* (with full concentration on Him alone).

"This is the first and great commandment.

"And the second is like unto it, Thou shalt love thy neighbour as thyself (All people are children of God. God is inside them as their souls and loving mankind is the same as loving God).

"On these two commandments hang all the law and the prophets (All the laws of God and the practices of the Enlightened Ones are based on fulfilling these two main laws)." See Mark 12: 30-33 for a similar report.

Mark 8: 29 To reach enlightenment we need to be led by someone who is united to the Christ Consciousness.

"And he (Jesus) *saith unto them* (his disciples), *But whom say ye that I am? And Peter answereth and saith unto him, Thou art the Christ* (Jesus the Christ, the one with the Christ Consciousness)."

Mark 10: 31 The time it takes for us to become enlightened depends upon our karmic load.

"But many that are first (first to come to the spiritual Path) *shall be last* (will find enlightenment delayed because of the bad karma they have accrued)*; and the last first* (and those who come later to the Path but have a light karmic load, will reach enlightened before them)."

Mark 14: 61 & 62 Jesus confirms that his duty is to lead his disciples to enlightenment.

"...Again the high priest asked him, and said unto him, Art though the Christ, the Son of the Blessed (are you the one with the Christ Consciousness?)*?*

"And Jesus said, I am: and ye shall see the Son of man sitting on the right hand of power, and coming in the clouds of heaven (and the proof of who I am is that you will see those for whom I am spiritually responsible becoming enlightened)."

John 3: 36 The person who strives for Christ Consciousness through the Master will become the immortal soul.

"He that believeth (in thought and effort) *on the Son* (the Christ Consciousness reflected in the Master) *hath everlasting life* (will realise that he is the immortal soul)*: and he that believeth not the Son shall not see life* (will remain subject to repeated earthly deaths of the body)*; but the wrath of God abideth on him* (and will continue to suffer under the Law of Karma as a result of his inevitable bad deeds)*."*

John 10: 30 In this simple verse Jesus sums up the state of enlightenment.

"I and my Father are one." Enlightened Ones are in complete unity with the Godhead and can exactly express the Divine Will.

John 13: 10 Jesus tells his disciples that they are free of karma but Judas is not.

"Jesus saith to him (Peter)*, He that is washed* (he that has had all his sins washed away by spiritual practice) *needeth not save to wash his feet* (needs only to wash his body)*, but he is clean every whit* (then he is clean inside and out)*: and ye are clean, but not all* (but there is one among who still has some bad karma)*."*

John 14: 6 Jesus, One with the Christ Consciousness, confirms that the Son is the gateway to the Father.

"Jesus saith unto him (Thomas)*, I am the way, the truth, and the life* (I, your Master, am one with the Christ Consciousness, the Son of God)*: no man cometh unto the Father, but by me* (no one can attain Cosmic Consciousness, oneness with God, without first attaining the Christ Consciousness, the gateway to God)*."* This statement is true in two senses: no one can reach God except through the Christ Consciousness, nor can a disciple reach God except through the agency of his Master.

John 15: 3-5 Jesus tells his disciples that they have reached an important milestone on the road to enlightenment.

"Now ye are clean through the word which I have spoken unto you (The Word I have 'spoken' to you out of the mouth of the Christ Consciousness has cleared all your remaining karmas).

"Abide in me, and I in you. As the branch cannot bear fruit of itself, except it abide in the vine; no more can ye, except ye abide in me.

"I am the vine, ye are the branches: He that abideth in me, and I in

him, the same bringeth forth much fruit: for without me ye can do nothing (Continue to follow the spiritual disciplines I have given you and tune yourself to the Christ Consciousness that is within me and you will reach enlightenment)."

John 16: 13 Jesus describes the benefits attained by meditating on the Word.
"Howbeit when he, the Spirit of truth, is come, he will guide you into all truth: for he shall not speak of himself; but whatsoever he shall hear, that shall he speak: and he will shew you things to come." In purifying the consciousness, the Holy Ghost brings the perfect guidance of the intuition and the power of Divine Sight.

John 17: 17 Jesus prays for the spiritual success of all those who follow his instructions to listen to the Word.
"Sanctify them through thy truth: thy word is truth (Enlighten them, Father, through the Holy Ghost, Thy True Word)."

John 20: 17 Jesus talks of the power over death enjoyed by Enlightened Ones.
"Jesus sayeth unto her (to Mary), *Touch me not; for I am not yet ascended to my Father* (I have not yet raised myself through the three stages, physical, astral and causal, necessary to be one with Cosmic Consciousness)*: but go my brethren,* (my disciples) *and say unto them, I ascend unto my Father, and your Father* (tell them that I am going into Cosmic Consciousness)*; and to my God, and your God."* The body can be reconstructed through the power of Cosmic Consciousness from whence it originally came.

Romans 16: 19 & 20 St. Paul assures the good people that their individual delusions will be overcome as they progress spiritually.
"For your obedience is come abroad unto all men (your perseverance in following the Path to God is well known). *I am glad therefore on your behalf: but yet I would have you wise unto that which is good, and simple concerning evil* (but I pray that you will become wiser to the difference between good and evil).
"And the God of peace shall bruise Satan under your feet shortly (The goodness of your right actions will dispel ignorance from your minds). *The grace of our Lord Jesus Christ be with you* (May the spirit of Jesus the Christ, our Master, help you and strengthen you by the power of the Word). *Amen."*

I Corinthians 3: 16 St. Paul states unambiguously that God is inside us waiting to be found.
"Know ye not that ye (your bodies) are the temple of God, and that the spirit of God dwelleth in you."

I Corinthians 15: 26 St. Paul says that death is overcome by achieving immortality in Spirit.
"The last enemy that shall be destroyed is death."

I Corinthians 15: 31 St. Paul confirms that by the blessing of his Master he is able to overcome ego and death.
"I protest by your rejoicing which I have in Christ Jesus our Lord, I die daily." 'I die daily' has two meanings: 'I am constantly killing off my ego as it arises'; and 'I daily practise transcending the body in meditation'.

I Corinthians 15: 50 St. Paul emphasises that only spirit can return to Spirit.
"Now this I say, brethren, that flesh and blood cannot inherit the kingdom of God; neither doth corruption inherit incorruption."

II Corinthians 3: 17 Unity with Spirit, God, brings freedom from the Laws of Karma & Reincarnation.
"Now the Lord is that Spirit: and where the Spirit of the Lord is, there is liberty."

II Corinthians 3: 18 St. Paul points out that through meditating on God we become One with Him.
"But we all, with open face beholding as in a glass the glory of the Lord (looking at the glory of the Lord, our true image, as in a mirror), *are changed into the same image from glory to glory, even as by the Spirit of the Lord* (we become identical to Him)*."*

II Corinthians 5: 6 & 8 Those transcending the demands of the body become focussed on the Lord.
"Therefore we are always confident, knowing that, whilst we are at home in the body, we are absent from the Lord (Now we know that too much body-consciousness takes our attention away from the spiritual path)*."*
"We are confident, I say, and willing rather to be absent from the body, and to be present with the Lord (we are willing to rise above body-consciousness into Spirit)*."*

Galatians 5: 22 & 23 St. Paul says that those who attain the fruit of Spirit are free of the Law of Karma.

"But the fruit of the Spirit is love, joy, peace, longsuffering, gentleness, goodness, faith,

"Meekness, temperance: against such there is no law (these do not attract any karmic reactions for they are divine qualities).*"*

Ephesians 6: 11 & 12 St. Paul advises on how to overcome the two satanic powers afflicting mankind.

"Put on the whole armour of God, that ye may be able to stand against the wiles of the devil (To overcome the evil forces do not dip only your toes in the lake of spirituality but your entirety).

"For we wrestle not against flesh and blood, but against principalities, against powers, against the rulers of the darkness of this world, against spiritual wickedness in high places (For our battle for liberation is against the satanic forces that create the Cosmic Principles of Duality and Individual Ignorance).*"*

Colossians 3: 9-11 The spiritual path converts man back into pristine Spirit where no differences occur.

"Lie not one to another, seeing that ye have put off the old man with his deeds (Don't lie to one another now that you have changed and have entered the spiritual path);

"And have put on the new man, which is renewed in knowledge after the image of him that created him (and by means of the Divine Knowledge have been converted into pure reflections of God):

"Where there is neither Greek not Jew, circumcision nor uncircumcision, Barbarian, Scythian, bond nor free: but Christ is all, and in all (where the Christ Consciousness in each one of you is common to all and recognises no divisions of race, status, religion, culture or anything else).*"*

I John 3: 8 St. John refers to the Cosmic Principle of Duality that is counterbalanced by the Christ Consciousness.

"He that committeth sin is of the devil; for the devil sinneth from the beginning (the illusion of duality, created by the Cosmic Satan, is inherent in the world). *For this purpose the Son of God* (the power of Christ Consciousness opposing duality) *was manifested that he*

might destroy the works of the devil (that men might turn towards God and be saved from captivity in the world)."

I John 5: 4 & 5 Being initiated into Spirit by the Master and having faith in the Path frees the disciple from the world.
"For whatsoever is born of God overcometh the world: and this is the victory that overcometh the world, even our faith (initiation and faith lead to liberation).
"Who is he that overcometh the world, but he that believeth that Jesus is the Son of God (does not a devotee achieve liberation by having faith that his Master is united to the Christ Consciousness)?"

Revelation 1: 8 The Lord states that He is the beginning and end of everything, the Supreme Consciousness.
"I am Alpha and Omega, the beginning and the ending, saith the Lord, which is, and which was, and which is to come, the Almighty." God is eternal and to be back with Him is the end of the great journey of our mortal existence. We came from God and are destined to return to Him.

Revelation 1: 10 St. John hears the mighty sound of the Word while meditating.
"I was in the Spirit on the Lord's day, and heard behind me a great voice, as of a trumpet." The Aum, Amen or Holy Word is the vehicle that carries our consciousnesses back to God.

Revelation 1: 12 & 13 St. John begins to describe the inner experiences leading to enlightenment.
"And I turned (I turn my attention from the material world to look inside myself) *to see the voice that spake to me* (to put my attention on the sound of the Word). *And being turned, I saw seven golden candlesticks* (and inside myself I saw seven sacred chakras shaped like candlesticks);
"And in the midst of the seven candlesticks, one like unto the Son of man, clothed with a garment down to the foot, and girt about the paps with a golden girdle (the candlesticks were in the middle of the light body of an angelic astral form shaped like a human being)."

Revelation 1: 19 & 20 The Holy Word informs St. John of the meaning of the astral form he is seeing.
"Write the things which thou hast seen, and the things which are, and the things which shall be hereafter (write upon your consciousness

The Truth Seeker's Guide to the Bible

and describe to others the experiences you are about to have);
"The mystery of the seven stars which thou sawest in my right hand, and the seven golden candlesticks. The seven stars are the angels of the seven churches: and the seven candlesticks which thou saw are the seven churches." The body has seven sacred centres called chakras. The shape of each chakra is similar to the old fashioned candlesticks in use at that time. They are centres of whirling energy which support the functions of the body. In the centre of each chakra is the star-like force of Divine Light. The chakras and 144,000 energy sub-centres have to be spiritualised in order to reach enlightenment, which is the process St. John recorded in the book of Revelation. See Revelation 7: 4 and 14: 1 below.

Revelation 2: 7 Whoever overcomes the world will have a purified Tree of Life, fit to express spiritual perceptions.
"He that hath an ear, let him hear what the Spirit sayeth unto the churches; To him that overcometh will I give to eat of the tree of life, which is in the midst of the paradise of God." The chakras lie within a three-fold network of physical, astral and causal channels making up the Tree of Life. See the section called 'The Tree of Life'.

Revelation 3: 12 & 21 Jesus tells St. John that those who become enlightened need not reincarnate again.
"Him that overcometh (He that overcomes the temptations of the world) *will I make a pillar in the temple of my God, and he shall go more out* (need not leave the heavenly realms again and reincarnate on earth)*: and I will write upon him the name of my God* (the Holy Word)*, and the name of the city of my God* (his entire bodily city will be spiritualised)...."
"To him that overcometh will I grant to sit with me in my throne (on the throne of Cosmic Consciousness)*, even as I also overcame, and am set down with my Father in his throne."* Here Jesus is confirming what every Master tells his disciples: I was once an ordinary mortal like you, lost in delusion, but through my Master I escaped from mortal consciousness into Cosmic Consciousness. You can also reach enlightenment like I have.

Revelation 7: 4 The Angelic messenger confirms the number of Nadis which must be purified.
"And I heard the number of them which were sealed: and there were sealed an hundred and forty and four thousand of all the tribes of the children of Israel." There are 74,000 minor energy points in the body each with a positive and negative charge, making up the 144,000 energy points in man's Tree of Life which must be spiritualised before he can become enlightened.

Revelation 14: 1 The Truth-Seeker reaches enlightenment when his Nadis are purified in his Tree of Life.

"And I looked, and, lo, a Lamb (the Christ Consciousness) *stood on the mount Sion* (descended from Cosmic Consciousness), *and with him an hundred forty and four thousand, having his Father's name* (the Word) *written on their foreheads* (resounding at the Christ Centre in their Single Eyes)." God supplies Cosmic Energy to the human body through the Christ Consciousness and 144,000 minor centres, the Nadis, comprising the Tree of Life and consciousness in man. The Nadis have to be purified in the stream of the Cosmic Aum or Amen (his Father's name) for man to become enlightened.

Revelation 21: 7 God tells St. John that anyone mastering the spiritual path will inherit all the qualities of God.

"He that overcometh shall inherit all things; and I will be his God, and he shall be my son." As a child of God, a spark of the Divine Consciousness, man is set to inherit all his Fathers powers, the gifts that he gave up automatically when he fell into mortal consciousness.

Revelation 22: 1-5 St. John experiences the state of consciousness of the enlightened man.

"And he (the angel) *shewed me a pure river of water of life* (spiritual energy flowing out of God to maintain the human body and soul), *clear as crystal, proceeding out of the throne of God and of the Lamb* (out of Cosmic Consciousness into Christ Consciousness).

"In the midst of the street of it (in the midst of the stream of it), *and on either side of the river, was there the tree of life, which bare twelve manner of fruits, and yielded her fruit every month* (within the clear stream of God-consciousness lay the purified Tree of Life which yielded the fruits of Divine Realisation in the appropriate way and at the right time)*: and the leaves of the tree were for the healing of the nations* (and the perceptions 'hanging' from the Tree of Life were put there for the purpose of spiritualising all people).

"And there shall be no more curse: but the throne of God and of the Lamb shall be in it; and his servants shall serve him (When each person's Tree of Life has been spiritualised, the Satanic Powers of Cosmic Duality and Individual Ignorance have no more authority)*:*

"And they (the devotees of God who have pure Trees of Life) *shall see his face* (shall see His form of Light)*; and his name shall be in their foreheads* (and they will hear the Holy Word when they focus their meditative attention on the Single Eye).

"And there shall be no night there; and they need no candle, neither light of the sun; for the Lord God giveth them light (and they shall live in and by the Divine Light): *and they shall reign* (and shall be in Cosmic Consciousness) *for ever and ever."*

The Final Word.

A recurrent theme in the teachings of the Masters is that this world is not our real home. We are only temporary earth dwellers waiting for God's call to go back to our Celestial Home. The journey back is the Path. The tools for doing so are meditation, devotion, and service to mankind in a spirit of love and faith. Nothing less will do. God can be attained only by wholehearted effort. The end result is enlightenment. But the Masters also warn that even these tools, by themselves, are not enough. The effectiveness of any spiritual practice depends on God's Grace. But it is also true that the flow of God's Grace depends almost entirely on the devotee engaging wholeheartedly in his/her spiritual practice.

The process of enlightenment is to gain control of the body, senses and mind; transform the ego into the soul; and resolve the soul back into the Godhead. Sure progress is guaranteed to those who follow their Master's instructions with loyalty, love, faith, persistence, and with complete surrender to the Divine Will.

A Truth-Seeker progresses towards enlightenment through various stages well-documented in authentic spiritual literature. The first benefit experienced by the ardent meditator is a slowing down of the mind, accompanied by increased feelings of peace, love and joy welling up from unknown depths within him. The loud voice of the ego begins to give way to the Silent Voice of intuitive guidance, the voice of God speaking through the soul. When the mind has become still and able to focus on the Single Eye between the 'little hills' in the forehead, the Divine Word and Light manifest, drawing the meditator's consciousness further inward until it merges with the Christ Consciousness. And, as the focus rises even higher to the 'mountain top' of the Crown Chakra, the soul eventually realises its oneness with the Absolute Godhead.

In much the same way that Creation is projected forth out of the action-less God, appears for a time as the visible Universe and then withdraws back into its Source after it has served its intended purpose, the soul of man emerges from God, manifests for a time in various human bodies and then completes its cycle by merging back into the Infinite from whence it came.

The discovery that Jesus shares the title of the 'Only Begotten Son of God' with many other great spiritual personages, in fact with all Enlightened Beings, might come as a shock to some of his most ardent followers. Regrettable though that might be, in actuality it releases Jesus from the human-prescribed limitation of 'The Messiah of a chosen people' to that of a World Teacher who brought God's universal and timeless message to all mankind irrespective of the religion of their birth. Rather than diminishing the stature of Jesus, the Perennial Philosophy as taught by today's Enlightened Ones reveals Jesus to be a very special person, a true Son of the all-embracing Cosmic Being: one who dared to overcome the world and, in doing so, showed every one of us the way to be like him. Since *'the foundations of the world'* Enlightened Ones have been incarnating with the express purpose of leading God's children back to Him and they will continue do so *'till the end of time.'*

Jesus, Christian Avatar, a Son of God:

Think not that I am come to destroy the Law, or the prophets: I come not to destroy but to fulfil.
(Matthew 5:17)

Krishna, Hindu Avatar, a divine incarnation:

O Arjuna! Whenever virtue declines and vice predominates, I incarnate as an Avatar: In visible form I appear from age to age to protect the virtuous and to destroy evildoing in order to re-establish righteousness.
(Bhagavad Gita IV: 7 & 8)

Mira, 16th century Indian warrior-princess, the ideal devotee.

The Perfect Master has revealed
Mira's Lord to her.
Mira, separated since eons,

He has brought back home.
(Mira, 16th century Indian saint)

Love is what we are and ever will be. The consciousness of man can be measured according to the degree of his narrow self-interest. As he grows in maturity his horizons expand to include all humanity, all saints and all nature. The Perennial Philosophy reveals that the real goal of evolution is not material development at all. It is the evolution of consciousness from its first expression as primitive life to total awareness of itself as the universal Self behind all life.

Acknowledgements.

References of appropriate spiritual literature and sources of information appear below under 'Recommended Reading' and 'Recommended Sources of Spiritual Information'. Rumi's quotations are taken from *'Whispers of the Beloved'*; Ravidas' from *'Guru Ravidas'*; Mira's from *'Mira: The Divine Lover'*; and those of Kabir, Dadu and St. Pipa from *'Kabir: The Weaver of God's Name'*. Quotations from the two SRF publications by Paramahansa Yogananda *'God Talks With Arjuna'* and *'The Second Coming of Christ'* are acknowledged in full in the text.

This book has been written with deep gratitude to that noble soul Paramahansa Yogananda and the organisation he founded, the SRF; to my own Enlightened Teacher; and to all the Enlightened Ones of all cultures, races and creeds who have graced this world in order to free its bewildered captives from bondage. Ignorant we may have been. Ignorant we might still be. But the glory of this earthly drama we are so engrossed in is that enlightenment is just around the corner, so close that it is only a hairsbreadth away. Praise be to the Masters and to the ever-loving God who continues to send His Emissaries of Light into this dark world.

Recommended Reading.

Be As You Are: The Teachings of Ramana Maharshi Edited by David Godman. Penguin Books, London.

Forty Verses On Reality by Sri Ramana Maharshi. Translated by Arthur Osborne. Mountain Path Journal of Sri Ramanasramam.

God Talks With Arjuna by Paramahansa Yogananda. Self-Realisation Fellowship, Los Angeles, California.

Guru Ravidas by K.N. Upadhyaya. Radha Soami Satsang Beas, Punjab, India.

Kabir: The Weaver of God's Name by V.K Sethi. Radha Soami Satsang Beas, Punjab, India.

Meister Eckhart: Mystic as Theologian by Robert K.C. Forman. Element Books Ltd, Longmead, Dorset.

Mira: The Divine Lover by V.K Sethi. Radha Soami Satsang Beas, Punjab, India.

Rumi: Whispers of the Beloved by Azima Melita Kolin and Maryam Maki. Thorsons, Hammersmith, London.

The Holy Bible: King James Authorised Version of 1611. Oxford University Press, London.

The Holy Man and the Psychiatrist by Samuel H. Sandweiss. Sri Sathya Sai Books and Publications Trust, Prashaanthi Nilayam, India.

The Second Coming of Christ by Paramahansa Yogananda. Self-Realisation Fellowship, Los Angeles, California.

The Sufi Doctrine of Rumi by William C. Chittick. World Wisdom Inc., Bloomington, Indiana.

The Yoga Sutras of Patangali by Alistair Shearer. Rider, Random House, London.,

Recommended Sources of Spiritual Information.

Ocean Research Library Computer Programme. www.bahai-education.org/ocean .

The Divine Life Society. Sivananda Ashram, Rishikesh, India. Founded by Swami Sivananda; www.divinelifesociety.org .

The Divine Light Mission/The Prem Rawat Foundation. Founded by Prem Pal Singh/Prem Rawat; www.maharaji.net and www.tprf.org Home Page.

Sri Sathya Sai Baba Organisation. Prashaanthi Nilayam. P.O. 515134, Anantapur District, Andhra Pradesh, India. www.sathyasai.org .

The Self-Realisation Fellowship. Founded by Paramahansa Yogananda, 3880 San Rafael Avenue, Los Angeles, California 90065-3298; www.yogananda-srf.org .

The Radha Soami Satsang Beas. P.O. Dera Baba Jaimal Singh, Dist. Amritsar 143 204, Punjab, India. www.rssb.org .

Sri Ramakrishna Centre. 17 East 94th Street, New York, NY 10128, USA; www.ramakrishna.org .

Ramana Maharishi Ashram. Sri Ramanasramam, Tiruvannamalai, South India, 606 603; www.ramana-maharshi.org .

SYDA Foundation. Founded by Swami Muktananda; 32 Cubitt Street, London WC1X 0LR; www.siddhayoga.org.in .

Printed in the United Kingdom
by Lightning Source UK Ltd.
122462UK00002B/1-39/A